The Saskatchewan

Rivers of America Books

already published are:

KENNEBEC by Robert P. Tristram Coffin
UPPER MISSISSIPPI (New Revised Edition, 1944) by Walter Havighurst
SUWANNEE RIVER by Cecile Hulse Matschat
POWDER RIVER by Struthers Burt
THE JAMES (New Revised Edition, 1945) by Blair Niles
THE HUDSON by Carl Carmer
THE SACRAMENTO by Julian Dana
THE WABASH by William E. Wilson
THE ARKANSAS by Clyde Brion Davis
THE DELAWARE by Harry Emerson Wildes
THE ILLINOIS by James Gray
THE KAW by Floyd Benjamin Streeter
THE BRANDYWINE by Henry Seidel Canby
THE CHARLES by Arthur Bernon Tourtellot
THE KENTUCKY by T. D. Clark
THE SANGAMON by Edgar Lee Masters
THE ALLEGHENY by Frederick Way, Jr.

THE WISCONSIN by August Derleth
LOWER MISSISSIPPI by Hodding Carter
THE ST. LAWRENCE by Henry Beston
THE CHICAGO by Harry Hansen
TWIN RIVERS: *The Raritan and the Passaic*, by Harry Emerson Wildes
THE HUMBOLDT by Dale L. Morgan
THE ST. JOHNS by Branch Cabell and A. J. Hanna
RIVERS OF THE EASTERN SHORE by Hulbert Footner
THE MISSOURI by Stanley Vestal
THE SALINAS by Anne B. Fisher
THE SHENANDOAH by Julia Davis
THE HOUSATONIC by Chard Powers Smith
THE COLORADO by Frank Waters
THE TENNESSEE: THE OLD RIVER, *Frontier to Secession*, by Donald Davidson
THE CONNECTICUT by Walter Hard
THE EVERGLADES by Marjory Stoneman Douglas
THE TENNESSEE: THE NEW RIVER, *Civil War to TVA*, by Donald Davidson
THE CHAGRES by John Easter Minter
THE MOHAWK by Codman Hislop
THE MACKENZIE by Leslie Roberts
THE WINOOSKI by Ralph Nading Hill
THE OHIO by R. E. Banta
THE POTOMAC by Frederick Gutheim
THE SASKATCHEWAN by Marjorie Wilkins Campbell

SONGS OF THE RIVERS OF AMERICA, edited by Carl Carmer

RIVERS OF AMERICA

EDITED BY *Hervey Allen* AND *Carl Carmer*

AS PLANNED AND STARTED BY

Constance Lindsay Skinner

ASSOCIATE EDITOR · JEAN CRAWFORD

ART EDITOR · FAITH BALL

THE SASKATCHEWAN

Marjorie Wilkins Campbell

ILLUSTRATED BY

Illingworth H. Kerr

RINEHART & CO., INC. , NEW YORK , TORONTO

PRINTED IN THE UNITED STATES OF AMERICA

TO

G. A. C.

1916–1948

Contents

III. Waterway

Preface

Most people who know the Saskatchewan know only parts of it. They know their own farm or city, their own stretch of mountain or muskeg. They know the homesites of their friends or the places they go to on business or on their holidays. Few have visited the sources, the tributaries, both branches, and the main river. Few are familiar with its entire history. Those who do know the Saskatchewan story well have given the same warning, freely and often:

"You're going to have some time trying to satisfy all the people on *that* river!"

Actually I haven't tried to satisfy anyone except myself. And even there I am short of the mark. Disregarding the literary angle, there are the facts of two hundred years, well over two thousand miles, the discovery of about a third of the North American continent, and the change-over from a primitive, nomadic Indian society to the way we live today. This Saskatchewan River story is told by one who grew up in its country and then moved sufficiently far away to see it in perspective. The material included is that which I like out of the rich mass available, which to me gives a fairly comprehensive picture of the people over those two hundred years and two thousand miles. It has been kept almost entirely within sight of Saskatchewan water. It is my version.

Marjorie Wilkins Campbell
Toronto, 1949

I

Highway

THE
Saskatchewan
RIVER
JANNAND
ALBERTA
BRITISH
COLUMBIA
Peace R.
Lesser Slave L.
Athabasca R.
Athabasca R.
McLeod R.
Pembina R.
Fraser R.
JASPER PARK
JASPER
VICTORIA
ST. ALBERT
N. Saskatchewan
EDMONTON
Quesnelle L.
150 MILE HOUSE
Athabasca Pass
Snow Dome
Columbia Ice Fields
Mt. Saskatchewan
ROCKY MTN. HOUSE
BANFF PARK
PALLISER RANGE
BEAVER
LAKE LOUISE
BANFF
GLACIER
Thompson R.
KAMLOOPS
CALGARY
Red Deer
Upper Arrow Lake
Okanagan Lake
Fraser R.
E.P. RANCH
PEKISKO
Bow R.
KASLO
Kootenay Lake
NELSON
Crows Nest Pass
Old Man R.
LETHBRIDGE
VANCOUVER
VAN. I.
ROSSLAND
Columbia R.
VICTORIA
CHIEF MTN.
GLACIER PARK
WASH.
SEATTLE
TACOMA
KALISPELL
IDAHO
SPOKANE
MO

Hudson Bay
FORT CHURCHILL
Churchill R.
YORK FACTORY
Nelson R.
Hayes R.
Shamattawa R.
God's Lake
Island Lake
Pike R.
Wollaston Lake
Lake Athabasca
Reindeer Lake
North
W
E
S
SASKATCHEWAN
CUMBERLAND HOUSE
THE PAS
R.
Saskatchewan
Carrot R.
Cedar Lake
GRAND RAPIDS
Lake Winnipeg
FORT PITT
PRINCE ALBERT
NIPAWIN
FT. LA CORNE
CARLETON
NORTH BATTLEFORD
BATOCHE
BATTLEFORD
EAGLE HILLS
SASKATOON
Swan L.
MANITOBA
Touchwood Hills
Last Mountain Lake
Dauphin Lake
Lake Manitoba
Winnipeg R.
R.
Saskatchewan
ELBOW
Qu'Appelle
R.
WINNIPEG
PORTAGE LA PRAIRIE
R.
Assiniboine
BRANDON
ST. BONIFACE
Red R.
SWIFT CURRENT
REGINA
Cypress Hills
CANADA
UNITED STATES
GRAND FORKS
MINOT
NORTH DAKOTA
Missouri
R.
BISMARCK

CHAPTER ONE

Geography Lesson

THE Saskatchewan, they say, drains the Rocky Mountains into the Atlantic Ocean. The statement is true, allowing for the exaggeration natural to so much space. Actually the North Branch, or the main river, rises in the Rockies some three hundred and fifty miles northwest of the international border at Montana, races for a thousand miles downhill to Lake Winnipeg, where it flows through the northern end and continues under the name of Nelson to Hudson Bay. Hudson Bay is North Atlantic water.

On the map the Saskatchewan sprawls like a big wobbly Y generally pointing northeast from its sources along the Rocky Mountains. The North Branch forms one arm of the Y, the South Branch forms the other, and united they make up the base.

While its primary source is the Snow Dome in the Columbia Icefields from which waters flow to the Pacific, the Arctic and the Atlantic, the North Saskatchewan starts as an icy cascade at the foot of Saskatchewan Glacier. Even though it is six thousand feet above sea level, Mount Athabasca towers as high again on one side and Mount Saskatchewan reaches almost as far on the other. Deep in the valley between these giants the tiny icy stream gives little indication of the strong river it eventually will become. The only hint is its quick meeting with Nigel Greek, the first of many streams it gathers into its channel. Some of these are mountain streams which any tourist on the Banff-Jasper Highway may see for himself, since mountain highways naturally follow the valleys cut by swift rivers.

Nigel Creek plunges so precipitously at Panther Gorge that many women and some men won't risk looking over its rocky ledge, even with the protection of the bus driver's steady arm—if they travel by bus—and the count of passengers is not all dry humor. Motorists traveling in their own cars may be divided into two groups after they have left the wonders of Columbia Icefields or the beauty of Peyto Lake—those who can bear to look down from a great height and those who dare not.

The North Saskatchewan quickly disproves the theory that all glacial water is green, as is the case with its sister stream below Bow Pass, the Bow River, a source of the South Branch. Pale putty is the color of the North Saskatchewan in the mountains, and often lower down on the prairies, when it is not a cascade of white lace, misty as a spider's web; or so vast that you bend backward to see to the top of it. For the Saskatchewan up near the icefields is heavy, and opaque with the limestone it is continually washing away from the rocks along its course. Where the Alexandra River comes in from the west the gravel flats are littered with bits of whitened driftwood resembling bones. Here it is known as the Graveyard. In early summer the water is such a raging torrent that nothing has a chance to start growth in this gray valley between towering Mount Coleman to the east and the bulk of Amery to the west. Yet by autumn the river's spring surging has settled down to a steady, swift flow. Perhaps it is the rush of spring water that carries the seeds of fringed gentian down from the glacier's edge to the rapids at the mouth of the river, a thousand miles away, gentians as blue as the dry skies above the length of the mighty river. The Saskatchewan carries many things along with its countless tons of gray silt. Seeds of fringed gentian and gold particles are two that are rarer; and so more precious.

The young Saskatchewan increases quickly with the union of the waters of the Howse and Mistaya rivers, not far to the west of the bridge known as Saskatchewan Crossing. Howse River flows from a group of rushing mountain streams in the vicinity of the famous Howse Pass, in the Great Divide, over which David Thompson toiled in 1807 on his way to explore the Columbia River, some thirty miles to the west. The Mistaya valley provides tourists on the Banff-Jasper Highway with some of the finest scenery in the Rockies, and the river gathers up the waters of Peyto Lake, at the foot of Peyto Glacier, to flow north at the dividing height of Bow Pass. For many a decade Mistaya's dramatic plunge down Mistaya Canyon has awed travelers who made the long trip by pack horse up from Lake Louise station, the nearest accessible point to the railway, and, until 1942, the nearest by road.

The main sources of the North Saskatchewan are the vast glaciers, remnants of the last ice age that covered most of the North American continent. Snow covered, split by crevasses in August, only rarely is the actual ice visible, and then it is blue-green, and marked and polished like fine marble. Acre after acre, hundreds of feet in depth, the glaciers fill in and soften the valleys between mountains so high as to delay the sunrise and hasten the moment when the sun finally dips behind them. Down in the valleys, where commences the young river—and it is a young river geologically speaking—moose feeding in the lush Waterhen Lakes of the Mistaya

River valley will be blurred in semidusk while sunrise or sunset flares brilliant above the rocky walls of the valley. Time was when the Waterhen Lakes were well named, when this valley was a regular flyway for millions of migratory birds, now lured these fifty years or so to the grainfields of the foothills.

It is cold up there, even at the 6,000-foot altitude where much of the river takes form. Above the tree line, at the actual sources, summertime is a brief disturbing season in the long, cold, and generally brilliant year. Seasoned guides in Banff National Park claim that one becomes accustomed to the altitude. They ought to know. The mere visitor never quite knows whether it is altitude or more majestic beauty than he can appreciate that makes him feel so breathless. But anyone who has been awed at the sources and then followed the Saskatchewan to its mouth understands and easily excuses those characteristics of mild exaggeration and not so mild optimism which have become associated with its country. For the river has left its mark on man at least as much as man has left his mark on the river, and this will continue to be so, even when the most ambitious plans for utilizing its waters for power and irrigation have been accomplished.

Well down in the foothills the Saskatchewan takes in the Brazeau and then the Clearwater rivers. At the confluence with the latter the explorer David Thompson stayed at Rocky Mountain House and made his plans to reach the then mythical western sea with the gap in the mountains through which the Saskatchewan flows ever beckoning like an open door.

Below Rocky Mountain House the river flows on and down through the deep channel it is still cutting, past the city of Edmonton; by Fort Pitt, once an important pemmican-distributing point in the fur trade days; on to the Battlefords, where it gathers in the historic Battle River of Indian war fame, and so to Prince Albert and its meeting with its greatest tributary, the vast South Saskatchewan. The Forks, as this great meeting of the waters has long been called, was once the site of the first white man's house built up the river. No one knows for how long before that year, 1749, Indians met there in the spring, or parted in the autumn to go on their lonely trapping expeditions. The river doesn't tell all it knows.

For the most part, the North Saskatchewan flows through forest and park land. The South Branch is the main watercourse for the entire prairie proper. Down its deep and sometimes gorgelike valley races enough water each spring to irrigate millions of acres of land that know recurrent cycles of severe drought. Farmers and ranchers and town dwellers hesitate to cross its shuddering bridges during the raging torrents of spring and early summer. Gazing at the low waters of August they wonder if the river could possibly have been so high when the ice went out.

Though the Saskatchewan has always been variable, its low waters provided the Indians and the fur traders, and even the early settlers, with an opportunity for reasonably safe fording. Today, with bridges to cross, some folk wish a little of that lost water could be stored for use during dry spells; others are busy making surveys and striving to persuade Parliament to grant the necessary funds to transmute wishes into water.

Some sources of the South Saskatchewan rise in Montana, below the border between Canada and the United States of America, the 49th parallel. An international water commission handles the ticklish problems concerning the amount of water that shall be available to the state of Montana and the province of Alberta. The St. Mary, the Belly, and the Waterton River start in the mountains of Glacier National Park, while the Old Man, the Highwood, the Little Bow, and the Bow rise on the eastern slopes of the Great Divide in southern Alberta. There is often a little local discussion as to how the Belly and the Bow got their names. Some argue, without an intimate knowledge of history, that these words are adaptations of French words used by the early voyageurs of the fur trade, "le beau" to the right, and "la belle" to the left. But since these waters were scarcely known to the voyageurs and not at all suitable to the canoe, it is more reasonable to assume that the Belly was named for or by the Gros Ventre, or Big Belly, Indians, and the Bow for beautiful Bow Lake up above Lake Louise, which is actually bow shaped. Banff is on the Bow River and the Highwood boasts as its tributary Pekisko Creek where the Duke of Windsor's famous EP ranch is situated.

The South Saskatchewan actually starts where the Old Man, having gathered up the St. Mary, the Belly, and the Waterton, joins the Bow in southeastern Alberta between the cities of Lethbridge and Medicine Hat. Already the combined waters have cut a valley hundreds of feet below the prairie level, a valley crosscut by coulees and, where it is not too steep, covered with the only shrubs and trees known to the Indians in these parts before the coming of the white man and his carefully tended windbreaks and parks. But the South Branch still has another strong stream to swell its floodwaters. Turning sharply at Medicine Hat, it angles northeastward to the border between the provinces of Alberta and Saskatchewan and in a deep, impressive valley unites with the Red Deer, which, too, rose in the mountains, close to Bow Pass. It is strange that these rivers, rising so close to each other, spread out across the foothills and the prairies, only to unite again in the wide main Saskatchewan at the Forks east of Prince Albert.

There are two cities whose homes and parks and places of business cluster along the banks of the South Branch, Medicine Hat in the province of Alberta and Saskatoon in Saskatchewan. Medicine Hat is just within the vast area blessed by the ever-incredible, ever-welcome chinook. Because it has so much natural gas its street lights for years were never turned off, day or night. There is much controversy as to how Medicine Hat received its name. The Geographic Board of Canada points out that the name and site appeared on a North West Mounted Police report for 1882. Sir William Van Horne of the Canadian Pacific Railway also is given credit for naming the new town in 1883, after hearing an Indian legend, the one about the brave who eloped with the youngest and comeliest wife of an important chief; when, after a couple of moons, the wife became lonesome for her own people she dreamed that the wrath of her former husband could be appeased by the gift of a war bonnet made from the tail feathers of seven eagles.

Another popular version is that the name Medicine Hat is derived from the Cree *muskike ustotin*, which means medicine hat or bonnet. Long, long ago, before the white man came, there was a Cree warrior who owned a magic war bonnet; when he wore it he was always victorious in war and successful in the buffalo hunt. What he had not realized, and what has taken the white man many bitter years of trial and error to realize, is that no one can count too much on the effect of prairie winds; even the chinook dries the moisture from the soil, and some winds are whirlwinds. It was a whirlwind which caught up the warrior's bonnet just as he was about to lead a party of Crees against their traditional enemies, the Blackfeet, camped near a ford on the river. Fortuitously the wind tossed the bonnet into the river and the warrior, brave as he was and quick to plunge after it, never recaptured his bonnet. The cunning Blackfeet took advantage of the sudden demoralization of the enemy and captured the Crees and the bonnetless warrior. From that day, so runs this particular legend, the place has been known as Medicine Hat. But sentimental as it is, the legend is scorned by poetic old-timers, who see in the hills east of the city the very shape of a medicine man's bonnet.

Saskatoon is a city with an air, a string of beautiful bridges across its wide stretch of river and a university whose founders had the good sense to organize a faculty of agriculture along with their arts. Like all the cities of the Canadian

West it is new, so new that its public services are all modern. The university, scarcely thought of at the turn of the century, is housed on a planned campus and in buildings constructed of handsome cut gray stone. Originally started as a temperance colony, Saskatoon's chief reminder of those first lofty intentions is, in 1949, a single street called Temperance. It has one of the most beautifully situated hotels in the country, the Bessborough, named for a one-time governor general and topped with a billowing plume of smoke and steam which is invaluable to the citizens of Saskatoon. To know which way the wind is blowing, and the direction of the wind may mean a storm or fine weather, perhaps even disaster or success for a year, they consult the Bessborough's smoke plume. You can see it for thirty-two miles. Only the deep valley of the river breaks the prairie's flatness.

The country across which the giant letter Y has been etched isn't really flat. It only appears so when you stand on the plains of the three prairie steppes that rise from Manitoba to Alberta, the plains referred to locally, and affectionately, as having a "40-mile horizon." It is flat in these areas, as flat as any table. Yet always the river is flowing downhill, when it isn't actually rushing. Folks who live on the rolling grass or park lands can't bear the flat plains. Those who enjoy far horizons, uninterrupted except by grain elevators and telegraph poles, wonder, sympathetically, how people anywhere else have enough room to breathe. But the same water flows by all of them, and they love it.

This, then, is its geography. It is still cutting its course, and full of meanders, because it has not yet found its level. It is still working hard, shifting tons of rock and soil every day, making rich river bottoms and smoothing away sharp bends—when it isn't making new ones. At a point on the united river, near the Manitoba-Saskatchewan border, an average of eighteen million acre-feet of water flow past each year. The weight of this flow is calculated to be fifty-six million tons a day, though this is most unevenly divided over the year. Spring floods bring many times the average acre-feet. In late summer folks comment on the rising sand bars.

"Never saw so many sand bars, this time of year," they opine August after August. "The river must be low!"

Obviously the Saskatchewan is not a good river for boats. Its depth is seldom more than twelve feet, often less. There are sand bars and shoals to complicate navigation. There are rapids. But it had its day as one of the greatest highways of discovery and commerce on the continent, perhaps in the entire world. A swift, glorious, unforgettable day. It did nicely for canoes; great flat York boats managed because they were built to suit its terms. There was even one brief era when steam and paddle wheels were talked about and a few boats built, just before the railways came. It makes one of the stories which scientists would list as negative information.

You can't make a picture of the real prairies without adding a focus, a human being or something he has made, such as grain elevators, telegraph poles, or a town; or an animal. You can't picture the Saskatchewan without people. Not a lot. Never vast crowds. Just a few here and there, once in a while or once in a few hundred miles lured somehow to its banks or on to its treacherous waters, hopeful, questing, willing to strive. And so much depends upon the extent to which they are willing to strive. If that willingness is adequate, the Saskatchewan will see that they make good. Not that there is any magic about it, except the magic of opportunity and optimism and always another horizon for those who have a longing for new horizons. It was something of this that attracted the discoverers and the fur traders.

Some discoverers and fur voyageurs using it as a highway thought it might be the Northwest Passage. From the day the main river was traversed by young Louis-Joseph de la Vérendrye in 1749 until settlers began to arrive in the late nineteenth century, peltries of fabulous wealth were floated down its comparatively shallow reaches; along its shores men fought bitterly for right of way.

It took a little rebellion to mark the transition from the culture of the red man to that of the white. History books call it the North West Rebellion and in 1885 the Canadian government hanged the leader, Louis Riel, a métis, or half-breed.

When the explorers and traders had had their day there came a hiatus in the Saskatchewan's story. The pioneers found the river handy for watering stock, sometimes for local barging, often on hot days for swimming within the protection of a sand bar. But they were too busy herding cattle or breaking soil to give much attention to a river with a deep valley and a lot of shifting mud shoals. They had to contend with catastrophes of drought and weather and low prices. They had to keep themselves comparatively sober when surrounded by the heady wine of success during years in which the Canadian West produced more wheat gold than all the gold mined in the world. They were busy building roads and schools, houses and grain elevators. They had to adapt the seeds of grains and of trees to their own climatic conditions. Not even wheat is native to the Saskatchewan River country.

A polyglot of human beings was lured to its banks. Mr. Clifford Sifton's "Man in the sheepskin coat with the big, broad wife" was often nearest neighbor to the younger son of the British aristocracy and his unaccustomed-to-work lady. Slavs and Magyars, Mennonites and Mormons, Swedes and Scots and Frenchmen—and, of course, the half-breeds who sprang from those many and often successful marriages which took place in early days without benefit of book and bell—they were neighbors. A neighbor might be thirty or fifty or a hundred miles across the prairie or bushland; but if he were your nearest neighbor you got to know him.

Now, once more, the river has come into its own. The period of trial and error has not passed, but it is passing. Men and women and children have learned how to live on the Saskatchewan as they have had to learn to live everywhere else on earth. History is repeating itself, with variations. The fur traders used the river as it was, a highway suited to the means of transportation of their day. It gathered men and their supplies and carried them slowly up, but more quickly and more easily downstream to the east. With the new era man is again using the river.

Irrigation is on every lip in the South Saskatchewan country and on many in the north. Growers of the world's best hard wheat do not want irrigation. They know that only the combination of comparative drought and high temperature can produce the precious life-giving gold. But there are those who want crops other than wheat, coarse grains and vegetables and small fruits, which in turn need water. People living in the great gateway to the north, Edmonton, are in the market. So they all look to their river and its tributaries.

The Saskatchewan way is not a soft way; it makes men and women of character, or it breaks them. Some of them have been forced to leave on account of drought, ill-health, or their own ineptitude. Some have taken and are taking to other parts of the world their heritage of courage and resourcefulness and the vision that is born of far horizons and rugged living. Often, when people get old, they seek an easier climate only to spend their time in getting together to talk about the good old days.

Like the stars in the belt of Orion, which it reflects, the river cuts across the central provinces of Canada. Its basin forms a large part of that territory to which Frances Shelley Wees refers in her prose poem entitled

Geography Lesson

Here is Canada, here is a map spread out upon the page. Can you name its bright boundaries? Do you perceive the depth of its coloring? Do you know its dimensions?

It is a broad, clean country stretching between two islands.

On the west, on the edge of the sunset, the Island of Vancouver lies in the froth and lace of the Pacific. Rugged and rocky, dotted with black lakes, it holds the wilderness still in its heart. The tribal gods of the Indians guard the silence lying behind the cities. The bear roams its hills, the soft-eyed deer hides in its forests until the logger comes with his great shining tools to cut away the shadow.

On the east, facing the foam of the grey Atlantic, is another Island. It has no wildernesses, no tree grows there without being known, no dell holds strange flowers. It is an old island, and covered now with peace. Its children leave it as young robins leave a nest that has grown too small. The Indians called it the Cradle in the Wave; it is a gentle cradle now, it rocks softly and slow.

Above it, in the surge and swell of the cold dark water, is that new found land. Hidden in fog, encircled by ocean, it long lay proud and alone. Now its once empty air flashes and beats with a myriad bright new wings.

Between the islands is the great sweep of the mainland. When you look at the map, look with dreaming eyes; the country is wider and deeper and bigger than any map could show.

It holds the Rockies; they are like giants sleeping under a ragged green blanket piled with snow. Some day, you think, watching them crowd up against the sky, some day they will wake, or turn in their dreaming, and shatter the world.

It holds the prairie. The prairie is the home of wonder. The world bends away from you there, as you stand on a grassy knoll, as you stand with your hands filled with the pale early flowers and stare and stare into the distance. The world bends away too far, to the very bowl's edge of the sky. You can see into the sky; when the northern lights flash in the summer darkness, you can see the gates of heaven behind the glittering bars.

This is the geography of Canada, the islands, the mountains, the plains, the strong rivers.

The old provinces in the east have geography, too, but you can scarcely see it for people. The old provinces cannot be thought of as geography. They lie in our minds as history, they lie in our hearts as home. They are our proud past, and in them still grows, slow and strong, the old mother-root of our proud future.

This is something, a very little, of Canada. It is bounded on the north by gold, on the west by the East, on the east by history, and on the south by friends.

It is our country.

CHAPTER TWO

Saskatchewan

THE Indians called it "Kisiskatchewan," the river that flows rapidly. For many years they talked about it to the white men who came in ships to Hudson Bay and by canoe up the rivers and lakes to the east. Down its swift waters they brought peltries to barter for tobacco and brandy or rum, bright beads, and the iron that shoots fire. It was the highway to the great Manitoba, the water of the prairies, and the lake the merry singing Frenchmen called "Ouinniping," the way that led from the plains of the buffalo and the land of many fur-bearing animals. The Indians talked of vast mountains toward the setting sun and a far-off blue water.

Not every white man's ears were open to the sayings of the red men. But some listened. Some, coming to the New World from the Old, dreamed day and night of finding a passage to the Western Sea. Some, also coming to the new land from the old, dreamed of a more immediate and a more personal reward, a fortune from furs. A few combined business with altruism and sought to make the fortune while they were searching for the Pacific Ocean.

Usually it was the French who came up the rivers and lakes by canoe. The English arrived in great white-sailed ships chartered by the group of London traders known since 1670 as the Company of Adventurers Trading into Hudson's Bay, anchoring at the new forts of York, Prince of Wales (now Churchill), and Albany. It was not by accident that the French strung their posts along the routes used by the Indians when bringing furs to the English. The trade was a lucrative one.

Characteristically the English didn't go to seek the Indians and their rich cargoes. They adopted the attitude that "with civility and good usage" the Indians would come to them. The French, on the other hand, troubled themselves to win the loyalty and friendship of the red men. They provided feasts and entertained at the long ceremonial gatherings the Indians loved. They gave them gifts. To a large extent they lived their kind of life. They got a lot of furs.

With a big investment in the land some Englishmen began to realize that more than civility and fair play was required. Also, some of them saw that the life the French were living close to the Indians was greatly to be preferred to the austere English relationship of master and servant. One such was Henry Kelsey, who may have been more Irish than English from his scant records.

Henry Kelsey had entered the employ of the Hudson's Bay Company as a mere boy, back in 1684. He had seen service along the forts of the bay with des Groseilliers and Radisson. According to old company records, he was "a very active lad, delighting much in Indians' company, being never better pleased than when he is travelling with them," a man rare among the Englishmen of his day. He learned to speak the Cree language fluently, and could make his way in Assiniboin, the tongue of the people "who cook on stones." In common with many a Frenchman before him, and later, he liked Cree women. To Kelsey it was perfectly natural to travel with the Indians, to go inland with them and persuade them to "work beaver."

The trip from York Factory led along the accustomed route of wide rivers and narrow lakes well known to the Indians who brought furs to the white traders. After many days of travel Kelsey came with them to a wide river with many white rapids, a river which the Indians called Kisiskatchewan. They paddled out into the wide, swift-flowing river and Kelsey made a base camp, calling it Dering's Point, after the then deputy governor of the Hudson's Bay Company. He was the first white man to visit the Saskatchewan. The year was 1691.

Kelsey's canoes were heavily laden and the Indians told him of fine hunting grounds to the south, down toward the land of the Assiniboin (or Sioux). Kelsey, with more wisdom than foresight, decided not to paddle against that mighty current, and cached his heavy cargo, to return for it later. Apparently he spent a pleasant enough year with the Indians. They took him out to the prairies where the men hunted buffalo and the women made pemmican for the winter's food supply. Emulating the French, Kelsey gave the natives gifts with much ceremony. The first trip of a white man to the Saskatchewan, even though it is not certain that he actually traveled on the river, seems to have been mutually satisfactory. He returned to the fort in the spring with a good fleet of Indians, the desired furs, and the news, which must have reached French ears, that the Saskatchewan was indeed a vast river, so vast that it might reach the Western Sea. The English may have heard but they did not heed his news. Much later someone named a lake in his memory.

Pierre Gaultier de Varennes, Sieur de la Vérendrye was a Frenchman with very good ears. La Vérendrye had served

France well, in New England, and later in Europe where he was wounded at the Battle of Malplaquet in 1709. Because of these services and because he was profoundly interested in the search for the Western Sea he was granted the monopoly of the fur trade in the Northwest and set out from Montreal in June of 1731. Unfortunately for him, however, his government did not see fit to finance his projected explorations and he had to pay his own way, largely from the fur trade with the Indians. His position was far from easy. The two projects, exploration and the development and maintenance of a paying fur trade, did not combine well. La Vérendrye was continually forced to show that he was not neglecting the one for the other. In Montreal the businessmen who had backed the venture were bitter in their accusations, while the good will of the government cooled as the western passage failed to materialize. Truly his precarious position could not fail to sharpen his ears.

Broadly, the English had established their fur posts to the north along Hudson Bay, while the French strung theirs like beads along the rivers and lakes from Superior to Winnipeg. Perhaps the trip of young Kelsey was having some effect. Perhaps there were other considerations. But La Vérendrye began to be a little more aware of those English forts which were also fur posts. Spurred, on the one hand, by necessity for curtailing the activities of the English so as to retain his own fur trade and, on the other, by the sharp goading from Montreal and Quebec, La Vérendrye still had his own great desire to discover that western passage. When, after many long and successful exploration trips, he had to return to Montreal to defend his position he left his youngest son, Louis-Joseph, called the Chevalier, in command.

Louis-Joseph was educated to command under such circumstances as prevailed around Lake Winnipeg in the seventeen-forties. As a boy he had been trained in mathematics and drawing so that he could make maps of the country he explored. With his older brother he had made a trip of incredible hardship and daring up the Missouri to what they thought was within sight of the Rocky Mountains. He had survived a massacre at Fort St. Charles. He had his father's happy faculty for winning the affection of the Indians, and he spoke Cree well. In fact he was an adopted son of the Crees and had wintered with some of them at the lower part of Lake Winnipeg. He knew the land of white water at the mouth of the great river sometimes known as the White Water, sometimes as the Pascoyac, the Saskatchewan.

Winnipeg is a very large lake, the largest in any of the provinces of Canada. Young La Vérendrye spent much time exploring its low shore line, especially in the vicinity of those beckoning rapids above the mouth of the river that leads to the west. He explored the rivers and smooth lakes so as to avoid the rapids and founded a fort at the confluence of a small, less-turbulent stream with the Saskatchewan, calling it Fort Bourbon. It was there, in the spring of 1749, that he prepared for the voyage that his father could not then take, but which he, Chevalier Louis-Joseph, would gladly undertake for the honor of the name of La Vérendrye and on behalf of King Louis XV. He had the assurance of the Indians that, with comparatively light loads, they could travel it for many moons' paddling. With high excitement he embarked on his great adventure.

This trip was to be the culmination of all the voyages his father and he and his brothers had taken and had talked about, ever since Louis-Joseph was a child. It was the one voyage, above all others, most likely to bring to the family of La Vérendrye the distinction that their intricate fortunes demanded. The young man thought of the delight with which he should journey east to Montreal, of the scene when he should tell his father of this vast highway to the west.

The river was very wide, the current strong and fast. Paddling against it was slow and laborious work. One must think of the ease with which heavily laden canoes could make their return. One must think, too, of the vast lands to be explored, lands rich with beaver, those darkened with buffalo, of the places where the tribes rode fleet-footed horses and never used canoes. So Louis-Joseph told himself as his men dug paddles into the strong current. He knew now why some Indians called it white water. Like lace it swirled against its low-wooded banks, no dream under the clear summer sky but probably the reality for which he had been born.

The men sang with the strong, digging rhythm of canoe-men pulling against the stream. What a country! What a river! The Crees had brought back copper when they traveled north to the land of the Dogribs. There was game aplenty, moose and fine deer, and fish in the river. Louis-Joseph de la Vérendrye was making the observations which Governor-General La Jonquière would shortly use in his report on the Discovery of the Pascoyac, 1749.

"The river [Pascoyac] is the most convenient route by which to pursue the discovery of the western sea from the ease with which you can transfer your effects thither by canoe, get guides there easily and have always the same tribe, Cree, to deal with as far as the height of land, which is not the case by the prairie road. There you encounter different tribes, all enemies, and different languages, causes of hindrance and difficulty which occasioned considerable expense formerly."

If only his father were with him on this route! But he would be next year, or the year after.

Day after day the canoes struggled up the river, their progress not fast because the current was so strong, yet every day a little nearer their objective. La Vérendrye made careful notes and drew his maps. He chose a possible site for a fort on the waterway where the Indians could be prevented from taking their furs to the English at Forts York and Prince of Wales. It was called Pascoyac. Traveling many leagues they finally came upon a great disturbance of the waters and the river divided into two, one branch apparently going due west, the other to the southwest. It was the Forks, the spring rendezvous of the Crees, the place where they went to deliberate whether to trade with the English or the French.

With a La Vérendrye on the river, the first white man to voyage even to the Forks, there was no doubt as to which country would get the bulk of the fur that year.

Louis-Joseph did not go beyond the Forks. Joyfully he headed his canoes downstream, east to Montreal to tell his father the great news of the Saskatchewan.

The news of a probable route to the Western Sea, certainly of a route to the great mountains, came just in time for the elder La Vérendrye. He died before Christmas in the midst of preparations for the next summer's trip which, he was now certain, would take him right to his goal. Grief stricken, the son at once petitioned to return, knowing full well the importance of the discovery of the river to the fur trade, anxious to learn what was at its source. Unfortunately for him, neither he nor his brother was appointed successor to the Sieur de la Vérendrye who had been so devoted a servant of France. Louis-Joseph was not allowed to return to the Saskatchewan as its discoverer. He died embittered and poor, the victim of a colonial minister who had not the king's interest in the western posts, perhaps the victim of the times.

Had those in authority in New France recognized the greatness of the Vérendryes, either as fur traders or as explorers, the Saskatchewan River might well have had a different story to tell of a different people. Who knows? Even one strong fort, such as the one at Pascoyac which La Vérendrye's sons were building when he died, might have held the fur trade for the French against the English.

The Sieur de la Vérendrye's command went to an officer who had been in charge at Michilimackinac, Jacques Repentigny Legardeur de Saint-Pierre, who could not speak Cree and who had not La Vérendrye's understanding of the Indians. But even he could not disregard the challenge of the discovery of the Saskatchewan. He dispatched a party of ten

Frenchmen in two canoes westward in the spring of 1751. Their instructions were to establish a fort some three hundred leagues west where, it was believed, they would be close to the sources of the Missouri and rivers that ran west to the sea. This venture fell far short of its mark, for, like that of Louis-Joseph de la Vérendrye, it got little farther than the Forks, where, instead of a great fort three hundred leagues west, they built a small fort and called it La Jonquière. A couple of years later another French party under Chevalier de La Corne paddled up to the Forks and built another fort, calling it La Corne, an outpost for the growing fort of Pascoyac.

In the space of three years three Frenchmen had made the trip up the Saskatchewan to its forks, but so far no white man, French or English, had penetrated to the mountains of which the Indians so often talked. The Indians were given to tall tales. Who knew but what these mountains were fabrications made to entertain the white men! Who knew but what western seas were the same!

There was more at stake, immediately, than finding the mountains or even the western sea. The erection of Fort La Corne threatened drastically to curtail the quantity of furs that would reach the English, still clinging to their forts along Hudson Bay. The new French fort completed a string of fur posts all the way from Rainy River to Lake Winnipeg and right up the new river, the Saskatchewan. The Company of Adventurers back in London found their dividends slipping. That was signal enough.

James Isham, governor of Fort York, heard from London. He was the right man to hear from London, too, because he had more than once remembered Kelsey's unique trip with the Indians. He had wondered whether survival for the English company didn't depend on going after business instead of waiting for business to come to the bay forts. Something had to be done to offset the effect of good French brandy. When Governor Isham heard that a French post was to be built on the Severn, right across the English life line, he called for volunteers to go into the country of the beaver and other fur-bearing animals, right to where the Indians would be trapping. In 1754 Anthony Henday volunteered.

Henday had come from the Isle of Wight. Company records show that he had made his living smuggling, at which he might have done very well if he hadn't had the misfortune to be caught. While smuggling wasn't frowned on socially in England at the time, it brought a penalty of outlawry. The Hudson's Bay Company may or may not have known of the outlaw sentence. In any event they hired Anthony as a laborer, adding a bonus for his netmaking skill. He turned out to be "a bold and good servant."

They tried him out carefully before sending him off among the Indians as a representative, even though his rank was that of servant. The French had always employed gentlemen for such duties. After a spell dragging the measuring wheel and doing some general surveys about the bay, Henday was outfitted and on June 26, 1754, sent off with a band of Indians who came to trade with the Hudson's Bay Company. They had come all the way, so they said, from the land of the Blackfeet, the Earchithinues, or stranger Indians, from the land below the great mountains where there are no canoes and where the Indians ride horses. The English didn't believe the story about the horses.

These trading Indians adopted Henday like a brother and their leader, Conawapa, became his close companion. They took him to the Saskatchewan by one of the easiest routes from York Factory, avoiding the rapids at the mouth and entering the large river by the smaller Summerberry River, not far from Pascoyac. Henday visited Fort Pascoyac (The Pas), the first Englishman to visit one of the French forts on the river. He had been instructed to keep a journal and in it he wrote:

On my arrival two French men came out, when followed a

great deal of Bowing and Scraping between us, and then we entered their fort (or more properly a Hogstye) for in short it is no better: they have neither victuals nor drink. Except a little Ruhigan [dried meat]; they are very lazy, not one stick of wood anigh their house; They asked me where the letter was. I told them I had no letter nor did not see any reasons for one, but that the country belonged to us as much as to them: he made answer it did not, and that he would detain me there, and send me home to france. I said I knew france as well as he did and was not afraid to go, more than himself, which made Monsieur a little Cooler.

However, this historic visit on the Saskatchewan turned out to be not too unfriendly. Henday wrote that "the Master invited me to sup with him and was very kind; He is very Genteel, but the men wear nothing but thin drawers, & striped cotton shirts ruffled at the hands and breast. This House has long been a place of Trade belonging to the French, & named Basquea. It is 26 feet long; 12 feet wide, 9 feet to the ridge; having a sloping roof, the walls log on Log; the top covered with Birch rind, fastened together with Willows."

There were three apartments, one each for trading goods, furs, and dwelling. Actually it was not more than three or four years old. It was the only real building on the Saskatchewan.

Next day Henday gave the Master two feet of "Brazile" tobacco, and received in return a gift of dried meat. Apparently, though, the three canoes only paddled a few miles up the river at that time, cutting off into the smoother waters of Saskeram Lake to avoid the strong current of the river where it bends north. Henday might have gone on, but his Indians found signs indicating that their families were in the valley of the Carrot, a tributary of the Saskatchewan to the south. The pull of kin was stronger than the pull of the river. Canoes were abandoned, soon the families were reached, and everyone hurried on to the rich hunting grounds of many berries and moose and red deer.

It was a land of plenty, probably in the parkland of what is now Saskatchewan province, and south of the river. Then, it seems, the parkland reached farther into the prairies than is the case today. Henday and his Indian friends did a lot of hunting. They celebrated their reunion, too, with feasting, those gargantuan feasts which the Indians manage when they have plenty to eat, and of which Hudson's Bay Company men often wrote "You can never fill an Indian." There was drinking and conjuring and much talking and visiting with other Indians, never very many, for actually the Indian population was incredibly small in comparison with the expanse of its hunting grounds. Once when Henday met two tents of Assiniboins he told them who he was and took great pains to invite them to come to his forts to trade. But they were independent. They told him they were well supplied by the French. Such contacts Henday noted in his journal, as he had been instructed to do, along with comments on the weather, the country, and the food supply. He soon found that he could not do all this and keep up with the other men without the assistance of a squaw.

He wrote "I am not behind, thank God, a good stomach, and as I am looked on as a Leader, I have Ladies of different ranks to attend me; please to observe the men does nothing but hunt, and we Leaders hath a Lady to hold the thogin with water to our heads when we drink."

Henday's particular lady not only carried much of his luggage, but she was invaluable in keeping him informed as to what the Indians were saying and planning. She seems to have been a congenial bedfellow, especially on cold, dark winter nights when blizzards howled out of the north. Such relationships were not allowed by the eminently proper and austere Governor and Company of Adventurers Trading into Hudson's Bay, individually living in warm beds in warm houses. Even the governor in his cozy fort at York Factory at the mouth of the Nelson River omitted all mention of such comforts when sending on his report to London. Doubtless it was as well that Henday made his own decisions on that long trip into the completely unknown and, by white men, unexplored territory of the West. He had been instructed to live like an Indian. He did.

By the 17th of August Henday and his Indians had traveled hundreds of miles across the bushland and some prairie and came out upon a vast river, the south branch of the Saskatchewan. He called it the Waskesew, or Red Deer, the Assiniboin equivalent of the Opah, their name for the united Saskatchewan.

It was a fine sight to come upon, after having traveled across the prairie. Henday stood on the high banks and looked across the deep valley to the distant plains, the first white man to do so. He saw the deep, muddy reaches, shining as they do in the clear, bright air. The riverbanks were covered with birch, "poplo," hazel, elder, and some fir. The river was very wide, the current fast and strong. They had no canoes in which to cross, having left them far behind on the banks of the Carrot. But the Indians had been this way before. They soon made bumboats.

Choosing willow from the riverbanks, they fashioned frames which they covered with cured moose skins. There was not much to carry across but themselves and Henday's notebooks, compass, and gifts. When they had crossed, the bumboats were abandoned as the canoes had been. Beyond the river there was an abundance of game, moose, in the woods along the Battle River, which the Indians knew, buffalo on the prairies. No great game hunter anywhere in the world could have had a better time than Henday. The sport was royal.

Hunting as they went, the party traveled southwest, Henday noting the rivers they crossed, all tributaries of the Saskatchewan, for the Indians knew their way up and down them to the great river. Toward the middle of October they crossed today's Red Deer, "another vast stream," and a tributary, and soon after met a party of Blackfeet. Henday had reached the country of the Earchithinues. He had made another record. The Rockies were over his right shoulder, the still far-off mountains that lifted the horizon from the foothills into the very clouds. That was cause for rejoicing. For the white man it was more. Anthony Henday, outlawed smuggler, servant of the Hudson's Bay Company, the only white man in at least a thousand miles, knew what it meant, even though he was a fur trader and not an explorer.

Henday's Indians knew the Blackfeet. They had many good times together. But Henday didn't let his good times make him forget his duty to his masters, the company. He went to call on the leader of the Blackfeet, a combined business and social call.

The chief received him cordially. There were two hundred tepees in the main Blackfoot village, placed in parallel rows. Young Henday marched down the space between the tepees, well aware of the black eyes that watched from every dark Indian face. None had seen a white man before. At the end of the street stood the chief's lodge, large enough to seat fifty persons, well decorated according to the owner's rank with a sizable string of scalps at the entrance.

The chief made the sign of welcome, and Henday entered. He sat down beside the chief on the sacred white buffalo robe.

They smoked in silence, several pipes going the round of the chief and his guest and the council. After a time boiled buffalo meat was brought in. The guest was given ten tongues, the choicest part, as his portion. When the ceremonies were over he formally presented his message through his interpreter; Henday was fluent in Cree, but he had not the language of the Earchithinues.

He said "O chief, I have been sent by the great leader who lives by the great waters to invite your young men to come to him with their beaver skins and wolf skins. They will be given in return powder, shot, cloth, and many fine beads."

The chief replied through the interpreter that the white

man's fort was far off and that his young men knew not the use of paddles. While he was courteous, he was obviously not greatly impressed. Henday was invited to return next day.

Again he repeated his invitation. He promised the young men every kindness, much goods in exchange. But the chief remained calm and aloof. Again he told Henday that the white man's forts were far away, and that his people could not live without the flesh of the buffalo. He pointed out that he had heard that people who journeyed to the forts of the white man sometimes went hungry, that some failed to return.

Anthony Henday knew that the old chief spoke the truth. He had done his best, and he had been well received. Now he must leave without any promise that the Blackfeet would come down to Fort York. But the mountains to the west had made a deep impression on him. Solemnly he took his leave of them, standing on a little knoll. Like the Indians, whose ways were becoming so familiar, he addressed the Rockies, the *Arsinie Watchie*, saying farewell, and that he would not again see them this year.

He struck off north, hoping to secure furs and canoes when they came to the great river of which the Indians told him and down which, so they said, he could travel to the great water of the prairies, Lake Winnipeg.

There was deep ice on the North Saskatchewan when Henday finally reached it. For many miles he and his Indians traveled on it till they came to the place where canoes could be made, a great meeting place, possibly the Thickwood Hills.

Spring is a momentous time for the Indians. From their hunting grounds each family journeyed to the spring rendezvous. As the ice melted and the river opened many canoes appeared, each laden with bundles of furs. Still awed by the magnitude of the river, Henday was almost equally awed by the wealth of pelts that confronted him. Business began to look up.

On the 23rd of April, 1755, he made a great celebration

in honor of St. George's Day. The Indians did not know St. George, but they were always ready for a feast. They admired Henday's flag and listened attentively to the story of his patron saint. They ate enormously. There was much drumming and dancing, and many long after-dinner speeches. This was what the Indians loved. Henday knew that St. George was merely an excuse. He realized, too, that feasting and dancing would attract more furs than all the civility in the world. When he was ready to start his journey downstream he had a flotilla of sixty canoes.

It was a great moment for a mere servant of the Hudson's Bay Company paddling with his Indians in so vast an array, down the wide reaches of the river, under the high banks with the clear blue sky above. Spring was in their blood. Tall trees and shrubs made the islands pleasant. The waters were fast and carried much sediment. Even though the canoes were low and heavily laden, paddling meant little more than steering. They carried food in abundance, pemmican prepared during the winter, fresh moose, and red deer venison. They carried a vast wealth in beaver and marten from the woods Indians, fox and bear and wolf from the prairies.

The trip downstream was swift and comparatively easy. In an amazingly short time they came to another great river which the Indians identified as the Waskesew, the south branch of the Saskatchewan. Just below the mighty confluence there was the French post of La Corne. Henday's flotilla of canoes spread along the shore, and Henday went to call on the governor of the French post. Perhaps he wanted to show off to these Frenchmen, to let them see his vast wealth in furs. Perhaps it was the longing to speak to another white man, for he had not seen a white man for almost a year. The French, too, were eager to welcome him.

He wrote in his journal "The governor came with his hatt in his hand, and followed a great deal of Bowing and Scraping, but he neither understood me nor I him, he treated me with 2 glasses of Brandy and half a Bisket; this evening he gave the Indians 2 gallons of Brandy, but he got very little trade."

There were but six men in the small, primitive fort, and they lived up to the French tradition of friendship with the Indians. In time the brandy did its work, as the French had intended. Next day there was more, ten gallons in all, adulterated with water. Ten gallons of brandy, even when adulterated with Saskatchewan water, went a long way. So did the trading between the Indians and the French. Henday noted that, when intoxicated, the Indians "traded cats, Martens & good Parchment Beaver skins." The French turned down the less valuable wolves and dressed beaver.

"I am certain he hath got above a thousand of the best skins," wrote Henday.

It was four days before he could coax his Indians away from the pleasant company of the French. Out again on the swift river, now with much lower banks, they shot the rapids and paddled on toward Pascoyac, where, after his experience at La Corne, Henday expected more trouble with the French. He was not mistaken. He realized now that the French were instinctively friendly and hospitable where the natives were concerned.

At Pascoyac Henday was invited to breakfast with the master, who took trouble to show the Englishman his "brave parcel of Cased Cats and Parchment Beaver." There was more brandy and much good fellowship. Henday could have had a very pleasant time had he not feared what was happening to his pelts. The Frenchmen were gay. The Indians were happy. The lone Englishman had to exert every shred of tact and persuasion he possessed, hoping to remain on courteous terms with his hosts and yet at the same time to draw off his Indians —and their cargoes.

He wrote, later: "The French talk several languages to perfection; They have the advantage of us in every shape, and if they had Brazile tobacco, which they have not, they would entirely cut off our trade."

Henday must have given devout thanks for that tobacco. It saved the trade. In spite of French brandy he had some seventy canoes with him when he finally reached his destination.

He had traveled well over two thousand miles, the first white man to traverse the united Saskatchewan. He took great care to tell Governor Isham of the Hudson's Bay Company what a vast and pleasant river was the Saskatchewan, and about the game and furs to be found along its course. He told him much of the Rocky Mountains, the *Arsinie Watchie* of the Crees. But when he told the governor about Indians who did not use canoes but who rode everywhere on fleet-footed, well-trained horses, the governor thought it was nonsense and refused to believe it.

Henday and others made several trips on the Saskatchewan during the time of the Seven Years' War. Very few Englishmen were molested by the Indians, though quite a number of Frenchmen were killed and some French posts were burned. While the political fate of the country was being settled in Prussia, on the Plains of Abraham outside Quebec, at Fort Duquesne, and on the high seas, the personal fate of Frenchmen and Englishmen on the Saskatchewan depended largely on squaws and brandy. A white man, as well as an Indian, needed a squaw to do his carrying. But the French, much as they were liked, were a little reckless about women, as well as about brandy. At times they took what they wanted and the Indians took revenge. Characteristically the English were a little more prudent—and perhaps a little less ardent. Securing their young women by purchase and with consent of the parties interested, they also secured a degree of protection from the band of Indians concerned.

CHAPTER THREE

Beaver

KING Charles II of England, like others in his day, made great use of rivers. When, in 1670, the group of adventurers headed by his cousin, Prince Rupert, petitioned for a charter assuring them exclusive trade in the rich furs of certain territories in North America, he granted them that territory which is drained by the rivers flowing into Hudson Bay. King Charles knew little of the extent of the territories concerned. Neither, for that matter, did the petitioners. Most of it was yet to be discovered and the Saskatchewan, the highway of discovery for much of the land in question, was not traversed by white men for some eighty years. The grant turned out to be one of the most valuable in history. Among many other rivers, the Nelson flows into Hudson Bay. Down the Nelson flow the waters of the Saskatchewan and down the Saskatchewan came the furs, not only from the Saskatchewan River country, but from the Peace River, the Athabasca, and from the Mackenzie basin. It was a kingly grant, that territory to be known as Rupertsland, almost half a continent.

Kings and princes did things handsomely in the seventeenth century, as was their privilege. English kings in particular were given to granting sweeping patents to merchant adventurers, grants which, over the years, paid good dividends in one form or another. The English fought for their life lines. They learned early, too, that trade with relatively fair treatment of those who do the work of trading pays much better than waging wars. The group of men who won the monopoly of the best of the North American fur trade were typical Englishmen of their day. They had a bright star on their horizon, the hope of finding a route to the western sea —and more business.

But while trade is essential, kings and statesmen need a loftier means to their ends. The stated reason for this particular grant was that the Governor and Company of Adventurers of England Trading into Hudson's Bay—to give them their full and original title—were financing exploration which would be carried on in the name of England; at the time an adventurer ventured capital in a business enterprise. Few men connected with the company were adventurers in the same sense and to the same extent as were their opponents who eventually appeared in Rupertsland or the Northwest. What the Hudson's Bay Company really had, the quality that made it great and able to withstand a couple of hundred years of competition, was a rather unexciting though thoroughly British ability to hang on in spite of all odds.

The terms of the charter were twofold. There was, of course, the monopoly of trade through Hudson Strait; there was also exclusive possession of any territory to be reached through the strait which it might subsequently lead to, providing such territory did not already belong to some Christian prince. As was common at the time, the company was to assume sole responsibility for governing the new territory, a feature which greatly relieved the motherland and had much to do with the terms. No one could inhabit such territory as might be discovered without consent of the company. Other traders were barred. And the price? The "yielding and paying yearly to us and our successors . . . two elk and two black beaver whensoever, and as often as we, our heirs and successors, shall happen to enter the said countries and regions hereby granted." The ancient obligation was fulfilled when King George VI and Queen Elizabeth visited Canada in 1939.

Stars are remote. While the star that led the servants of the company was the hope of finding a route to the Western Sea, beavers on a river were more readily accessible. It was the small, flat-tailed, industrious beaver that discovered and opened up the Saskatchewan, just as that rodent had led to the discovery of many another North American river. "The colder and the farther north the better" was a known yardstick for beaver quality. Down along the Upper Mississippi traders had found beaver, a little light as to shade, a little thick of skin. From the north, Indians brought much superior pelts, very dark with rich long guard hairs and very fine down. At Michilimackinac and Grand Portage, the two great inland centers of the fur trade, these facts were discussed, possibly with more enthusiasm and understanding than at the factories along Hudson Bay.

Perhaps even the beaver might not have led to discovery of the Saskatchewan so soon had it not been for the eighteenth-century fashion in hats, those wide, fur-felt hats which had long been the rage in the capitals of Europe and the British Isles. The fine hairs of the beaver have many barbs when seen under a microscope, a feature very desirable in felt making for hats. Coat beaver played a part, too, but coats are utilitarian. Fashion is far more fickle and effective. Its place in world discovery must not be regarded too lightly.

Previous to the coming of Europeans there were probably ten million beaver in North America, the number steadily increasing, because beaver, if left alone, increase at the rate of about twenty per cent a year. They migrate little, do not hibernate, and can live in the coldest climate. Small lakes and slow rivers well wooded with birch, poplar, cottonwood, and willow form their natural habitat.

The life and habits of the beaver are a study at least as provocative as that of the ant or the spider, and apparently more useful. The beaver is a monogamist. The young are born in May, averaging from two to five to a litter, and though they are weaned at six weeks, they stay with the mother for a year. Thus a beaver lodge houses several animals of varying ages. In years of abundance there are from ten to fifty beaver per square mile. The Indians trapped them for food as well as for clothing. Mature animals weigh about fifty pounds and although the meat is fat, hungry Indians don't mind that. They, and white men too, consider beaver-tail soup quite a delicacy.

So long as the Indian was armed merely with sticks and stone axes the beaver in his sturdy lodge had a good chance for survival. Iron and guns, coupled with the keen rivalry of competing interests, were almost disastrous. The hunt went on even during summer, when the rivalry was at its height and when the pelts were by no means so valuable as in winter. Lodges were broken through, dams were destroyed, burrows laid dry, and since the beaver takes two years to mature his fate was certain. Trappers gradually killed off the beaver in the East. They pressed farther west and north in search of new rivers. As the distance increased, and new rivers were found, so their need for organizing the transport of trading supplies increased. The fur trade became big business.

With French opposition removed, the Hudson's Bay Company might well have decided to sit back in its factories along Hudson Bay and await its trading Indians in the lordly manner to which it was accustomed, not concerning itself too much with discovery so long as the dividends remained high. That was, in fact, just what it was doing, not by plan so much as by lack of plan. Down east, in the settled parts of Canada and the English colonies which were so soon to become the United States of America, very real adventurers were making very real plans. Some, having been to the territory of Rupertsland during the French regime, were unwilling to acknowledge the English monopoly.

Hudson's Bay Company men who traveled the linking lakes and streams of the Saskatchewan valley during the first twenty-five years after its discovery were referred to as servants. Most were, indeed, servants of the aristocratic English firm rather than employees. Year after year several were sent out with known bands of trading Indians, safe because of the company's treatment of the natives, just, though economical to the point of parsimony. A few colored beads and kettles bought a lot of beaver from savages unfamiliar with the glamour of white man's ways, a fact which, adjusted cautiously to meet the demands of the years, kept the company solvent and eventually absorbed its more adventurous opponents. The caution was shown also in the written instructions handed to each servant as he left York Factory for the year's trip inland. In 1763 one Joseph Smith slowly read and reread his instructions—or commands—before starting out with his Indians:

> You are to take Particular Care that the way of Liveing of those People you are going with be no Inducement to You to Forget your Duty to God . . . You are not to appropriate to Private Trade and what Furrs you Trap, Catch or Shoot, or what you have any Claim to Otherwise, you are on Your arrival back to this Factory to Deliver them up to the Chief to be Sent Home in your Name to the Company. You are to Encourage the Indians to get all the Furrs They can, and use your Best Endeavours to prevent their going to Warr. You are to make Inquiry & get what Intelligence you Can of the approaches of the people of Canada, how far they have Penetrated into the Country, and what the Chiefest of the Persons Names are that advances into the Inland Country to Trade. Lastly we wish you Health and a safe Return with a great Number of Indians and Plenty of Furrs.

As he paddled up the river and hunted and trapped with the natives Smith heard that "the People of Canada" were reported to be in some parts of Rupertsland. When, on infrequent occasions, other bands came his way he questioned them carefully. Yet though he smoked with several bands, trapped during the long, cold winter with his own people, and met others as usual in spring to make bark canoes for the trip down to the bay with the furs, he encountered none of the men from Canada or, more specifically, from Quebec or Montreal or Albany. Had he lived a few years longer Smith would have had an exciting report to give at the end of each trip. But the wish for health and a safe return was not fulfilled. He died on his way home, perhaps as the result of cold and exposure following some minor ailment, possibly from a more serious condition; in those days on remote rivers a man had only his own physical resources with which to combat disease. Smith's Indian leader delivered his furs to the factory, and the company gave to his canoemate and her child their value in "Necessaries for their Support."

The year 1766 was a momentous one for the servants who wintered with the natives as well as for the company. At least four of them spent the fall and winter on the trapping and hunting grounds. Edward Lutit traveled several days' paddling up the North Saskatchewan with Assiniboins, the first of the servants to winter with this band. Another servant, James Allen, was in the area a little nearer the Forks, while William Pink hunted buffalo to the west of the South Branch and Isaac Batt was down near the old French house at Pasquia. None of these servants were traders. They merely traveled with the Indians, urged them to trap furs and to bring their laden canoes down to York Factory. They did well, too. In the spring of 1767, 156 canoes sped down the swollen river, laden with 31,640 "made" beaver. Briefly, the servants tasted power in that swift, thrilling voyage, and one, at least, remembered the taste and liked it. Thirty-one thousand "made" beaver represented a small fortune. There were pelts other than beaver, but from the early days prime beaver had been the unit of barter for the fur trade; other skins were valued as so many for each "made" beaver, as, too, were trading goods.

In 1766 also "Franceways" appeared, but not as a servant. François le Blanc had been west during the French regime, probably as a voyageur. Now he returned as master of his canoes and cargo, valued at £2,400! Franceways was soon followed by others who paddled up the streams and toiled over the portages from the east. The struggle on the Saskatchewan had commenced.

The servants were quick to use the term "pedlar." As servants of a company with a monopoly they felt superior to trespassers no matter how daring or independent the trespassers might be. In a manner typical of the English caste system they made much of the difference between going to the Indians to persuade them to trap and "peddling," as they called the Canadian way of direct barter.

Franceways was not greatly troubled by such niceties. He had been on the Saskatchewan before. With the attitude of one who has reason to believe in squatters' rights, he regarded the river as his to trade on at least. He had been well outfitted by Isaac Todd and James McGill of Montreal and he had brought his men and canoes up the long and difficult waterways known only to the French voyageurs. He was one of the lords of the lakes and forests, proud and arrogant.

The fur traders from Canada and the Hudson's Bay Company were rivals from the start. It was not a mere rivalry of conflicting interests, either. There was that distinct difference in character of the men involved. On one hand the devil-may-care independence of the pedlars, on the other the humble-servant-of-a-great-company attitude of the company men. William Tomison, destined to become a familiar figure on the river, showed something of this attitude in his written description of Franceways:

His dress was a ruffled Shirt, a Blanket Jacket, a pair of Long trousers without stockings or Shoes, his own hair with a hatt bound about with green beinding, a poor looking Small man about fifty years of age; he Seemed to have great Command over the men; he lay in the Middle of the Canoe with his wife and Son.

William Pink also met Franceways in the spring of 1768 and the meeting is not the cordial one to be expected between two white men in a land occupied almost solely by Indians. Pink had spent the winter with his Indians, trapping and gathering food supplies, a long, hard winter, most likely without meeting another white man. Franceways was better off, having his own countrymen as canoemen, though he, too, could have given the excuse that he could not speak Pink's language. Probably the two exchanged greetings. Possibly they smoked and ate together. But excited though he must have been, Pink doesn't mention such interesting details in the dutiful account in which he refers to Franceways by his Indian name, Saswe, or Shash:

This day as we were paddleing Down the River, I See all of a Sodon on the North Side of it some of the people of Canada and a Little up from the Rivers Side I see thare house the has made up of Poplo wood. They are consisting of Twelve Persons in Nomber, the chiefest persons Name is Shash, the are all French men that are heare upon the account that the English did not know the way. I find that the are intended for to Gow something fother up the River this sommer and thare the are intended to Bild a house propper for them, the are Expecting 2 canewes more up this Sommer, and Seavrel of them are Englishmen that are with them the say.

Franceways' house, "made up of Poplo" wood, was near Pemmican Point, probably about a hundred and seventy miles above Pasquia, or The Pas, and these were the first Canadian traders whom Pink had seen in his two years on the river. He soon met more. Several days' paddling downstream, he came upon another canoe, very large and containing eleven men, all French traders engaged by Franceways. There must have been over twenty men at the post at Pemmican Point that year. On reaching Pasquia, Pink met his fellow servant, Isaac Batt, camping with thirty tents of Indians, and heard that there were other peddlers on the rivers to the south, which might be reached by way of the Saskatchewan. Pink's hand, unaccustomed to writing, must fairly have trembled with the importance of all he had to set down for the information of his masters:

With 240 Canews of Indians in Company With mee, Likewise three other English I find that a bout halfe a Mild below this place [The Pas] thar is the Ruens of an Old French house Where the French has Been Gone for a bout 7 Yeares.

I Has Heared Sevrill times this years of the people of Canadae being Comeing hear a Gaine to Repare it for Staying at a Gaine as the French did. But now the Indains Say it of a Sortanty they Say thare is five Large Canews of them will be thare this Sommer or Rather in the fall.

Pink went with his Indians and the furs to York Factory and returned almost immediately for the next winter's trapping. By the time he reached Pemmican Point the pedlars had left, but farther up he came "to the plase whare they has bilt anoather house" at Nipawin:

We came to our Famelyes inland Tenting opposite the ruens of the Upper French House, consisting of fiftey tents and a little below this on the opposite side thare were tenting thourtey tents whare to more Englishmen came with thare Indians to thare Fammelyes.

Though his trip and those of the other servants up and down the river was a once-a-year event and Pink, like many of the others, had much to say about the weather, his journal here and there is brightened with bits of momentous news. The year after he had passed Franceways' two houses, he

Canyon Below Saskatchewan Glacier, North Branch

noted that "heare is one Englishman with 12 French men With hym his Name is James Finlay from Montreal he came up with Three Canews to this house . . ."

James Finlay was well outfitted and had financed his own expedition. Coming up the river he had left men and canoes with supplies at two other points where they might intercept Indians going to the bay. Pink reported to his masters: "They Say the has Liberty to Come or Gow as Far as the chueses in to the in Land countrey."

This was indeed a threat to the company's monopoly.

Ferdinand Jacobs, governor at York Factory, wrote to his superiors in London that "he [James Finlay] says he has a right to Come and Trade within 50 Leagues of the Company's Forts, and if the Company had 50 men inland they should not hinder him. The above Mr. Finlay made an offer of £25 pr. Ann. to some of your Servants and would pay their passage to Quebeck, and gave Pink the Following Directions where to Apply. You will Direct your Letters to James Finlay, Merchant in Montreal; To the care of Messrs Hunter & Bailey, Merchants in London."

Pink turned the written instructions over to the governor, who sent the scrap of paper on to Hudson's Bay House in London.

With Franceways and Finlay on the river, the company's returns of made beaver were reduced almost to a third. Governor Jacobs sent the bad news to London. He even suggested building a house on the river, perhaps at Grand Rapids, astride the pedlars' carrying place.

Opposition from the natives below Lake Winnipeg prevented canoes getting through to Grand Rapids next year. Up went the company's returns to normal, 34,000 made beaver. The respite was brief. Thomas Corey, heralding a long line of Scotsmen on the Saskatchewan, built a "decent Kind of House, Stockaded round" at Cedar Lake, two days' paddle below Pasquia. Corey had with him thirty men, including himself and his guide, and an adequate supply of

"Spirituous Liquors." He was by no means a literate man, but he knew how to handle Indians. He even won to his side Chief Wappenassew, long considered invaluable by Governor Jacobs. The company governor and his men resented the familiar treatment that Corey accorded the chief.

> The Canadians . . . tried every means to attach him to their Service, and they have succeeded. He lives in Their House in the Winter, dines at Table with the Master, and his family are clothed with cloth & no favor refused. In return he intices the Indians to resort thither, and he Convoys the large Canoes up & down to Michilimacinac & in great Measure prevents the numerous Tribes through which they are obliged to pass, from molesting them.

Corey's arrival at Cedar Lake with his canoes was no mean accomplishment. Along the rivers and lakes and carrying places from Grand Portage other traders had tried to pass hostile bands of Indians, some losing their lives as well as their cargoes. Corey got through. From his time on, the way from the St. Lawrence to the Saskatchewan was open.

Corey met the Indians' increasing demands for presents, being a sound student of human nature and recognizing the trading value of rum, tobacco, and guns. Company men regarded his largess as "giving abundance of goods for nothing and trading at a cheap rate," especially when they watched the seven canoes loaded with beaver that Corey sent down to Grand Portage. They could not pay such high rates and survive.

Corey sent at least two letters to the governor of York Factory. In one he referred to Wappenassew, the useful chief whom he had lured away from the company. He wrote: "Wabunashui Desired me to let you know that he Dwoe knot go to See you this Springe But Send his pipe Stem and Will go to the Grande portage with me if you have ane thing to Send him you may Send it by the Bellhom."

In another letter he said: "Dear Sir if ane of my men

Shold Com to your fort I Should Be Glade if you would Send them Prsners to London as the have Robed me of a Consetrabel Sum in Goods and I will Pay ther Passage if ther his ane thing in this Part of World that I or ane of the Gentelmen of this Compane Can Sarve you we will Dwo all in our Power . . ." Corey meant that last part, too.

The company's governor and servants were irritated by the changed attitude of the natives. They were shocked to realize that the Indians weren't even denying that they had traded their prime furs with the pedlars. That, to the company, was unspeakable disrespect; it bordered on sacrilege.

Corey spent only two winters on the Saskatchewan, but they were highly profitable; on his returns he was able to retire to the East and set up shop in a comfortable manner. The year 1772–73 brought growing pedlar opposition. Besides Corey and Franceways, there was Barthelemi Blondeau, who, like his fellow Frenchman, had been supplied by the merchants McGill & Todd of Montreal. They had some forty canoes between them. There was also William Bruce, an independent trader, and the Frobisher brothers, members of a keen family of traders and businessmen who were to make their presence felt throughout the fur trade. Between them, these men from Canada built houses along the main river from Grand Rapids to near the Forks. The Frobishers had a small "log tent" at Whitey's Narrows, just east of Cumberland Lake, and on the path of Indians coming down from the Churchill. Corey had already shown evidence of an improved supply line. He had connections with a fort out on the buffalo plains from which he was supplied with pemmican, and his own men had an excellent fishery on Cedar Lake. The existence of the Hudson's Bay Company was threatened.

Legally its monopoly was sound. But there were delicate considerations to be thought of before demanding the arrest of the pedlars, and sending them to London for trial. The

Mother Parliament had another offspring to whom it looked with great hope, the new colony of Canada. Very strong feeling existed in Montreal and Quebec, especially among the French, that the entire Northwest was theirs, including the area granted to Hudson's Bay Company as a monopoly. The governor and directors of the company deemed it wise not to insist that the Proclamation of 1763 tacitly admitted the monopoly by not mentioning it, and by omitting to point out that "the west" which had been granted to Canada was in reality that area adjacent to the Great Lakes. The French had been there first and had had their string of fur forts. In London Canadians might arouse too much sympathy. The company astutely decided against open warfare. At long last it gave consideration to the carefully worded letters from its respectful, humble servants, the governors in the forts along the bay. They noted, in particular, the need to supply the natives "with Necessaries; Ammunition, Tobacco, and Brandy, the Principal Articles; without the latter the Indians would not resort to your house if they could procure it elsewhere . . . the Brazile Tobacco would be a strong enticement . . ."

The company had never been generous with brandy. It was kept as a reward for Indian leaders, especially those bringing in food. Tobacco had served to keep trading rates down and dividends up. The company's attitude toward brandy was sound. Alcohol, it had noted, rendered natives unmanageable and sometimes dangerous. Besides, it was costly.

Feeling comparatively secure in its short overland route, the Hudson's Bay Company had also regarded lightly the potential trading cargoes of the opposition. It was a shock to discover that one man alone, Blondeau, brought up three hundred gallons of rum and brandy and thirty gallons of wine, together with rifles, gunpowder, shot and ball, and other trading goods. The Frobisher brothers' cargo, in 1772, was valued at £1,500. The thirty-four rifles alone would be good for many bundles of prime beaver.

With characteristic caution the company decided to send

one of its most competent and trusted servants into the interior to make a survey. It chose Matthew Cocking.

Cocking set out with a carefully chosen band of Indians, following a waterway which brought them out near Pasquia. Beyond Pasquia the river makes a great bend northward, and this they avoided by paddling across low Saskeram Lake and back into the main river by a channel existing at that time. Cocking relied on his Indian leader's familiarity with the maze of channels. Had he had a map it would have been very unlike today's map. The only thing constant in this low country, which the river is gradually raising up with the silt carried down from the west, is change. Year after year the channels change.

Back on the main river Cocking passed the portage to Cumberland Lake and met several canoes of Indians who had been trading with the pedlars. Their presence stressed the importance of his mission. By that time it was August and the river was getting lower; here and there shoals appeared. Gradually, as the days were paddled away, the banks became higher, looking, perhaps, higher than they actually were, because from a canoe even 50-foot banks look high. Cocking noted several bottoms in the valley, wide open areas which would make fine house sites. On one of these was Franceways' house, though at that time of year the pedlars were absent. Farther up they passed the house of "One, Mr. Finlay from Montreal" near Nipawin, and in a day or so the tumbled-down ruins of La Corne's fort.

House sites on the river, whether those of Canadian traders or of the Hudson's Bay Company, were invariably places of great beauty, as well as of strategic value. A good view of the river was of supreme importance.

Nipawin, like Peonan Creek, had long been the place where trading Indians met their families. There, on a height of land, women and children and older men gathered when the young men were due to return. It was the scene of many reunions and feasts, and much talking and drumming and dancing before the families finally drifted off toward their hunting grounds. "Drifting" is the proper word, too, for the Indians were a leisurely people. The men had only to hunt, and fight minor wars occasionally. The women prepared the food and carried the tent rolls and other small burdens at their own pace. Smoking with them, Cocking verified his governor's estimate of the company's situation.

"The Indians," he wrote, "consider an Englishman's going with them as a person sent to collect furs & not as an encouragement to them to trap furs and come down to the settlement."

Cocking's travels took him across the prairies for a little distance, to the land where the buffalo roamed, and then across the wide South Branch in the area near where it flows to meet the North Branch, as the two arms of the letter Y unite in the main river. There he crossed to the wider North Branch and followed it for some days' paddling, hoping to meet bands of Indians who had not yet come to York Factory. He did meet some Gros Ventres (Big Bellies); one of the equestrian tribes who had been driven from their former hunting grounds near the rapids at Nipawin by the firearms of the Crees. But, while the Gros Ventres were friendly, they saw no need to make the long trip to the bay; they answered Cocking much as Henday had been answered eighteen years before.

The Indians always abandoned canoes when they decided to drift across the prairies or through the parklands in search of game or to trap beaver and other animals. When spring came Cocking met them near the site of the Fort Carlton of later years and there they built their canoes. All winter Cocking had urged any bands he met not to trade with pedlars and he continued his mission as the canoes swept downstream. If only he could lead down to the bay this vast flotilla, dotting the river like birds in the spring! But there was Franceways' post at Nipawin to be passed; Franceways would not be absent at this important trading season, nor without goods to trade. Franceways' post was a fine "plantation" of about twenty square yards, well stockaded and housing twenty men. Cocking's opinion of Franceways was much like Pink's. He wrote:

"He is an old ignorant Frenchman: I do not think he keeps a proper distance from his men; they coming into his apartment and talking with him as one of themselves. But what I am most surprised at, they keep no watch in the night; even when the Natives are lying on their plantation."

Franceways had no need to worry about his personal safety with an Indian chief's daughter as squaw. Any worry there might be was Cocking's. The Frenchman gave the natives four inches of tobacco. The natives made up a fine bundle of about a hundred beaver as a present for the pedlar. He rewarded them handsomely. They got four gallons of rum, adulterated with Saskatchewan water but strong enough to please their unjaded palates. Two of the Indian leaders were "cloathed with a Coat & Hat."

Poor Cocking had no rum and very little tobacco after his winter's hard traveling. In spite of living almost a year with the natives he still remained English and aloof. The Indians obviously preferred the methods and generosity of the Frenchman, with whom they traded some of the best of their furs.

Farther down the river were other pedlars, William Bruce at Pasquia and Corey at Cedar Lake, equally generous. Bruce had already dispatched two canoeloads of furs down east. He and Corey naturally got the best of the remaining beaver pelts from Cocking's Indians; they had many 90-pound packs to load in their canoes. Quite likely they got a good supply of pemmican, too, the staple food that would enable their voyageurs to travel quickly without having to stop to fish. Only sixteen canoes, with the less valuable pelts, remained to make the trip to the bay with the English servant.

Cocking learned, on his arrival at the home post, that

one of his fellow servants, Primo, originally a Frenchman, had deserted to the pedlars on the promise of a return trip to his native Quebec. The fact further colored his report. But even then the company's action was limited to sending three servants to notify the natives that it was planning to build a post inland.

Pedlars stampeded the river in 1773–74, and had it all to themselves. The English were too busy making plans for building a house and securing transportation to send out servants; perhaps they had at last realized that the practice had become useless. York Factory heard that sixty Canadian canoes had headed west, though some may not have reached the Saskatchewan. Blondeau moved up the river and, on a beautiful wide bottom adjacent to a vast beaver dam, built his post eighteen miles below old Fort La Corne. He was within easy reach of the prairies and the buffalo. The Frobishers occupied their own house and had outposts. Though Corey had made his fortune and left, his house at Cedar Lake was occupied by one of the Todd-McGill people. There was so much rum, such easy trading facilities that the Indians didn't bother to go all the way to the bay. York Factory's returns in made beaver plummeted down to 8,137! The new house must be manned by the best the Hudson's Bay Company could spare. Samuel Hearne was chosen.

Hearne had just returned from his magnificent trip of discovery to the Coppermine River, Great Slave Lake, and the polar shore, one of the few really outstanding discoveries made by the Hudson's Bay Company at that period. He was to have Cocking as his assistant, several servants, a carpenter, and many canoes laden with supplies. Various bands of Indians were chosen to take Hearne and his associates to the Saskatchewan, the company so far having been unable to make or secure canoes of their own.

Hearne traveled with five canoes, taking a few tools for building the house, 180 pounds of tobacco, some gunpowder and shot and balls, but only 12 gallons of spirits. He had learned while on the Coppermine trip to carry little provisions and to live off the country. This knowledge was to be taxed to the utmost at the site he eventually chose for the first company house inland. Cocking traveled with two English servants and his Indians, and had with him Hearne's precious medicine chest.

Hearne and his Indians took the watercourse from the bay that brought them out at Cumberland Lake. Here they portaged across the four hundred yards and paddled down the river toward Pasquia, the site tentatively chosen by the governor and Hearne. Hearne took a good look at Pedlar Bruce's house on the north bank, across from the Carrot River, and surveyed the prospects at old Pasquia on the south bank. He was not satisfied with either. So he paddled back till he came to the Tearing River, which used to flow into the Saskatchewan to the east of Cumberland Lake. There, on a fine bay, not far from the portage and with a good supply of wood at hand for building and fuel, he decided to erect his house, the earliest permanent settlement on the river. It was a sound, strategic choice, a trading crossroad for the northern half of the continent.

Three of his five consignments of canoes arrived, the last on the 15th of October. But neither Matthew Cocking nor Isaac Batt nor their canoes appeared. Their failure to arrive caused Hearne much worry.

Cocking and Batt were not without worry and discomfort either. Their Indians had taken another route, and when the two parties reached the river the natives decided to cross the prairies instead of going up to Pasquia to meet Hearne, as arranged. In spite of every known persuasion Cocking and Batt were deserted, though not without a promise that other canoes would be sent for them. When the other canoes finally arrived those natives couldn't resist the honor of taking a couple of traders to their own hunting grounds. The Englishmen were helpless. They went along for the winter and in spring made their way to the river as best they could.

They were a forlorn pair when they finally arrived at Grand Rapids. The river was swollen with spring floods and the water was white for miles. They could not expect to find any of their own people down so far at this time of year. They did not know whether the new house had indeed been built. All they knew was that they must somehow make the arduous trip back to the bay. It was then that Cocking saw the group of pedlars at the carrying place.

Cocking had not seen many pedlars before, never in the fine action of carrying their bundles at a portage. He stood in wonder, his own distress forgotten at the sight of those strong young men with their two 90-pound packs, trudging over the rough path with a fine swinging ease. He marveled at the quips that passed so lightly among them and to himself and his companion Batt. Most of all he marveled at the wide leather band across their foreheads, which enabled them to carry the heavy burdens on their backs with comparative ease. "Better than the Natives carrying across the Breast which gives pain in those parts, often spitting of blood."

It was Cocking's introduction to the tumpline, which was, so far as the fur trade was concerned, almost as important a discovery as the wheel to earlier civilizations. Cocking may well have been the authority for the advice the company's governor sent to London: "The Canadians are chosen Men inured to hardship & fatigue, under which most of Your Present Servants would sink. A Man in the Canadian Service who cannot carry two Packs of eighty Lbs. each, one & one half Leagues loses his trip that is his Wages."

While Cocking was so carefully studying the competent methods of the voyageurs, one of the pedlars, Charles Paterson, Frobisher's representative, had a little talk with Isaac Batt. He listened to Batt's story of what had happened during the winter, and then he made an offer the Englishman could not refuse. Perhaps Batt recalled that day when he had sped down the rivers with a huge cargo of furs, and the feeling of power that went with being more than a servant. Probably the sight of other men carrying burdens across a carrying place was less interesting to him than to Cocking. Batt had had a bad winter. When Paterson offered him £30 a year, all found, and the salary due him from the Hudson's Bay Company when he reached Grand Portage, Batt agreed. He signed on for three years, a gentleman now and no longer a servant. Later he returned to the company's employ.

Alone with his few Indians Cocking started off on the long and unhappy journey to York Factory. He would have nothing but failure to report to his governor. The only bright spot was the hope that up at Hudson Bay there might be some good word as to what Samuel Hearne had been doing at Cumberland Lake.

CHAPTER FOUR

With Samuel Hearne at Cumberland House

THE chop-chop of axes echoed through the woods and across the small, shining bay. Samuel Hearne's men were clearing a "spot of Ground to Build a Log Fort for the present." September had arrived and Hearne was well accustomed to the early winters and late springs at York Factory up on Hudson Bay. Though far inland now he was taking no chances of having to spend the winter without shelter.

Tents had been pitched on Saturday, following the careful search for a suitable site. On Sunday Hearne had his men at work helving axes. Sunup Monday saw them felling timber for the "log Tent" on the south side of Cumberland Lake, close by the short portage to the "Theiscatchiwan" River. It took Hearne, like everyone else, a little time to get on to the spelling of that word. Carpenter Andrew Garret and laborer Robert Longmoor had come up with Hearne. They did the building while the three other Englishmen cut logs. Though the first logs were felled on Monday, Hearne and his men moved in on Thursday evening. It was a quick job, perhaps too quick, because a new chimney had to be built on the 1st of October, "the old one being very Smoakey."

Later, too, round "loggs" were laid for the "floor and the carpenter fixed some little Conveniancies inside," including a table. A storeroom was built at the end of the log hut, making in all a structure 28 by 14 feet. But the living quarters were far too cramped for six men, with more expected any day. Another 16 feet were added. Hearne had the outside of the storeroom plastered with clay. The sun cracked the clay so badly that he feared rain might get in and spoil his valuable trading goods and the furs he hoped to secure, so the "People" were sent out to gather long grass for thatching. Hearne usually referred to his English companions as his "People."

He was soon trading with the first Indians to arrive at the post. On Monday, while the men were felling timber, eleven canoes of Grass River Indians came and pitched nearby. Hearne was able to procure some moose meat and a few parchment beaver. The Indians accepted a little tobacco, and after a couple of days' stay returned to their families. They were the forerunners of many who were to come right up to the present day. When others came with more moose meat, and because the weather was warm, "the People were Empd Drying of Meat to Prevent it from Spoiling."

Food was ever present in the minds if not in the stomachs of people living at Cumberland House. There were some fish in the lake, and in spring and fall geese, swans, and ducks appeared in clouds as they do today. But there was no great supply of moose or deer at hand. It would take time, Hearne knew, to get the Indians from the buffalo country to come regularly to his post with dried meat. There was no other food at all, no bread or cereals, only meat and fish and the wild berries that grew in abundance in summer. In August

Hearne and his companions Garret and Longmoor had lost their taste for berries. When they could find no game on their first arrival at the river they had been forced to live on wild raspberries and currants.

"Dureing the whole time we had nothing to Eat Except Berries," wrote Hearne in his journal, "which when eaten in so large a quantity as to stop hunger are of such an astringent quality (Espessually to Strangers) that me and my 2 men ware much desorder'd by them, at the same time hunger obliged us to have recourse to a still greater quantity let the Consiquence Prove as it may."

"Fresh gales at N W" with snow and sleet had occurred at least once when, on October 9, seven canoes of Canadian pedlars landed about a hundred yards from Cumberland House, the first white visitors. Hearne hurried down to meet them. To his amazement he saw the servant, Robert Flatt, who had been sent from York Factory with some of his canoes of supplies. Flatt was in strange clothes. He looked wretched.

The pedlars introduced themselves, Messrs. Joseph and Thomas Frobisher, with six large canoes, and Charles Paterson and Franceways. Joseph Frobisher had wintered not far from Cumberland House the previous year. Paterson and Franceways had come in their canoe merely to make a call. The Frobishers were going a little distance north to winter at Athapapascow Lake. The other two pedlars were going up the Saskatchewan; they had left their canoes down the river with William Holmes. But Hearne wanted to know what had happened to Flatt and the goods with which he had been entrusted.

The pedlars had come upon Flatt, far from his intended course, when their great flotilla of canoes and over a hundred and fifty men met at Grand Rapids. The Indians who had brought him from York Factory had taken all his cargo and abandoned him. Probably Flatt would never have been heard of again had the pedlars not come upon him, for in that vast wilderness of woods and water any man who didn't know how to look after himself was out of luck. Flatt, like all the company's servants up to that time, had depended on the Indians as guides and for providing and paddling canoes. He depended on them for food.

"Mess[rs] Paterson and Franceway took care of Robert Flatt," wrote Hearne, "and cloathed him very well, for the Indians had strip'd him almost Naked, the Masters ware all very kind to him but those above mention'd particularly so. I thank'd them for the care they had Taken of my man and offered to satisfy them for the Expense they were at in Cloathing him & which they declined accepting, saying he ware very welcom."

Probably Flatt's wretched condition was due as much to mosquitoes and flies as to shortness of food. On the lower river the air boils with mosquitoes in June and July. Stripped almost naked, poor Flatt suffered agonies.

The pedlars pitched their tents near the new house and invited Hearne to eat with them. He accepted and learned a lot from his competitors. Hospitality shared by these rivals was always accompanied by more or less restrained curiosity about the other's doings and especially about successes with the native. In 1774 the pedlars were speculating on just how far the Hudson's Bay Company would go. Company servants, like Hearne, tried to learn every secret of the Canadians' success, always handicapped by their orders about civility.

Hearne didn't come off too badly in his brief observations over the fish or gray goose or dried moose flesh. He discovered that there were the beginnings of a partnership or loose company of Canadians, because Paterson told him that he was in partnership with many others, who, with the exception of Franceways and Holmes, separated soon after they had reached the river. They worked far apart, too, so as to get furs cheaper and be able to secure food with much greater certainty than was possible in large groups of perhaps two hundred men.

Of far greater interest to Hearne than the difficulties of supply—he knew about that already—was the pedlars' mode of transportation. He compared the company's inadequate supply of two small canoes with

Their Cannoes [which] are 24 feet Long 4 feet 8 inches Broad and 1 foot 8 Inches deep, and are paddl'd by 4 Men—the Pataroon or Steersman of each Cannoe has £50 p^{r} an^{n}om, the foresman £40 and the rest of the Crew 20 and 25£ according to their goodness. 2 Men in Each Cannoe has £5 p^{r} An^{n} extraordinary for carreying and Mending it on all accations. By the Masters account, when they Embark at the grand Portage 65 or 70 Packs or Caggs, called by them Pieces, are Put on board each Cannoe, with Provisions for 10 weeks at least, which according to the weight of their Packs & c as also the Mens lumber, each Cannoe Carries upwards of 2 Ton. 60 of these large Cannoes came into the internal Parts of the Country this Year and were all in one Company when they found Robert Flatt.

Hearne later realized that the wages paid by the Canadians were not as high as he had at first understood, and revised his advice to the company a year later. But the price of articles which his men traded with the Canadians was exorbitant in his opinion, "a Gun 5£ New England rum 10 dollars p^{r} Gallon. Tobacco 6 Livers p^{r} lb, Cloth much inferior to the Company's both in Weadth and fineness 10 Livers p^{r} Yard, small knives like the Company's jack knives 2 a Doller and every other artical in Proportion."

Hearne recorded the pedlars' visit in his journal. "Weather moderate and Cloudy" went first, as befitting the importance of the weather; then the fact that the Canadians had all embarked and gone their respective ways: the Frobishers to their new house at Athapapascow, Franceways and Paterson rejoined the seven canoes they had left farther down the river. Bitterly at the end, he wrote: "The Indian Captain who brought me from the Fort and had been tenting by me Ever since, ware so affected by the smell of the

Canadians New England Rum that he and his crew embark'd and follow'd after them, before they were out of sight."

A day or so later several more canoes of Indians followed the pedlars. Others went off to their own wintering grounds.

That smell of New England rum troubled Hearne. He had lost much of his own brandy on the trip down from the fort when his Indians breached several kegs, and refilled them with water. This practice, they told him when he took them to task, had always been their custom.

Hearne's small canoes had brought down a few trading goods, less than three hundred pounds of tobacco, a moderate supply of ammunition and guns, a "Sean" net for fishing, a few yards of broadcloth, several kettles, spades, felling axes and augers, sixteen blankets, and a very meager supply of brandy and "white waters." He was still expecting Cocking and Batt with ten canoes containing, among other items, his valuable medicine chest and more brandy. Flatt's goods he knew to be gone. With great rejoicing he greeted the company's servant, Robert Davey, and five canoes bringing supplies which had come by boat from England, very late in the season. The governor at York Factory gave Davey a list of the goods entrusted to his care, adding that he had taken special precautions with the thirty-five gallons of brandy. They were in "7 Cags the Bungs seal'd with the Company's seal in wax."

But it was too much to expect Indians to carry kegs of rum across portages without enjoying some of the contents. There were many portages on the routes they chose. The old custom continued.

Hearne had no intention of putting up with the log hut indefinitely. There was to be a house worthy of a master and his men serving the Honorable Company. The temporary shelter was barely completed when the People were put to work felling timber, with the carpenter at the more professional task of squaring logs. The spot on which he proposed to build the "house Proper" was fine and level, and though not very high (none of the land in this country, except the Pasquia Hills to the south of the Pas, is much more than eight hundred feet above sea level), it had seldom "ben known to overflow by any of the Indians of the Company." The ground is stony with clay, and in Hearne's day the woods for a quarter of a mile about the site were straight pine with a little poplar and small birch. There was, as there still is, a fine view of the lake for several miles.

Though the work of felling timber must go on, some of the people had to be kept busy cutting and piling firewood. Never a day passed without noting the condition of the weather, from "thick" to "fine and moderate." And attention was paid to industry. It wasn't enough to assume that the men were kept employed. Each day's record showed what was being done and by whom.

Apart from cutting wood, working on the "house Proper" and hunting, men were engaged making fishing nets from twine which had been brought up for the purpose. Hearne was busy too. Every day there was a little trading, nothing spectacular, just a few canoes of Indians or a tent overnight. On October 20, with winter imminent, he notes: "this day Trusted the Indians in all about 200 Beaver in Amanition and other Necessaries, to support them Dureing the Winter."

The stern need for food and good pelts, as well as canoes which might be used for spring transportation, prompted Hearne's trust.

As cold "airs" continued to blow from the northwest and lakes and rivers might be frozen over any morning, the Indians gradually left the settlement until all were gone, "except two or three" women who stayed to make or mend snowshoes and do other similar chores for the Englishmen during the winter. There were, too, several York Factory Indians who were kept busy hunting game for food.

On Sunday, October 23, there were "Light airs from NW and cold frosty W^{r} this Morning when we arose we found all the Bays of the Lake froze over for near a mile from the Shore." Heavy snow fell next day. Hearne set the carpenter to work making snow shovels and had what he called a baracado built to the northwest of the house, a shelter of "brushy sticks, it laying very open to that Quarter." Whenever the weather permitted Hearne kept some of his men busy preparing timber for the house. All were occupied with the rugged business of keeping alive.

Game was scarce from the time the migratory birds had left. Day after day Hearne sent men out hunting or to look at the nets. The comments are uniformly stark: "Caught no fish," "Returned from hunting without any success." It was a rare occasion to write down "caught several fine fish." Men sent out "with tools proper for taking beaver houses" returned several days later having had to eat the few beaver they caught before they got back to the house. The arrival of a tent of Indians, whom Hearne had befriended when they were starving, "with a sled load of Moose Flesh" provided temporary relief.

Cumberland House was not the only area where food was scarce. In the middle of November five hungry Frenchmen of the Frobisher group called at Cumberland House on their way up the Saskatchewan. Already they had walked for twenty days without killing any game, and must go another eight or so. Nothing but the prospect of bountiful supplies at the upper post near the buffalo prairies kept them going for the next hundred miles. They told Hearne that Mr. Frobisher and his men were in great distress for want of food.

During the couple of days the Frenchmen stayed at Cumberland House Hearne fed them the same rations as his own men, "but two Scanty meals p[r] Day." He could give them very little to take on their long, bitterly cold journey.

On Christmas Day, 1774, his first Christmas on the Saskatchewan, Hearne wrote in his journal only: "Ditto Weather."

Weather was cold, and when the hunters returned with a few partridges or a "Phesent" everyone rejoiced. January was bad. Hearne tried still harder to keep his people occupied. Each day several were sent hunting or to look at the fish nets. A few cut firewood. Once he had the storeroom cleared of "ice and Rime." February started out even worse. On February 8 Hearne wrote that the scanty rations

> has accationed many grumblings among some of the men, but as from the first of the scarce times I stipolated myself to the very same allowance in every artical . . . This scanty way of living, at times, being so different from the sertin good allowance at the Factory is so alarming to my men in general, that it is with the greatest difficulty I can Perswade them from thinking that Entire famine must Ensew.
>
> Partridges, Rabbits, Fishs & c have entirely faild . . . however I'm not without hopes of some Reliefs before long as I daily expect some Indians.

The rations had been reduced to a small handful of dried meat and about four ounces of other meat each man a day in January. Later it became necessary to reduce them even lower. Occasionally an Indian arrived with a sledload of moose meat, and one predicted a deluge in the spring on account of the very deep snow. They had never seen such a bad winter. Later Hearne heard that Frobisher had eaten the few seeds he had brought with him to plant a garden, and that one of his (Frobisher's) men had been accused of cannibalism.

The cold, too, was severe. Robert Longmoor had both big toes frozen while hunting, and then Hearne thought once more of Cocking and longed for his medicine chest. For he "lay'd Robt Longmoor's Toes open which are froze to the Bone . . . and applied to it the inner Rind of the Larch Tree Root which is generally us^d among the Natives to stop or Prevent Mortification."

Day after day, following the operation, Hearne noted laconically "Longmore lame." But eventually Longmoor went back to work, about six weeks after his toes had been frozen.

In March Indians occasionally brought in or sent word of a little moose meat or a few "blathers of fatt." Some fish were caught, sturgeon and trout and pike. There was even a little trading of furs. And the sun was warmer. The long, harsh winter couldn't last much longer. Neither could the tempers of the men.

They protested when they were put to work building a "stage" above the ground, in case the predicted deluge should occur with the spring thaw and as the result of the record snowfall. They grumbled because, on a mild day, Hearne set them to work clearing the place for the "Proper house." When extra large logs had to be felled the protests of the men became loud enough to warrant mention in the journal:

> This day most of the People complained of the great hardship it ware to work the whole Day . . . but . . . finding it necessary for the good of the Expedition I commanded them to work from 6 till 6, and shall keep them at such hours tell the house is compleat[d] or Recieve orders from the Board to the contrary.

Probably that statement marks the commencement of labor troubles on the Saskatchewan.

April saw the Indians "halling of birch Rind" for canoes. The settlement took on a busier aspect. From daylight till dark the sound of axes echoed through the softening air and in the woods men's voices rang loudly. Hearne himself was doing a little trading with the natives, and on April 7 the sills for the new house were laid and the carpenter commenced building the walls, surely an occasion for a small issue of brandy.

When the first swans appeared over the lake, on April 10, many tents of Indians were eager to hunt. A week later Hearne traded eleven, and on the 18th the first gray geese flew overhead, a few at first, honking directions to their followers, and then more and more until they darkened the bay, either as a whirring cloud overhead or down on its blue waters. No one minded that the vast wedges pointed north. They came from the south, and with them they would soon bring spring. Of a morning ducks skimmed the waters in wide, quick-winged scallops and for a time the anxieties of hunger were past. The natives could prepare for their canoe building. Hearne could get his furs packed ready for the spring trip to Hudson Bay. His people were busy "shovling away the Snow and Rubbige from Round our Present Dwelling house" on days when the weather prevented work on the new house.

There was still cause for grumbling, in spite of spring's great stirring. Those timbers which had been felled in the autumn and had lain under snow all winter were wet, "which makes it bad to boar" holes. The logs were cruelly heavy to carry. But Hearne permitted no slackening, on account of either such handicaps or even bad weather. When the men could not work outdoors they were employed inside. As a result the walls were soon up and the upper floor "across and secured."

It couldn't all have been hard labor. There must have been some response among the people to the arrival of spring, to the ever-constant flight of wings overhead and the thrilling change of "airs" from the north to those from the south. There must have been a little betting as to when the ice would go out, as there is today on the Saskatchewan. In 1775 the big day was May 8, and at once the Indians started to pack up their tents.

All during the winter and especially from the moment they began to haul birch bark, Hearne had been endeavoring to get the Indians to build him some large canoes. He had traded goods with that in mind, and he had had many promises. Promises came easy when the weather was bitterly cold and bellies ached with hunger. Now they melted with the snow. Day after day Indians left, some without trading the few furs they had. Many who still stayed were openly waiting for the Canadians to arrive. Hearne's brandy was all gone.

The trading he did was only for necessities, but it brought him some pelts and a little much-needed food. His own people were busy with the house and the York Factory Indians could not supply all their provision needs. Though food was adequate now that winter was gone, the trading of "several geese and 2 swans" merited a place in the journal. Swans came high, one for a beaver, and cut into the settlement's profits. With swans that flew over in such numbers as to cast a brief shadow over the house, and geese whose honking turned the usual quiet into a noisy babble, Hearne still wrote daily, in his fine, flourishing hand, about the number of birds the home Indians killed, or which he traded. The cost seems to have worried him almost as much as did his inability to secure canoes. On May 25 he wrote a bitter entry into his journal:

> This day most of the Indians went away with their females Several of which Promoused to build me large Canoes and who I have been dayly giving them everything they ask^d for to Encourage them there to, yet, as soon as their own Cannoes ware finished, they all sot off to have a drink of the Pedlars Rum, some went to Pasquia, and some for the two Forbershers, whose Settlement lays at the back of Churchill, so that out of 6 large Cannoes which I Expected to have had made under my own inspection, I have but one.

Hearne watched the Indians pack up their tents and paddle away. More rum the company must have, and more and larger canoes. And there must be posts farther up the river. Already he could see the effect of the Canadian posts to the west, from where the furs came down the main river; to the north where the Indians came from the Churchill, and down at Pasquia and Cedar Lake where Canadian runners met the natives on their way from the South. He was able to trade one large canoe, and a few Indians from the buffalo country were persuaded to go down to York Factory as usual. The fur trade, though small, had not entirely vanished. Actually, it was an accomplishment to have secured any furs at all with only eight men at Cumberland House as compared with over a hundred and fifty Canadian pedlars up and down the river.

Work was going on well with the house proper. Because the "Pitt saw" had been sent in Cocking's canoes, and had not arrived, rough sticks had to be used for the floors until such time as another saw could be brought from York Factory. "Lower Floor Petitions & c" were erected, and a cellar dug for a magazine. Brush and small trees which obstructed the view of the lake were cleared. Hearne felt he could leave the work safely in the hands of Garret, with Slater and Flatt as assistants, while he made a quick trip to Hudson Bay with his few furs.

On May 29, with "Fine Pleasant Weather and Fair, what Furrs I've already traded being Packed, I this day about Noon ambark'd for the Fort in Company with 32 Cannoes of Indians, 17 of which are to accompany me to the Fort." The Canadians sent down to the St. Lawrence upward of forty canoes, each much larger than Hearne's, and well laden with prime furs.

It was a flying trip. Hearne arrived back at Cumberland House on August 18. Some of his Indians had deserted. He had had great trouble keeping the others sober. As on his previous trip west, the kegs of brandy were breached by the natives at carrying places and when under pretense of hunting. At only three days' paddling from Cumberland House he wrote:

I ware determined to undergo a Thousand difficualties extraordinary (if Possable) rather than put it again in their power to make a Dupe of me . . .

Brandy being the only thing that can raise an Indian's courage and thay haveing a good dose of it ware Just ripe for Mischief, and some of them began to toss about the goods and ware for staveing the Kaggs of Brandy & c in defence of which a scuffle ensued, and tho we ware of much inferior Number yet had greatly the advantage being all sober and they much intoxicated. We ware careful not to take any Affensive Weapons and only gave them a little old English Play, which had so good an effect that we soon drubed them into a seeming good humour again, tho some of them ware a little sulkey.

Hearne found on his arrival that 43 pounds of tobacco and 56 of ball were missing, and that some of his "Kaggs" were "full of fair water." When he tasted the others he realized that many had been opened and the contents now no stronger "than good grog." In all he figured he had lost half of the two hundred gallons he had taken from York Factory.

The house had progressed much further than his best hopes. Though the roof was not yet on, the People had moved in. Garret had procured leather tents from the Indians to protect the goods from the weather, which "is very bad being a constant heavey Rain and a Strong gale from the SE." Hearne lost no time in putting to use the new saw he had brought with him. At once a man was employed making a sawpit, and the rest carrying in timber ready for sawing boards. While Hearne outfitted the home Indians for their return to York Factory, the carpenter and two men were "sawing fether edged Boards for the Roof."

A fine, busy scene greeted Indians who came to tent and trade meat at Cumberland House that August of 1775. A few of the home Indians were making or mending nets, or fishing. Some were hunting. All the People were at work on the house. Gradually the roofs of the house and warehouse were "civered in." Men clambered up and down ladders. The ring of hammers echoed in the land where there was no sound other than that of birds, or the wash of the lake at night, and the call of men's voices. Only occasionally at that time of year was the voice of an Indian child or woman heard.

With the roof on, gathering stones and building the all-important heating and cooking units kept the men busy for days. There was a fireplace and chimney in the men's quarters and a fine one for the master, with the front enclosed with some boards which the carpenter had "plained." On October 2 the carpenter was able to nail on a "set of new Parchment windows," and the rest of the People were busy at clearing up the "Plantation and burning rubbage."

The first company house inland was completed. Once more the nights were cold and the wedges of geese headed south. Soon a warm house and a tight roof would be welcome.

But it was by no means the first house on the river, nor the farthest up. Though Hearne had not paddled west to see for himself, he had heard of the forts which Canadian pedlars had built at Nipawin and elsewhere. He had assured himself, and his superiors, he hoped, of the necessity for more brandy. But he also realized that transportation was a serious handicap to Hudson's Bay Company trade. The distance from York Factory to the Saskatchewan being so much shorter than the long trips the Canadians must make, he felt certain that with proper canoes the company could compete on a sound basis and even undersell the pedlars. But how to get the canoes? And a canoe, Hearne noted, "if Ever so good will not Serve 2 Year." The company must train men who could gather birch "rind," build canoes, and handle them. And make it worth their while. In no other way could the steady, high dividends demanded by gentlemen shareholders in London be maintained.

Hearne made a few inquiries while at York Factory. He learned that some of the Orkneymen working there "seem'd to intermate that 12£ per annum would enduce them to be actave and useful." Hearne was quickly realizing that the short distance of York Factory from the Saskatchewan was seriously offset by the skill and daring of the French-Canadian voyageurs. These men could build and repair canoes, and shoot the swift, frequent rapids that turned the putty-colored waters of the river to treacherous froths of white. They were almost one with the swift waters, as much at home and as familiar with their thrills and dangers as though they had been born on them, as indeed some almost were. They paddled and sang and had great races between individual canoes and brigades of five or six. The Orkneymen, strangers in a strange country, could not get the feel of the river; in time their half-breed sons might do better. Even Hearne missed some of the thrill of the canoe, perhaps because he was faced with so many difficulties. That may be why he suggested, for the first time in the company's history, that "light shells made of wood after the canoe form" be used instead of bark canoes. Of the small canoes which they had been using "50 of such vessels would not carry as much as ten of the pedlars' Cannoes, & at the same time each of them requires 3 Man, whereas the pedlars only have 4 in their large one's which carreyes 2 Ton of Trading goods, besides the Men, Provisions & other lumber."

Hearne learned from Frobisher that the Canadians didn't count on feeding their voyageurs once the houses were up and the firewood in. After that the men foraged for themselves, hunting with the Indians until it was time to make the long return journey home to Montreal or Albany the following spring. He learned, too, much more about the necessity for keeping the posts far apart so that there would be an adequate supply of furs and food for the natives as well as for themselves. The company must have more houses inland. But not until there were canoes or other means of transport. Dependence on the natives' canoes was uncertain and faced the possibility of great losses due to the easy Indian habit of stealing. The resultant costs not only ran away with the company's profit, "but," wrote Hearne, "render the Company^{s} Servants the make game and laughing stock of every trader from Canada"!

Hearne realized that there should be another company post above Cumberland House, up "Theiscatchiwan" River near Paterson, Holmes, and Pangman's houses, and at least another near the Frobishers'. He was preparing the way for his company to lock horns with the Canadians. It wasn't his fault if the Englishmen and Orkneymen lacked initiative and authority to come to grips with men like Peter Pond, Alexander Henry, and the Frobishers.

CHAPTER FIVE

Peter Pond

PETER POND was a typical, enterprising Yankee. In a day when white North Americans lived mostly along such populated rivers as the Kennebec, the Hudson, and the St. Lawrence he followed other rivers from his home in Milford, Connecticut, to Methye Portage and the Athabasca. He was one of the men who, literally, put the Saskatchewan on the map.

Pond traveled almost the entire way from Connecticut to the Athabasca by canoe. On the map a line drawn between the two points angles right across the continent. It was a trip which demanded a man who could write "from the fifth gineration downward we ware all waryers ither by sea or land," a man of resourcefulness and courage and endurance, a man of tough and resilient fiber. That he was hotheaded as well as being sensitive, and collected a few enemies, is to be understood. What matters is that he threaded his way through those intricate waterways for thousands of miles and over many years. He was two summers' paddling from home when he tracked up the Saskatchewan to discover Methye Portage and point the way to the arctic and the Pacific.

That was an up-and-coming lad. He started life in a poor family and died poor and old and obscure. But in between he packed enough thrills for a dozen hot westerns. After he retired he wrote his narrative, full of phonetic spelling and colored with exaggerations. But vivid! "Beaing sixteen years of age I gave my parans to understand that I had a Strong Desire to be a Solge." At twenty he had received a commission in General Amherst's army, came through the campaigns of Ticonderoga and Niagara, and witnessed the surrender of Montreal. He could speak Indian dialects and some French, the latter probably learned while guarding prisoners of war, and he knew how to command men. Had the war not ended and had he had a little better education he might have become a great soldier. Instead he became a great fur trader and explorer.

Pond knew the fur trade, having served his apprenticeship at Michilimackinac and on the Mississippi. The army and two voyages to the West Indies had given him some knowledge of astronomy and navigation. He had learned that voyageurs paddled on their stomachs just as much as armies marched on theirs. In his early thirties Pond was well equipped for his many trips up and down the Saskatchewan.

By 1775 he was at Grand Portage, the great inland center of the fur trade, an old-timer and a man of some celebrity in the Northwest. At that time the term Northwest wasn't applied to much of the territory that is now Canada. Pond was one of the men who were to extend it by way of the Saskatchewan to the Athabasca and beyond. He was well known at Albany, when that Hudson River town was the business center of the fur trade, and as well known in Montreal when the business moved to the St. Lawrence. He knew the fur trade from trapper to buyer.

Pond was the sort of man to hear about the fine pelts Finlay and Thomas Corey and the Frobishers had brought down from the Northwest. He was, which was equally important, one of those men who like to see what is round the next bend in the river. The prospect of keen competition with the famed Hudson's Bay Company was a fine fillip. He set out from Grand Portage with two canoes and seven men for the trip to the Saskatchewan country.

In autumn great storms blow across Lake Winnipeg, often referred to by early fur traders as the Sea Lake. One of these storms delayed Peter Pond's canoes. That year, too, winter set in earlier than usual. By the end of September he realized he was farther north than he had ever been. Already small lakes were frozen over and in the woods snow lay inches deep. Skirting the shallow shore of Lake Winnipeg he was overjoyed to meet up with a large brigade—the canoes of the Frobishers and Paterson, Alexander Henry and his companion Cadotte. Like his own men, each voyageur was paddling against time and freeze-up. Together the thirty canoes manned by a hundred and thirty men swept up the two miles of comparatively smooth water at the mouth of the Saskatchewan until the roar of the rapids forced them to track.

Success of each fur-trading enterprise depended on reserving all available space in every canoe for trading goods, and living off the country. Pond, like the others, had obtained sufficient wild rice at the foot of Lake Winnipeg to last until he reached the Saskatchewan. As a result of being delayed by the storm, that was almost all gone. Like his companions, the need for food worried him almost as much as the proximity of winter. Game or fish they must have. But not until the rapids were passed.

For part of the way the men tracked, that heart-bursting, backbreaking labor so well known to canoemen in the fur trade, and for which the Saskatchewan is justly damned. For hundreds of miles above Cedar Lake there are new shoals every year. Rapids occur round every other bend in that river which is all meanders.

On bad rapids, such as those at the mouth of the Saskatchewan, voyageurs used long ropes with a wide band across the chest and shoulder for tracking, hauling the craft from the shore if possible; if they couldn't trudge along the shore they waded in the icy water, often up to their armpits. In October winds and water are cold. When all thirty canoes had been hauled up the minor rapids they were unloaded and the 90-pound packs carried, two or three to a man, over the 2-mile portage. By the time they had moved forty tons the men were warm and their clothes dry. They were ready to repair their canoes, push them into the water, and get wet again to their knees while reloading. Only the hardiest young men survived from year to year. Even they were old at forty, and content to settle down in the St. Lawrence villages from which they had come, eager to tell and retell tales of their adventures to wide-eyed families, cozy about the winter's fire.

Losing no time Pond and the brigade pressed on to Cedar Lake and a good sturgeon fishing ground. So great was their need for food that seine nets with large meshes were strung between canoes.

There is scarcely a spot high enough to pitch a tent between Cedar Lake and The Pas, but at this late season little time could be spent in tenting. Beating the ice was the prime concern. Twenty-six days after touching paddle in the Saskatchewan the flotilla reached Cumberland House. Though not welcome guests the masters were received by Matthew Cocking, now Hearne's successor, "with much civility." From Cumberland House the party broke up, the Frobishers and Henry going north; Pond, being a new trader and having only two canoes this year, went south to Lake Dauphin in the buffalo country, while the others continued up the river. Once again they had Cumberland House surrounded.

That year, and the subsequent two years, which Pond

spent on the Saskatchewan, marked him as an expert organizer of the all-important supply line. At that time the fur trade was the major industry on the continent. Powerful business interests in Montreal were handling the trade between that center and Grand Portage on Lake Superior, along the vast waterway of rivers well suited to the large transport canoes of the East. Grand Portage was the great inland distributing center. An intricate system of financing trading supplies and the sale of pelts had been developed but as new territories were reached and the distances increased new methods of competing with the short summer season had to be developed.

Traders to the Saskatchewan set out from Grand Portage in early June. Even with large outfits they could get as far as Cumberland House before freeze-up without too much hazard. But if, as Pond did with superb skill during his second year, they should penetrate farther upriver the time was very short. Pond built his first post on the Saskatchewan far above the other Canadians at the mouth of the Sturgeon River, beyond the Forks and near the site of the present city of Prince Albert. His men could not get as far as that in a season and hunt their own food as well. To speed up the trip Pond engaged Indians to supply his canoes along the way. He traded wild rice at the foot of Lake Winnipeg. On the lower Saskatchewan he obtained buffalo meat. His own post was situated where the buffalo prairies came up to the wooded fur country. Pond also had made arrangements with the old Albany firm of Phynn and Ellice, recently moved to Montreal, for trading supplies to be forwarded to Grand Portage and to handle the sale of his pelts. He had not pushed farthest up the river without first securing his life lines.

Of course he didn't have the farthest post up the river, and the best furs, to himself for long. The Hudson's Bay Company, finding Cumberland House inadequate to prevent Canadians from securing most of the best pelts, built a second post, Hudson House, a little above him. During the first year

Pond did extremely well, but the second year he felt the pressure of competition. He had heard about the fabulous wealth in fine furs to be obtained farther north. Because of his great success that first year several of his associates pooled their trading goods and invited him to try his—and their—luck on the Athabasca. Or it may be that Pond suggested this move. He ever had his eye on new horizons. Frobisher had tried to paddle through to that river of which the Indians had so often spoken, and failed. With a new base on the Saskatchewan, near Cumberland House, Pond took his four canoes to Ile à la Crosse and the Athabasca. There he commenced looking for new rivers.

That first post of Pond's on the Saskatchewan, usually referred to as the first Sturgeon River fort, was the scene of many great plans. Probably it was a log shack with a crude fireplace for cooking and warmth; Pond had only seven men and could not have brought up much equipment. The site was a beautiful one, opposite what was later known as Holmes Plains when that trader wintered there. Much of importance to the future of the northern part of the continent was planned at this post, referred to by Pond on his famous map as Peter Pond's Fort.

Winter on the Saskatchewan is long, its days are comparatively short. Pond must have spent a lot of long evenings thinking about what lay up the river to the west and along its connecting waterways to the north. On his crude table and with only the flickering light of the fire, he labored with his quills, drawing the first known map of what is now Canadian and Northwest Territory. Ink frozen, paper scarce, handicapped by a lack of education and with no educated companions other than the rare visits of men like Joseph Frobisher, it is amazing that he kept at it. An occasional Cree girl may have interested him, but it is likely she was sired by a chief who knew the difficult waterways followed by tribes to the north, or by one who had talked to those who knew the tribes familiar with the Rockies and that far-off "blue water." No new Indian came to Pond's Fort to trade without having to answer a lot of questions.

Frobisher spent some time at Pond's Fort. Probably the greatest fur trader of his time and the first to recognize the necessity for a partnership to curtail the high costs of the trade, Frobisher undoubtedly told Pond about his winter at Ile à la Crosse far to the north and of stories he had heard from the Indians of a great frozen sea beyond the mighty river that is now known as the Mackenzie. There must have been great excitement at the Sturgeon River post when a letter arrived by Indian carrier from Thomas Frobisher wintering at Ile à la Crosse. This was probably the first letter to be received on the Saskatchewan. From its bearer Pond would get some idea of the terrain crossed. He never could talk to an Indian from strange country without wanting to see that country—and its rivers—for himself.

Pond not only pushed on beyond the known territory at Ile à la Crosse, but he penetrated to the beautiful Methye Portage and down the Athabasca, which he spelled "Araubaska." Pond's spelling makes what remains of his narrative almost as interesting as the incredible facts it includes. As has happened too often with others, the careful, labored record of his journeys and explorations was partly destroyed as waste paper; his life on the Saskatchewan can only be pieced together from the writings of other men. But he was considered sufficiently important by his contemporaries to appear frequently in their narratives.

Sir Alexander Mackenzie, who was his pupil during a winter on the Athabasca, apparently remembered only the uneducated, rough man, old in the fur trade. It is unfortunate that Mackenzie did not recall more of the man so well informed in matters of moment to the traders and explorers of his day, of his tireless questing and the development of strategic caches of food. Doubtless Pond was difficult at times. Yet often he must have been irritated beyond endurance by those of his fellow white men who took to themselves Indian leisureliness as well as Indian girls. Views which did not coincide with his own drew stinging retorts. But it was an era needing strong men with strong convictions. No one need be surprised that Pond was implicated, though acquitted, in two murder trials.

For thirteen years Peter Pond traveled the Saskatchewan, though he never mentioned the word on his one surviving map. Pond marked on that map: "This river is called by the Indians Pasquia." He knew it had two large branches, and that they came from the mountains. It did not occur to him that either branch might lead to Captain Cook's Pacific Ocean, of which he heard while in Montreal on a visit. But he did think that there must be some connecting waterway between the Saskatchewan and the rivers to the north and "Cook's River" to the west. He drew a map which he hoped to present to the empress of Russia, in the event of being able to reach Russia by some northwest passage.

It is interesting to picture Pond tenting on some pleasant bit of the river at night, or nooning, as he traveled this principal highway of his day. Others might struggle up or sweep down its broad current without seeing the high banks below the Forks, the lovely beaver meadows at Nipawin, or the blue ridges of the Pasquia Hills beyond the monotonous expanses of low shores below Cumberland House. But not this enterprising Yankee; he saw everything, and remembered what he saw.

Sir Alexander Mackenzie and Alexander Henry the elder, as well as Henry the younger, have received much more credit for exploration in what is now the Canadian Northwest, probably because the passage of a few years had drawn attention to the territory. But neither of them would have survived to write their narratives without pemmican. All later fur traders and explorers owe Pond a monumental debt of gratitude for developing the supply of pemmican from the buffalo prairies.

A man doing hard work out of doors and having nothing else to eat needs at least twelve pounds of fish a day. Pemmican, especially when cached at strategic points, not only added miles to each day's paddling, but widened the vista of new rivers. In no time it became indispensable.

Today a recipe for pemmican is as hard to come by as the product itself. In the days of the fur trade it was common knowledge among Indian women who spent week after week turning thin strips of buffalo meat over the drying fire. The hunter's responsibility stopped when he had killed game. His woman or women hauled in the carcass, dressed and cut up the meat, and dried it. When it was completely dry the women pounded the strips to powder, using a hollow log or a buffalo hide, depending on their location. They sewed other hides into bags, hair side out. Each bag was filled about three-quarters full with powdered buffalo meat, the other quarter was melted fat, poured on top. If the camp happened to be near a thicket of wild saskatoon berries, in they went, after the manner of all good cooks. That was pemmican.

It kept well through the heat of summer. It was light and convenient to carry. Given five or six pounds a day, plus a tot of rum, a man could paddle from dawn to dusk. He could carry two, and sometimes three, 90-pound packs of furs across a portage. He could stand heat and cold and bitter winds. Moreover, he was merry and sang as he paddled.

They say pemmican, comparatively fresh and well made, was delicious, as well as sustaining. Caches dug up in recent years look like a rough ball of weathered concrete, the buffalo hide covering having long since rotted away. Ironically these caches suggest one explanation for the huge quantities of rum that Peter Pond and his contemporaries poured into the fur trade. But that was after the supply lines had been developed. Before any fur traders could rely on their food caches they must know that they could rely on the natives—an uncertain factor on the Saskatchewan in 1775.

CHAPTER SIX

Chatique

THE brigade of heavily laden canoes bucked the strong current and a stronger northwest wind. The foremost steersman squinted ahead for shoals and limestone rocks. With shoulder muscles all but inured to fatigue canoemen dug into the choppy waters.

"La rivière du Pas!"

There it was! The chanson broke on the frosty air as over a hundred voyageurs counted the score and more of conical tepees clustered on the small ridge where the Pas River flows into the Saskatchewan.

"Sacré!" exclaimed the foremost Frenchman.

"They look well armed," cried Joseph Frobisher. The wind carried his words back to his brother Thomas and their partner, William Paterson, to Alexander Henry and Jean Baptiste Cadotte and Peter Pond and to their voyageurs. They were all experienced fur traders, the Frobishers and Paterson having been to the Saskatchewan the year previous, 1774.

Pond and Henry had been on the Mississippi for years, Pond penetrating farther inland than any other white man of his time. Cadotte's wife was daughter to a Saulteur chief down on Lake Superior. There was only one thing to do—pull in at the Indian village with no sign of fear. These natives might be friendlier than some who, in previous years, had prevented other fur traders from reaching Saskatchewan.

By the time the first canoe touched shore the chief was there with his followers, all armed with bows and arrows and spears. The white men looked at the buffalo-hide tepees and saw the Swampy Cree markings on them. They looked at the enormous chief, a man over six feet tall, somewhat corpulent, and as Henry described him, "of very doubtful physiognomy." Gravely they returned the chief's grave greeting.

"Towaw. Utumi' showao!"

The chief was "Chatique," Chá Chukew, the Pelican. He was a chief of some renown, cunning and hotheaded, well aware of his power. With much Indian ceremony he invited the white traders to his tent. Alexander Henry was not too certain of Chatique's intentions, but thought it wiser to comply than to refuse. Though they were a hundred and thirty white men, with arms, and the Indians had but bows and arrows and spears, they were strangers in a strange country, a country where they hoped to winter and to trade.

They entered the lodge. Instead of receiving the usual ceremonial peace pipes the white men found themselves surrounded by armed warriors. It was a tight spot. But Chatique made a fine harangue. He was glad to see the white men. The traders were told that the young men of the village as well as Chatique himself "had long been in want of many things of which we were possessed in abundance." Though the portly Indian used nice, ceremonial language, he did not mince matters. He made it very clear that he had the white men in his power, a fact which they fully realized. He told them that if they did escape and get up the river he could easily kill them on the way down. They knew that too. And having some knowledge of Indians it was no surprise to hear that, under the circumstances, he expected them to be exceedingly liberal with their presents. He was helpful on one point at least; he told them exactly what he wanted: "three casks of gunpowder; four bags of shot and ball; two bales of tobacco; three kegs of rum; together with knives, flints and some smaller articles."

The traders looked at one another while the Indians looked at them. Not only was their personal safety at stake and that of their men, but they had an investment of many thousands of pounds in those thirty canoes. Each trader hoped to make at least ten times his investment on his winter's trading.

When they were told that assent to Chatique's demands was necessary before they could leave the tent, the white men agreed—quickly, and possibly without much ceremony. After that, the pipe of peace was passed.

Doubtless that pipe of peace was smoked with as little delay as the niceties of the situation would permit. The air in the tepee was stifling. Once the pipe had been smoked they were comparatively safe; nothing could be more unforgivable under Indian code of honor than treachery to a guest with whom the pipe of peace had been smoked.

The voyageurs in charge of the canoes never let their eyes leave the doorflap of the chief's tepee. Their fellows, having less responsible duties and possibly more irresponsible temperament, likely passed their time in the pleasures of the teepee. Cree girls measured their social prestige in terms of their relationship with white men. At that moment, at Chatique's village, Messrs. Frobisher, and Paterson, Henry and Cadotte and Pond were in no mood to be interested in either squaws or the relationships of their men with squaws. They wanted to quit the place at once. Peremptorily they summoned all their men as they sorted out the plunder demanded by Chatique, fearful that the strong man would find some means of satisfying Indian honor and at the same time increasing his demands. Across the river the wind blew a bitter reminder of their race with winter. Ceremony was reduced to a minimum as the canoes pushed off, the Indians too hilarious over their booty to notice any omission.

But Chatique wasn't through. The flotilla had gone a bare two miles when he was seen paddling quickly after them. As the traders' canoes closed in for safety the big chief cut in among them, standing up in his canoe, spear in hand. He wanted one more keg of rum, and he would put to death the first who opposed him! To have killed this daring robber, wrote Henry, "would have been attended with very mischievous consequences." Chatique got his keg of rum, the fourth that day, all concentrated high wine. Saluting them with a derisive Indian cry he swung about his canoe and paddled swiftly downstream to his cheering warriors.

It wasn't often that fur traders on the Saskatchewan were treated in so highhanded a manner. On the comparatively few occasions after this when trouble did occur too much rum was to blame, especially when it happened to be accompanied by a white man's behavior similar to that of Chatique. The only other excepting cause was license concerning women.

Probably the next time fur traders stopped at the Pasquia fishing grounds they found another Indian village or no village at all. The Indians frequently moved their camping grounds, sometimes following game, sometimes for sanitary reasons, or because of a mere whim. But the mouth of the Pasquia, like that of the Carrot not far to the west, is a natural choice for tenting or townsite. For many years The Pas Mission gave the place its name, combining a French and an English word. When the railway finally threw a huge bridge across the Saskatchewan on its way to Churchill on Hudson Bay, Le Pas or The Pas—it is given both French and English spelling by the Canadian post office—became one of the most northerly and important towns in the country. It has been called Fort Pascoyac, Basquea, and Pasquia. Probably it got its name originally from the Chevalier du Pas who was with

La Vérendrye; in some early records the river is referred to as La Rivière du Pas.

With both French and English being used all the time, and both mixed with a certain amount of Cree, words were easily confused. The old Hudson's Bay *Herald* claimed that English settlers had naturally translated du Pas into "of the Pas." Du Pas might have been a better name for the town, Le Pas, "the step," having no particular meaning, and The Pas even less. But there it is, on all the maps, on railway timetables and airway schedules. The town's most enterprising newspaper of today, the *Northern Mail*, places itself in The Pas, Manitoba.

Today, near the sometime site of Chatique's village, the whistle of a large, modern sawmill cuts the day into tidy portions, a great change from the casual living of the natives. The Pas' stores outfit Indian trappers and big mining men and scientific expeditions into the Far North, which is just beyond. Small, handy Tiger Moth planes and huge Norsemen transports settle their pontoons on nearby Grace Lake. After freeze-up they switch to winter landing gear. Where the early traders and Indians hauled their heavy sledges great tractors today skiff up the snow and ice.

There is change and not so much change. Beady-eyed Cree youngsters, running about Henry Kelsey's monument in the modern town, wear factory-made pants and slacks instead of deerskin. Their mothers still have soft voices and comfortable, plump bodies. Probably it isn't fair to suggest that their fathers don't like work any more than did Chatique's warriors just because they have taken so completely to the motor canoe in summer and the tractor in winter. Though there are reserves, many Indians have bought off their treaty terms and live in the town. Indian and white children may have the same education, and in many cases it is difficult to tell whether a youngster is more Cree or more white.

The Pas is an important distributing timber and fur center, linked to the outside by a railway and a road and by air; famous for its Dog Derby and its Northern Lights and its warm hospitality. Should any modern Chatique try some highhanded holdup plunder he would soon find not only the Royal Canadian Mounted Police waiting for him, but the familiar, blue-uniformed officers of the law known all across Canada. While The Pas has to concede to Cumberland House the honor of being the first permanent dwelling place on the Saskatchewan, it is the oldest transient site. Its strategic natural position has changed the romance of transiency for the security of increasing business and an attendant prosperity. The future of The Pas is more important than the past. Yet in common with every other community along the Saskatchewan it has tall tales and true tales to last through a thousand and one long northern nights.

CHAPTER SEVEN

The Nor'westers

WHEN the Hudson's Bay Company took to inland trading its servants tactfully dropped the derisive word "pedlar." They were great hands for the niceties of decorum. They also had to keep face with those lords of the lakes and rivers, the Nor'westers, swaggering up and down the Saskatchewan. They had to justify their own part in the ruling against the use of force, a ruling which probably contributed as much to their feeling of inferiority as did their English upbringing. So the opposition, the men who came up by the long canoe routes from the east, came to be known as Canadians whether they were citizens of Canada or of the new republic, the United States of America. On their part *Canadians*, French, English or American, cared very little what they were called by the servants of the Honorable Company. Theirs was the real Northwest spirit. They were masters of the birch canoe, the finest canoemen the world has seen. They could travel by snowshoe when winter turned the streams to ice and covered them with snow.

From the start they had the advantage of the Hudson's Bay Company, those Nor'westers. The rhythm of the rivers was in their blood. As lads they breathed the very air of adventure, waiting for the moment when they would be old enough to join the brigades. They were tough and lusty and cavalier. It was only after a few generations on the rivers that the Hudson's Bay people began to catch their spirit. When they did catch it, when they, too, felt the rhythm of the rivers merge with their inherited caution, a quarter of the continent was theirs. In the meantime the Hudson's Bay Company generations that lived through the changes knew plenty of heartache and embarrassment.

That little group which pooled its trading resources on the Saskatchewan and sent them off with Peter Pond to the unexplored Athabasca gave birth to as powerful an opposition as the continent has seen. The cost of transporting rum and other trading goods from Montreal to the Saskatchewan and beyond was enormous. Coupled with increasing competition it could become ruinous without some form of co-operation, as those keen traders well know. Time and again they tried to tighten their loosely knit partnership, never with much success. Yet the Nor'westers surmounted all difficulties. They built an empire which spanned three thousand miles before, like a Greek tragedy, the very qualities that made it great brought about its downfall. The fur trade owed much to the good start it received from the Yankee acumen of Pond and Alexander Henry and the sound business experience of the Frobisher brothers; almost as much as to the voyageur.

Pond had appreciated the necessity for an adequate supply of "dry'ed meat, pounded to a powder and mixed with Buffaloe's grease, which preserves it in the warm seasons here." As the number of traders on the river increased, the need for pemmican and pelts increased proportionately. And as independent traders competed for the Indian trade the price of beaver went up. The Indian was no fool, though eventually he, too, suffered from the evils of competition. Gradually a loosely knit partnership, the North West Company, was formed. In 1779 it had sixteen shares, not all the interests involved being concerned with the Saskatchewan trade. At that time the Mississippi was still the continent's top fur-producing area.

The simple business of one man with a few canoes of trading goods changed quickly, the Saskatchewan trade being lucrative. By 1779 the industrious little beaver had lured fur traders to build forts as far as the Eagle Hills, up near the confluence of the Battle River, five hundred miles above Grand Rapids. There was constant jockeying for position. The Canadians added two more forts to that at Sturgeon, which they referred to as the Lower Settlement. The Upper Settlement was at Eagle Hills until another was built farther on. William Tomison, in charge inland for the Hudson's Bay Company, decided to build close to the Canadians and sent Robert Longmoor off with 2,406 "made-beaver" worth of goods for that purpose. But with the English company's usual bad luck or bad management of the period ice on the river prevented him from going beyond the Canadians as planned. He had to accept the offer of one of their unwanted, half-finished houses for the winter, they having used most of the suitable building timber of the vicinity. The Nor'westers kept Longmoor under close observation all season.

The Hudson's Bay Company didn't have a chance that year. There were three Canadian trading posts nearby, with ten shacks belonging to independent traders. Up at Eagle Hills Peter Pangman, ever in the lead, built himself a fine fort below the Battle River, in country as beautiful as there is anywhere. With him he had five or six other traders, all well supplied with trading goods and rum. Longmoor soon discovered that the traders had bought up all the food supplies readily available in a rich area. When he had to send men in search of Indians who would hunt, the prices were unconscionably high. The natives had gauged the value of competition.

It was an intolerable winter for the Englishman. He was on the track of some of the best trading Indians so far met on the river, with valuable furs from the Thickwood Hills and the Sturgeon River to the north and enormous food supplies from the plains across the river to the south. But he had to pay such high prices for his buffalo meat that his beaver currency must be hoarded. He had little rum. Optimistically he tried to make the utmost of his tobacco, sending men out with it on the theory that, having smoked, the natives would come to him to trade. Again he found that his opposition had been there before him. Too often his men returned with the tobacco and their few trading goods. The natives had already smoked with the Canadians.

The few tribes free to smoke with Longmoor's men might have passed the Nor'wester houses had it not been for the smell of rum, irresistible on the clear, cold air. Protests were useless, the Canadians being well within their own laws; they had laid down that any native who drank their rum automatically owed them furs. And an Indian always drank. Having twelve men to every one of the Hudson's Bay Company, the Nor'westers distributed a lot of rum without too much trouble.

So far as Longmoor was concerned, that winter the villain of the piece was Canadian William Holmes, justly reputed to be a tough man living a tough life. Holmes readily used force on natives who tried to go to the Hudson's Bay Company house, "the English being their friends." On one occasion when a considerable band approached Longmoor's house, Holmes sent out his eighteen men with pistols and tobacco—and ten gallons of rum. It was unfair. But it worked. The natives enjoyed the sample of rum, and Holmes took care to remind them of the Nor'westers' ruling. To make certain that they would trade he locked up their horses and kept them within his stockade until the pelts were all in his hands. Later when Longmoor tramped over to the Canadian's house to lodge a formal protest, Holmes apologized. Doubtless he also offered Longmoor a generous "drachm" of rum. The Nor'westers were like that.

Holmes could beat up a Hudson's Bay man one day and send an apology to Longmoor the next. It was easy to explain that his men had been drunk. Quite likely it was true. What mattered was that he got the furs. The Nor'westers had to keep pelts always in mind. They were building a vast trading empire, and the cost was high.

No man trading on the Saskatchewan could quite forget the high cost of furs. Behind the Canadian traders, back in Montreal and at Grand Portage, there was the sharp competition of their various backers. Charles Grant, reporting to Governor Sir Frederick Haldimand on the fur trade on April 24, 1780, is authority for fixing the annual return of "Furrs to Great Britain" at £200,000 sterling, and the value of each canoe at £750 at Grand Portage. In London the Honorable Company, with its own superior kind of decorum, was keeping a close check on dividends. It was gloves off on the Saskatchewan.

To put up some competition, the Hudson's Bay Company, under Tomison, built Hudson House, between the Canadians' Upper and Lower Settlements. The site was strategic, on the wide stretch of river between the present cities of Prince Albert and Battleford. Behind were fine fur tracts; before lay the buffalo plains. And up and down the river Tomison could watch the Canadians passing between their posts. The Canadians watched him, too. They noted his new house, 37 by 27 feet, with a stockade and a plot dug for the first garden on the river. Soon they, too, were planting turnips and radishes. But few of them emulated Tomison so far as to read prayers in their posts on Sunday. Perhaps they blamed the omission on their lack of a Church of England Prayer Book, which no Hudson's Bay Company post ever lacked for long. Quite likely formal prayers did not go with the cavalier conscience of the typical Nor'wester; in the early days canoemen received a blessing before leaving the St. Lawrence and that had to last until they returned, some seventeen months later.

Upper Settlement was a frontier of the frontier. The natives along the Battle River and up the Saskatchewan were comparatively numerous. They trapped fabulously rich fur fields; and they quickly acquired a taste for rum. They flocked to the forts at the mouth of the Battle, and the rum, well diluted with Saskatchewan water as became their inexperienced palates, flowed almost as free and as fast as the river. The traders lost their heads in the face of so much cheap wealth. Yet the pelts were not quite so cheap as they appeared. Part of the unwritten cost was the extreme nuisance of drunken Indians about the forts. Many a lusty Nor'wester sickened of begging, half-drunken natives offering their women for grog.

At the Upper Settlement an Irish trader, McCormick, to get rid of the "importunities of a native" put a little laudanum in his grog to keep him quiet. One dose of laudanum might have done little harm, in spite of McCormick's overbearing manner toward even important Indian chiefs, but for the coincidence of another trader's giving the same native another dose of laudanum. The combined doses were fatal.

Fortunately they were comparatively rare, those white men who had no feeling for Indian dignity. Rum was far less disturbing when served with an appreciation of native thought and psychology. McCormick made the mistake of assuming that he had "put the savages in their place." During the winter there was no outward sign of reprisal, even though the Irishman swaggered about the fort, too often issuing commands with his sword in hand. When spring came five tents were pitched on the hill behind his house and, to pick a quarrel, a horse was stolen. McCormick roared his threat to kill every Indian if the horse was not returned at once. The natives replied that they, too, could shoot. Even then trouble might have been averted if the trader had listened to an old

Indian who warned him. Insolently McCormick refused to smoke with the old man. He told his interpreter to tell him he should "put on Petticoats that he was an old woman and he would cut his tongue out," and went on with his pleasant morning task of sorting pelts beside the river.

McCormick ignored the natives' folding their tents. He showed no interest when they came and watched him, these silent red men who could stand still and inexpressive for so long. Suddenly a shot rang out, and McCormick's interpreter lay dead. Another shot felled a white man. At once the fight was on. White men fired from the corners of their houses. Red men fired from bushes and the hill. Soon only two white men were defending the place, the rest having taken shelter in the houses. The two ran up a flag of truce, and the Indians settled for all the rum at the post, some two hundred gallons. In the end the white men lost most of their trading goods, too. They were lucky to escape with their lives. The natives were too drunk to be alert when a survivor pushed a canoe into the Saskatchewan under cover of darkness.

There was great excitement when word reached Middle Settlement next day. The Canadians blamed the Englishmen for instigating the trouble. Philip Turnor, up at Hudson House to survey the river, resented the false accusation. But he thought it proper to defer settling the latitude and longitude of the Upper Settlement for the time being.

Hotheaded as usual, Nor'wester Holmes sent for Turnor and Longmoor and, though they had eaten together on several occasions, informed them that he was much set against them and "likewise every Englishman upon that spot . . . and if the People which was at the upper settlement was killed they would not let one Englishman pass." Later Turnor heard that three of Holmes's men swore on a Bible that not one Englishman would pass the Sturgeon River.

Turnor decided that departure was the better part of discretion and prepared to return to Cumberland House until the trouble had subsided. The Canadians thought even less of the English for his decision. Yet, when Turnor needed another canoe, one of the Canadians provided it. Well he could afford to, for Turnor estimated that the Canadians' rum that year had cost the Hudson's Bay Company not less than two thousand made beaver.

Philip Turnor and his men "dropped easily down the Saskatchewan river," coming eventually "to the other Branch which comes from the South being a bold river but no traders ever going up that branch out of leed of Indians." That day he found the river "very crooked leeding from SSE to NNE, current strong, the Land on both sides bold in some places covered with Pine, but mostly with small poplar." It was Turnor's first trip downstream.

In this section the river meanders so much that its canoe distance must be at least twice its air distance. Flying down it you cannot see a straight stretch anywhere, and the outer curves, high and eroded, look like nothing more than the back of a horned dinosaur, an effect which is missed from water level.

The disaster at Eagle Hills put the traders on their guard without relieving the rivalry between the Canadians themselves or between them and the Hudson's Bay Company. But it did give Tomison a break when he went up to Hudson House the following year. Because the Canadians, as cautious as Turnor, were staying away from their Upper Settlement, Hudson House enjoyed a brief period of good trade.

That brief period of good trade gave Tomison little peace from the opposition of Holmes. Holmes could play many games. He tried sending his runners to steal furs from Indians staying at Hudson House and then laying the blame on the servants of the Honorable Company. If he had not overplayed his hand, Tomison might have fallen for his next move, information that the natives had burned Cumberland House. Tomison ignored that though he sent one of his men to Cumberland House for definite information. It was, as he expected, a hoax.

Encouraged by their success at Eagle Hills the natives burned one Canadian fort at Sturgeon River and made an abortive attack on Hudson House. Fortunately Longmoor had been on the lookout and had had the gates closed. He waited while a hole was hacked in the gate and broke the first gun barrel that came through. Later he disarmed each Indian who appeared, threatening that if a single Englishman were killed not an Indian would survive. When the Indians were finally quietened Longmoor locked up their leaders in the kitchen, and commenced trading. As soon as trading was completed he released the prisoners, greatly increasing the company's prestige; the natives respected forceful justice. That year between Hudson and Cumberland Houses the returns in made beaver were fifteen thousand. That year, too, Longmoor secured ten canoes, one of them very large. Hudson House was near Thickwood Hills and a good supply of birch. Doubtless the Nor'westers enjoyed many a race with those canoes.

The entire fur trade suffered what appeared to be a serious blow in the winter of 1781–82 when smallpox ravaged the native population. Strangely very few white men caught the disease, though several of their young squaws died. Hudson's Bay Company servants tried to combat the disease, "smoaking everything . . . with Flower of Sulphur." Dutifully they cared for their own natives as well as possible, and buried the dead when there were no Indians left to perform the gruesome task.

The epidemic brought horror to the clean spaces of the Northwest. With no immunity the Indians fell like flies under a strong insecticide. When they could no longer move, either from disease or from hunger, their dogs devoured them in their teepees. Fear, not often known to the natives, drove those who did survive far from their accustomed haunts. Few were left to hunt and trap and paddle their canoes down the river in spring. Few of those who survived came to trade.

Looked at nearly two hundred years later the smallpox

epidemic appears to have saved the lives of a lot of white men, especially Canadians, from an increasing Indian hostility. A few seasons of scant trapping permitted the beaver population to increase greatly.

Hard times fell upon the Saskatchewan. The Canadians found their first North West Company did not work out so well as they had hoped. They were not sufficiently organized to withstand even a temporary depression and the so-called partners were far too individualistic to work together. They were in the throes of reorganization.

The Hudson's Bay Company was no better off. The War of American Independence reached the very shores of Hudson Bay when the French sided with the Americans. The French fleet burned Fort York to the ground and blew up the fortifications at Fort Prince of Wales. No supplies got in to the servants that year. The following year a ship did reach the bay, but so late that Tomison, who had gone down for the all-important trading goods, had to return before its arrival. Inland posts had nothing to trade, not even for food. Proud Tomison had to face the ignominy of going to the Canadians for ammunition. He was in no position to compete with the renewed energy of the opposition when the Canadians finally returned to the river reorganized, in force, and with plans to explore the rich trade of the Athabasca. From 1783 until 1785 the Honorable Company paid no dividends. It was a sharp reverse from their usual ten per cent. On the Saskatchewan it meant short rations for all servants.

The Nor'westers scorned men who would accept such handicaps instead of foraging for themselves. Their independence was arrogance to the Englishmen, especially William Tomison, brought up in a tradition of duty to his superiors at whatever personal cost. The Nor'westers never got to like Tomison, if indeed anyone could like that dour, just man except his mother, and perhaps his wife; probably Tomison never had a wife or even an agreeable squaw to share the burdens of a stern opposition. The Canadians didn't try to

Badlands on the
Red Deer River

discover whether he was sensitive and shy or just plain difficult. Tomison was often the butt of their ribaldries.

Peter Pangman, who made the Saskatchewan his particular fur trade area, was a typical Nor'wester. Even the Saskatchewan was hardly big enough for Pangman. He pushed farther up the river than any other man of his day. In 1790 he saw the mountains and cut his name and the date into the bark of a huge pine, at the site that eventually became Rocky Mountain House. Like many a Nor'wester he was a natural leader. He knew what he wanted, and how to get it. He possessed few of the characteristics of practical co-operation. In the earlier days Pangman "tented without the palisades," from time to time because he could not or would not agree with his fellow Canadians. Pangman brought an echo of the war in the United States to the Saskatchewan.

Down in Detroit the strong firm of Gregory & McLeod realized that war and the opening up of the Mississippi country to settlement indicated a move. Pangman persuaded them to transfer their capital from the Mississippi to the Saskatchewan and to trade in opposition to his erstwhile partners, the North West Company. The break did not last long and after a few years it became apparent that the costs of increasing opposition were insupportable. In the meantime Pangman's new connection added more posts to the river and reached out to fresh beaver meadows. It also brought to the Saskatchewan several young and enterprising newcomers, among them Alexander Mackenzie.

Pangman struck out boldly up the South Branch, just as he had penetrated farthest up the North Branch. His house at Fort des Iles, some forty miles up the South Branch, was a good trading move. To it came the Indians from the headwaters of the Carrot River, from the Thickwood Hills, and from the Sturgeon River. Here the two branches of the Saskatchewan are very close together. It was a natural meeting place, with the all-important buffalo on the adjacent plains.

Pangman's move resumed and accelerated the jockeying

that had gone on prior to the smallpox epidemic. At once William Holmes built near him. Not to be outtraded, Pangman sent a man to tent beside Holmes's post near the Battle River. Tomison of the Hudson's Bay Company, having trading goods at last, built a house beyond Pangman's. It was on a beautiful island, near the present Gardepuy's Crossing. At once both Pangman and Holmes abandoned their South Branch houses and built near Tomison. Tomison dispatched servants, in the old Hudson's Bay manner, to live among the natives up near the Battle River. He and Pangman agreed to unite strengths should Holmes get rough with either of them. They were all warming up for the struggle.

New traders building posts along the river confused the natives. One, Donald McKay, came up from the depleted Nipigon country. McKay pushed up the Saskatchewan to well beyond the Battle River and built his post at Pine Island, right in the midst of many tribes. In no time there was a minor land rush to the beaver meadows of Pine Island. Tomison, who had long felt that the Hudson's Bay Company needed to be located well up the North Branch, erected Manchester House on the island. Pangman at once crossed the narrow space between the two great branches, and made for Pine Island also. The North West Company followed with a lone trader named Champagne, making five competing posts on the one island in the Saskatchewan.

Beaver abounded, that winter of 1784–85. The natives had come back in numbers. Trading was brisk with five posts for them to visit, though the Hudson's Bay Company continued traditionally careful with rum.

The Indians soon learned to shop around. They traded where they could get the best terms, usually the most rum. Pangman and McKay and Tomison and the Nor'wester watched one another like cat and dog, and they all watched the lone trader. Servants were sent out with tobacco and rum. Persuasion often became confused with force. "It is not possible to please the natives when there is so many houses to go to, the Canadian giving the same quantity of Liquer for 20 skins that they used to give for 50," fumed Tomison, having to go right into his neighbors' forts more than once to wrest from them pelts which were his by right of smoking.

Every trader sent out wintering parties with goods. The natives rapidly became independent. When the Nor'westers dispatched Edward Umphreville to build a post fifty miles farther up the river, in the midst of untouched beaver country, lies and intimidation and good, healthy hoaxes became more common than ever. One day Tomison and McKay were told that Indians who had accepted their tobacco were trading with Umphreville. Umphreville himself may have started the story, or possibly the enterprising Pangman. But though Tomison and McKay sent off messengers to intercept their fur-bearing Indians, none were seen. It was a typical joke, that 50-mile return trip in the bitter cold of winter and through heavy snow.

For a time Pangman's Fort and Manchester House remained the main posts on Pine Island. Pangman's Fort was 160 feet square, palisaded, with the customary two gates, the main gate opening on the river. There was the wintering partner's house; the main building; a store; and the glacière where meat was piled in winter with water poured over it, thus ensuring a supply of frozen meat until the brigades were ready to leave in the spring. The houses for the men were echeloned across the fort, so that Indians entering by the main gate were gathered in a triangular court where they could be kept under observation in case of attack. Pine Island was in the midst of the warlike plains Indians to the south and west, the Plains Crees, Assiniboins, Gros Ventres, and Blackfeet; with the beaver-hunting Indians in the Battle River valley and up the north Saskatchewan.

Great ceremony attended the arrival of the beaver-hunting Indians. There were generous gifts of rum and clothing as became friendly, useful natives. The Plains Indians, on the other hand, though important for the pemmican they might bring, were treated with more respect than friendliness, their furs being less valuable varieties, coarse buffalo skins and wolves. They were warlike and strong and fearless. They resented the traders' gift of arms to the beaver-hunting natives.

At Manchester House on Pine Island, in 1788, the Hudson's Bay Company took one of its slow, deliberate steps toward catching up with the Nor'westers. There the first of the famous York boats was built. That clumsy craft, bowed at either end and shaped like a canoe but lacking all other similarities, greatly amused the voyageurs. Like the Honorable Company, it was slow, sturdy, safe, and enduring. Lacking entirely was any semblance of grace and beauty and speed, the qualities beloved of the voyageurs and extolled by them at the expense of the Englishmen. When spring came the Canadians glided gracefully downstream in their light craft, loaded with twenty-five pieces. The heavy York boat plowed down, manned by five men, but with forty pieces of cargo. That last item cheered Tomison. It was sound and economical. The Hudson's Bay Company men soon realized that a sail could be hoisted on their boat on open stretches of the river and on the many lakes near the mouth. And all unwittingly they got even with Canadians in what turned out to be as practical a joke as Holmes or Umphreville ever devised. To haul their boat over the long carrying place at Grand Rapids they cut and laid down logs.

Those logs were fine for rolling the heavy York boat, much easier than struggling to carry it over two miles of rough terrain, through a too-narrow path in the woods. With stout lines the crew trudged along, hauling their craft much as they tracked on the river. It was very fine. But when the Canadians came to carry their packs and canoes over the familiar portage they stumbled and fell and cursed, especially toward dusk when the path lay in the shadow of the trees. At every step the logs tripped them, often dangerously. The incident did nothing to improve relations between the Nor'westers and the English.

When Pine Island became a no man's land between the Plains and Woods Indians, Tomison decided to build Buckingham House still farther upriver. He left a small detachment at Manchester House to compete with Pangman, who, confident in his strong guard and his strong palisade, continued to distribute grog and collect pelts. Pangman's strength withstood more than one attack while the men at the weakened Hudson's Bay House were robbed of everything.

Characteristically Peter Pangman had trained his clerks to be on the lookout for signs of attack. When, in 1793, the natives dropped all semblance of trading and became insolent, one of his clerks quickly gave the alarm "To arms, men!" The post's triangular Indian court proved extremely valuable.

The Indians, as well as beaver, were now becoming a deciding factor in the location of trading posts. Grown arrogant as a result of their minor success at Pine Island they attacked the Hudson's Bay South Branch house next year. There little provision had been made for defense, the Englishmen feeling secure in their traditional attitude of fair play toward the natives. In a quick attack, when the post was lightly guarded, the house was burned, one of the two white men present killed, and most of the native women and children either killed or taken away. The North West Company post was attacked soon after but, having had time to prepare, was able to drive off the natives, who had lost a lot of their men and sickened of fighting for the time. The surviving servant at South Branch House hid in a cellar until the natives left, and made his way by canoe at night to Nipawin. The South Branch was abandoned for some time after that.

Relations between Hudson's Bay Company servants and Nor'westers, in spite of the common Indian hazard, became increasingly stiff. Without the stern competition of the fur trade they might have enjoyed one another's company very much. Even Tomison, when the Nor'westers had helped to put out a fire at Buckingham House, sent a note to the wintering partner in charge, John MacDonald of Garth, inviting all in his place to a dance. Doubtless Tomison provided plenty of buffalo meat and fat, some fine tongues and game, as was customary at such gatherings on the river, but he gave his guests only "a delicious punch" to drunk. Tomison could not be expected to serve rum indiscriminately even to men who had helped to save his house.

MacDonald and Tomison had much in common, especially a great liking for the Saskatchewan River country. But the strain of unequal competition was leaving its mark on the older man. Tomison's unbending stiffness irked the Nor'wester. MacDonald determined to "have it out" with the master of Buckingham House when, during a spell of drought, not infrequent in the West, Tomison forbade the Nor'westers use of a common well. Tomison pointed out that his company had dug the well. MacDonald insisted that a well belonged to anyone who needed water to drink. He went further. He told Tomison that either the Nor'westers got their water or Tomison would visit the bottom of the well. Long years of an embargo on force had its effect, and Tomison agreed. He always kept in mind the interests of his employers, no matter how personally irksome.

John MacDonald of Garth, so called to distinguish him from the other MacDonalds in the West, had been sent up to build Fort George, close by Buckingham House, over six hundred miles above the mouth. MacDonald described the site as being "upon the margin of a fine hummock of Pine—upon a rising Hill or Bank with the noble Saskatchewan in front." There were heavy woods on the banks to shelter deer and moose. There were rich, almost untouched beaver meadows nearby. Once more the fur traders had picked a site which was both beautiful and productive. As an old man

MacDonald remembered his busy days at Fort George and later, Augustus, with nostalgia, those days of hunting and making canoes and pemmican, of sorting and packing and pressing pelts, and, in spring, being "all afloat upon the Grand Saskatchewan, then at high water from the melting of snows from the Rocky Mountains & all its tributary streams."

Fort Augustus saw some rowdy, rousing times toward the end of the eighteenth century, plenty of gaiety, plenty of meat and rum, an unparalleled abundance of unblushing crimes. In its heyday some eighty men were kept at the post, the large number necessary on account of the continued hostility of the natives and the developing competition with a new group under Alexander Mackenzie, the XY Company. Eighty white men, with their squaws and children and the natives who always adhered to a large post, created their own order of good times. Indians were always coming in with buffalo meat and pemmican and pelts. At intervals along the river horsekeepers' tents extended the territory of the community. Hay had to be cut. A garden was planted. Canoes were built for summer, snowshoes and sleds for winter travel. The Indian women were busier than they had ever been, preparing meat, tanning buffalo hides, and stitching clothes and tents, making snowshoes, pounding the endless dried meat for pemmican while they tended pots of melting grease.

There were two or three forts named Augustus, just as other forts were moved from time to time to keep up with the beaver though still retaining the same name for convenience. Tomison built the first of the Hudson's Bay Company's Edmonton houses up beside the second Fort Augustus, finding, as the Nor'westers had done, that the beaver of the Upper Saskatchewan surpassed all expectations in quality and quantity. It was said during those years that the beaver were so plentiful that women and children could kill them with sticks and hatchets. Yet the various traders had not yet reached beyond the hunting grounds of hostile natives. Danger was constant and there were some serious incidents. Once Tomison, refusing the demands of two natives who came empty-handed to trade, was severely stabbed.

Duncan McGillivray, nephew of Simon McTavish, well-known agent for the North West Company, was clerk and then senior officer at the upper forts. McGillivray pondered the increasing cost of competition as no previous Nor'wester had done. He realized that each leap up the river, each move by one or another company to be above the others, was extending the distance and cost to such an extent as to be ruinous to all concerned, excepting perhaps the Hudson's Bay Company with its shorter route to tidewater. McGillivray and the Hudson's Bay Company, with rare common intent, had discouraged and driven all independent traders from the river; there was little room for any man without powerful backing in those days of keenest rivalry.

As, once again, the latest and finest fur area was becoming depleted McGillivray pondered the possibility of union with the Hudson's Bay Company. The beaver and other valuable fur-bearing animals were being destroyed too quickly. Co-operation could bring an end to the indiscriminate destruction. It might be to the advantage of all concerned.

But as he pondered he also moved, another great leap toward the west, this time to the vicinity of the confluence of the Clearwater River with the Saskatchewan. In sight of the mountains, near the famous pine where Peter Pangman had carved his name, he sent John MacDonald of Garth to build the Nor'westers' Rocky Mountain House. Tomison soon arrived to build Acton House for the Hudson's Bay Company.

The site of the first Nor'western post in sight of the Rockies is commemorated by the restored chimneys of the fort where Duncan McGillivray, Alexander Henry the younger, and David Thompson spent their most fruitful years in trading and exploring. The Canadian Historic Sites Plaque reads:

Built in 1799 by the North West Co. David Thompson wintered here in 1800–1801–1802, 1806–7 & from here he set out in 1807 for the discovery of the Columbia River. It was for over seventy years the most westerly & the most southerly post in the Blackfeet country and remained in operation until 1875.

The site of the restored chimneys of the fort was donated to the Canadian Historic Sites in 1931 by Mrs. Mabel A. Brierly, on whose farm is the site of the original post.

Here at the confluence of the Clearwater and the Saskatchewan, with the Saskatchewan gap beckoning, the hare and tortoise race between the two great companies continued, the ponderous, now well-established Hudson's Bay Company stopping for consolidation while the restless Nor'westers barely paused for breath before taking their next leap, the one before the last.

CHAPTER EIGHT

David Thompson and Alexander Henry the Younger

BY THE end of the eighteenth century the Saskatchewan was very much a highway. Trading posts mushroomed along its banks, usually at the mouth of some linking stream. Each spring Canadian fur brigades swept down for the two weeks of good times and business at Grand Portage. Late each summer, when the furs had been exchanged for trading goods and a few gaudy luxuries, they toiled west again. It was a masterpiece of disciplined organization, that annual trip to meet the proprietors at Grand Portage. The midcontinent rendezvous cleared the news for thousands of miles, news of wars in Europe and America, of fabulous fortunes in furs in the Northwest and rumors of Russian aggression from Alaska.

Only at Fort York, on Hudson Bay, was there any threat of a North American scoop.

Trade was the paramount traffic on the highway. Seldom did a true explorer stand out among his fellows like the bright shirt of a voyageur hoisted for a sail. In the motley groups on the upper river just after the turn of the century no one can miss David Thompson, sturdy and strong, more often seeking truth than pelts and pounds sterling. David Thompson is justly celebrated as astronomer, geographer, explorer, and discoverer, a man trained in the exacting service of the Hudson's Bay Company before associating himself with the prestige and the freedom of the powerful Nor'westers.

Thompson lived on the Saskatchewan as much as he lived anywhere during his most productive years. Using it as a highway he explored the vast territories on either side for hundreds of miles. At the upper posts of Fort Augustus and Rocky Mountain House he combined his duties as a bourgeois of the North West Company with work on his maps. Thompson's map of the Northwest embodies the knowledge of previous mapmakers, in this case Peter Pond, Philip Turnor, and Alexander Mackenzie. It covers so much more territory and has so much more original information that it places him among the great geographers of the world.

From the vast, blockaded fort at Rocky Mountain House the mountains were ever before him. Kootenay Indians came and went by the beckoning gap through which flowed the Saskatchewan. Duncan McGillivray and his fellow bourgeois, Alexander Henry, already had been up some distance, though not to the source. The half-breed Jaco Finlay, whom Thompson had sent out as a scout, made his way to the height of land, which was the Great Divide. Thompson could know no peace until he went to see for himself and, seeing, record his findings.

Thompson first came to the Saskatchewan in 1786–87 when he wintered with several servants of the Hudson's Bay Company at South Branch House. Fatherless at an early age, he was educated in the Grey Coat School in Westminster. His modest mathematical training brought him to the attention of the Hudson's Bay Company in London, seeking likely lads for apprenticeship as surveyors in Rupertsland. He was only fourteen when he left England to sail the North Atlantic to Hudson Bay. He never returned. A year or so later he was sent off to the Saskatchewan country, equipped by the Honorable Company, as befitted his future station, with "a trunk, a handkerchief, shoes, shirts, a gun, powder and a tin pot." The tin pot was his drinking cup. Any other clothes he might require could be secured from the skins of deer and buffalo, tanned and stitched by the competent, patient fingers of Indian women.

Thompson's education did not cease when he left the Grey Coat School. Perhaps it really started then, the liberal, practical education which enabled him to explore and map thousands of miles of territory hitherto untouched by the foot of white men. He traveled up the river to South Branch and Manchester Houses, eyes and wits sharpened by a youthful desire to become an explorer. The company's servant Mitchel Oman, who could neither read nor write, taught him how to live and travel in the Indian country. Their journeying was hard and slow. Oman had plenty of time to tell an eager boy all he had learned about the natives, about the ways of beaver, and how to handle a canoe on a rapid. Young Thompson welcomed each rest period when the canoemen smoked—and talked. He lay awake many a fine night rolled in blankets near the fire, while the river ran strong beside them and the sky was bright with its map of stars.

They were rare enough, those magic moments. Often the travel was all that a lad could endure. Clothing wet and cold, food scarce, tortured by mosquitoes and black flies—these were the regular conditions that threw into strong relief a young man's dreams, which in time forged schoolboy tales of adventure into reality. Because he was as much a poet as a potential explorer Thompson readily learned the intricate ceremony of Indian barter. At seventeen he headed his first small command of six men and wintered with the warlike Piegans south on the buffalo plains.

That winter stood Thompson in good stead during all the twenty-three years he lived in the Northwest. By learning native psychology Thompson not only enhanced his later prestige as a trader, but he assured his personal safety among tribes who were either traditional enemies or enemies as a result of the introduction of arms and alcohol. He had to learn when to give small gifts from his precious store. He must become familiar with plant and animal life, with the skies and their place in discovering locations of streams he encountered.

Philip Turnor, competent surveyor of the Honorable Company, took charge of the apprentice's scientific training. All through one winter at Cumberland House Thompson looked forward to accompanying Turnor on a long-planned expedition to the headwaters of the Churchill. The bright prospect of that expedition compensated for the usual short rations of the lower river and helped him to tolerate the pain and handicap of a seriously fractured leg. To his great disappointment the fracture was so slow in healing that he was not allowed to risk the long trip. Instead, the Honorable Company kept him busy trading in the muskrat country.

A change of governors denied Thompson many of the opportunities for exploration that were in line with the aroused policy of the company in London. Month after month he was kept trading and surveying in the dreary musk-rat country. He did survey the Saskatchewan from Bucking-ham House to the Forks, and resurveyed the main river. But that was old territory. Thompson longed to explore. Even-tually he obtained permission to explore a new route to the

Athabasca, though as a result of war in Europe practically no equipment could be spared.

For his trip to the Athabasca Thompson was obliged to build his own canoe. With two untried Indians he threaded his hazardous way for hundreds of miles up to the Athabasca and back. His reward was a curt note from the local Hudson's Bay Company governor that he cease his surveys and explorations. It was a cruel blow. Thompson remembered well enough the hardships and hazards of the trip he had so recently made. Well he knew the value to the Hudson's Bay Company of the new route he had opened to the rich fur districts of the Athabasca. He saw the supreme importance of further discovery. In all directions rivers flowed unexplored. To the west lay the mountains and the Pacific. No one knew the extent of the continent. And a shortsighted colonial governor ordered him to stop exploring! To have commanded the Saskatchewan to cease flowing was as senseless. Thompson was through with the Hudson's Bay Company. Boldly he went over to the Nor'westers. Exploration meant more to him than loyalty to any company.

The Honorable Company was affronted. It had increased his wages to sixty pounds a year. It had trained him under Philip Turnor, and presented him with his set of surveying instruments. His ingratitude was beyond comprehension, and completely unforgivable.

With the Nor'westers Thompson came to know the great highway better than any other man of his day. As a youth he had been jeered when he had steered his canoe up a false channel. While in the employ of the Hudson's Bay Company he had been far up the South Branch. He knew Cumberland and Hudson and Manchester Houses. Now at the great forts of the North West Company far up the river, at upper Augustus and at Rocky Mountain House, he made his plans to explore the headwaters of the Saskatchewan and, eventually, those of the Columbia.

In 1798 he had married Charlotte Small, daughter of an

Irish trader of good family and an Indian woman. Thompson's domestic life turned out well. He took his wife with him on most of his trips together with such children as had arrived. She was with him on his first trip to the sources of the Saskatchewan, toiling up the river by horse and canoe, their baby cozy and comfortable on her back.

Thompson was by that time senior officer at the North West Company's Rocky Mountain House. He had instructions from Grand Portage to cross the mountains and, if possible, head off the Americans under John Jacob Astor who were bending every effort to build a powerful fur empire on the Pacific. The big moment of his life had arrived.

Preparations for the trip were made during the winter of 1806–07 with the greatest secrecy. The Hudson's Bay Company had at last been roused to search for a route to the Pacific. By that time the race for trade had settled down to a stern struggle between the two major contestants. But initial success depended upon the Piegan Indians who jealously guarded the pass against the possibility of arms going to their defenseless foes the Kootenays. Under cover of darkness Thompson's supplies were taken upriver and carried on pack horses over circuitous land routes. Just when he was ready fate smiled on him.

"The murder of two Piegan Indians by Captain Lewis of the United States," he wrote in his journal, "drew Peagans to the Mississouri to revenge their deaths; and thus gave me an opportunity to cross the mountains by defiles of the Saskatchewan River, which led to the headwaters of the Columbia River." It was one of the greatest of those great leaps so often taken by the Nor'westers.

The going was tolerably easy until they climbed out of the foothills. Beyond the grassy slopes the mountains rose ever higher and more precipitous. Travel became increasingly difficult. In places the river was narrowed by the rocks to a foaming gorge. Far above them mountain goats and sheep scaled crags where it seemed impossible for any living creature to get a footing. Snow domes glistened in the morning sun or took on rosy shadows as the days lengthened. And all the time the little party struggled on, David Thompson and Charlotte with her baby on her back; Thompson's clerk, Finian McDonald; and the half-breed helpers. Their most important pack contained Thompson's instruments, his precious means of finding and recording their position.

Eventually they came out on a plateau where the air was dry and crisp, the famous grassy lands which Thompson called the Kootenay Plain because it was here the Kootenay tribes came to dry their supplies of woods buffalo and mountain sheep. The plain lying to the north of the river is famous for its abundance of game—moose, deer, sheep, and bear. It was about a mile wide, and "about two hours' walk in length." Beyond the plains the Saskatchewan narrows till it is not more than fifteen yards wide, a swift, strong current which had to be bucked to its confluence with the Mistaya, and, a little farther on, the Howse. There the main range of the Rockies lay ahead. There, too, canoes had to be abandoned.

The little party had reached the valley at the foot of the Great Divide. Here, to the north tower the mighty peaks that support the glaciers; from the south flows the Mistaya; ahead the Howse River courses down from its icy lake. Craggy rocks, wreathed by summer clouds, pierce the dry, blue sky. Streams cascade down sheer-walled valleys. Thompson and his wife had made the arduous, thrilling climb up the river from Rocky Mountain House, past the Palliser and Sawback Ranges. They had reached the very source of the Saskatchewan.

Thompson climbed up the Howse River to the Great Divide, where the world dropped away in some places even while at others great mountains, snowcapped, rose so high that he had to bend backwards to see their summits. There he came upon Blaeberry Creek, whose waters ran west. And there he made a simple prayer: "May God in His mercy give me to see where its waters flow into the ocean and return in safety." He stood at the place where the waters run west to the Pacific and east, down the Saskatchewan, to the Atlantic. He was on his way to explore the headwaters of the Columbia.

The prayer was answered.

Thompson's contemporary in the North West Company, Alexander Henry the younger, nephew of the Henry who came to the Saskatchewan with the Frobishers and Peter Pond in 1775–76, made the trip from Rocky Mountain House to the source a couple of years later. It was on February 3, 1811, "the weather clear and calm, thermometer 12° below zero, and the hour 5.30 in the morning," when Henry left Rocky Mountain House, at the mouth of the Clearwater River, with two men, each of them traveling by dog sled. That winter ice was piled up as high as fifteen feet on the river near the post, so that they had to travel part of the way on land. Eventually they reached smooth ice, and a fine trip they had, dogs running well, men warm and comfortable in moose-skin sleds and buffalo robes. Henry was interested to realize that the ascent, readily noticeable when the river was running, was barely discernible when frozen. That winter the weather was so cold that, though they traveled until 3:30 P.M., only one short stretch of open water was encountered, and that at the foot of a very strong rapid.

Alexander Henry was a born trader. The price and plenty of pelts meant as much to him as a new location on his map meant to Thompson. It was Henry who, traveling up the river, noted every item of value to a trader. Like Thompson, he kept copious notebooks. But while Thompson's journals are full of astronomical calculations and traverse tables of great scientific value, Henry noted the plentiful game along the river, especially when the going became too steep for sleighs and the journey had to be made on foot. In Henry's time, as today, the valley of the Saskatchewan in the mountains abounds with game—mountain goats, woods buffalo, grizzly bear, deer. Wolves and porcupine made it necessary to leave all meat protected on scaffolds. Henry noted that the flesh of mountain sheep is juicier than any other kind of meat in the country.

His journals make good popular reading, with colorful details about the natives and their customs; about the fur trade; of the lives of men engaged in it, and of their women. It is fine travel stuff, as well larded with fact as Henry's favorite wood buffalo were larded with good, rich fat.

Spreading out baggage and packs of trading goods to dry on a fine windy day is the sort of thing Henry noted. He could easily have been responsible for naming Calico Rapids, having seen yards of gaudy-hued calico drying on the shore; drying goods was a familiar scene on canoe trips, and one which took up a lot of time. There was always ample time, too, to note men gathering and eating raspberries, as well as the color of the rocks along the shore. Henry put his observations into written words. He saw trees and game and the changing color of water and sky. He suffered under the sting of countless mosquitoes on paper for posterity to read. As his steersman and bowman kept the canoe straight while the rest of the crew tracked laboriously up the river Henry could sit amidships dozing pleasantly or planning his campaign with opposing traders. After his canoes passed Sturgeon River and reached La Monte, the place where the wintering partner often took to horse while the men labored on the track lines, Henry went off for a bit of buffalo sport. It was a pleasant means of supporting his brigade. Characteristically on such an occasion, when a large band of unknown Indians approached on galloping horses he wrote: "We are determined to sell our lives as dearly as possible." Alexander Henry lived that way. He was a gregarious sort who thought it worth mentioning on paper that his neighbors, Messrs. Longmoor and Hallett of the Hudson's Bay Company, took trouble to call on him upon his return from the East. He liked to be liked.

Henry's great success as a trader depended largely on his understanding of the natives; he was on as good terms with them as Thompson generally, though less sympathetic and often irritated by their primitive ways. He didn't let his lack of sympathy handicap trading. It was not often that this strong trader was taken unawares by warring tribes, or taken advantage of by individual groups.

Henry ruled the natives with a strong hand. He had his forts well palisaded. Not more than thirty or forty principal Indians were allowed within his palisades at once, and then only after proper formalities. Young men sent on ahead for tobacco were received first, thus announcing the coming of the older men with whom trading was accomplished. There was a large keg of grog and tobacco for each tribe, the sort of gift calculated to woo those with valuable pelts. Often there was little rum and much Saskatchewan water in the keg, Henry nicely gauging the acquired tastes of the natives. He was responsible for what he called "Blackfoot milk," rum diluted with varying proportions of water to please new and uneducated palates, as well as hardened addicts, but without unnecessary waste. In the new post upriver four or five quarts of high wine, with water, were sufficient for a 9-gallon keg. Some tribes needed their Blackfoot milk twice as strong.

Buying cheap and selling dear came naturally to Henry. From the natives he secured dried berries, as well as pelts, pounded meat, grease, back fat, buffalo robes, and horses, all very cheap. "A common horse" cost a gallon keg of Blackfoot rum, two fathoms of tobacco, and a few minor items.

The Indians were often exasperating. When, as at Pine Island, it was necessary to ferry to the house all but the young men, who swam naked, the rest of the band invariably swarmed aboard until the ferry sank. Then they waited for the white men to start it. In vain were they persuaded to travel a few at a time; they were afraid they would never cross if not by the first trip. The ferrymen soon became used to it. When the ferry had been sunk by sheer weight of Indians they retired to smoke. When sufficient Indians wearied of waiting, and the ferry floated again, the white men quickly boarded and poled off. They had to do it that way every time, returning for the remaining natives as quickly as possible. So, in spite of his exasperation, Henry did business with them.

His swivel gun was a great precaution against possible Indian disturbance; he made a ceremony of firing it so they could see how it worked. The gun was regularly primed in their presence and kept pointing toward their encampment on the riverbank. Up among the well-fed Blackfeet and Piegans, life for white men was much more dangerous than farther down the Saskatchewan in the familiar Cree country. Minor thieving was a constant source of irritation. Nothing could be left safely about a post while the Indians were trading. Horse thieving was a common and dangerous practice, dear to the Indian heart. But Henry could deal with a horse thief when he had to, though he regretted having to execute one of them "with a discharge of 15 guns."

While Henry got on well with his neighbors, he enjoyed the satisfaction of convincing more than one Hudson's Bay Company servant "of his error in settling matters according to his own ideas of business." When it was prudent for white men to stick together Henry consulted his neighbors about the frequent moves of forts farther and farther up the river. He knew when to move a fort, too. Usually the supply of beaver dictated such a move, but the mood of the natives was important. If they promised trouble, a few men could be left with trading supplies to hold the old fort while a new one was being erected.

When a large post was moved upriver canoes, boats, horses, dogs, and women did the carrying. It was the sort of confusion from which Henry liked to ride away, leaving his subordinates to carry out his orders. By the early nineteenth century the equipment of a fort had increased to include articles of furniture and utensils not dreamed of a few years before. There was generally a pile of bales and kegs of trading goods and such essential equipment as the fur press. Each white man had his box or dunnage. Tea and flour had made their appearance. Few pelts would be moved upriver. They went downstream.

On shore the cavalcade straggled along, as slow as the slowest member. On the river canoes and boats had to be tracked most of the way. Both groups kept a constant watch for marauding Indians. Sometimes Hudson's Bay Company and Nor'westers moved together for added safety, though such a large group increased the strain on supply. Henry, concerned with getting his people to the new post of his choosing, rode the high riverbank, enjoying the lush spring blossoming of shrubs, on the lookout for buffalo and other game. He sought out growths of birch for canoes, and gum for sealing joints. Good building stone for his chimneys, logs for houses and stockades, natural hay meadows for his horses all caught his watchful eye. And all interested him as being essential to the big business of which he was an active director, a wintering partner.

Thompson and Henry were each a part of the vast and powerful North West Company whose prestige they enjoyed and enhanced. On the Saskatchewan they were more than spearheads. As Thompson took his findings and recorded them, Henry forged on with the increasing trade. They carried the Nor'westers over many vast leaps up the river, making famous for a time such forts as Vermillion and George, White Earth and Rocky Mountain House. There is little to indicate that they were ever close friends. Probably their interests were too divergent. But they forced their competitor, the Hudson's Bay Company, to such lengths of enterprise as to contribute in no small measure to the final oblivion of their own company. Thompson and Henry the younger were indeed two heroes of the rise and fall of the North West Company, two heroes whose story has the quality of Greek tragedy.

While Thompson and Henry were pushing their way toward the sources and beyond, other Canadians, notably Alexander Mackenzie, and his XY Company, challenged them ruthlessly on the Saskatchewan and far to the north and west. The years at the end of the eighteenth century and the beginning of the nineteenth became notoriously bloody.

CHAPTER NINE

XY Company

He was a bold man who, during the great days at the end of the eighteenth century, steered his trading canoe into the waters of the Saskatchewan without a nod of approval from the North West Company. The nod went to the Hudson's Bay Company with arrogant deference to the old monopoly. Besides, the English company was too slow to be really troublesome. Or so the Nor'westers thought. There was no nod of approval for other traders. They came at their peril.

The mere fact of reaching the great highway proved a man peer in courage and enterprise to those other lords of the lakes and rivers who so cavalierly regarded not only the Northwest as their own, but the St. Lawrence also. Back at Montreal they saw to it that little capital remained available for potential opponents, and only such trained voyageurs, guides, and interpreters as were drunken and unreliable. On the canoe routes, both east and west of the Great Lakes, those who dared oppose could expect to find huge trees fallen across narrow streams or to have their trading goods and canoes destroyed, their tents slashed to ribbons. The Nor'westers were unrivaled pranksters. They gloried in persuading the natives not to trade food with an opponent. They laughed uproariously at his discomfiture or, if he looked like a good fighter, offered him employment. With them, all was fair in love or the war that had to do with trade.

As a result few independent traders reached the Saskatchewan from the St. Lawrence. But there were firms who had been operating in the vicinity of the Great Lakes. Among them were Forsyth, Richardson & Co., of Detroit, and Parker, Gerrard & Ogilvy. Both firms sent canoes to the Saskatchewan. Both received the usual Nor'western treatment. Derisively the Forsyth outfit was dubbed the "Little Company" and the "Little Society." Its men were called "potties," from the French "potée," a small pot or measure.

But they were by no means "small measures," those little companies. Soon they made their presence felt. When the Little Society built a post on Fort Island the North West Company abandoned Fort George to move up beside them. Even the Hudson's Bay Company left Buckingham House to be near the opposition at what came to be known as Island Fort. The Ogilvy group built in opposition to the two older companies at Fort Augustus and Edmonton. They sent canoes to the Athabasca to compete for the rich furs in that richest of all fur areas, traveling up the Saskatchewan as far as the Pembina River confluence to take advantage of the abundant food supply and because they could not secure guides for the regular Cumberland Lake-Churchill River route. But the two new companies were short-lived. They found the cost of a four-way competition ruinous and joined together in the New North West Company, generally called the XY Company from the marks on its bales and kegs. The resulting three-way competition—Hudson's Bay Company, Nor'westers, and XY Company—marked the peak of bitterness in the fur trade struggle in the Northwest.

The union of the two small groups brought to them the distinguished leadership of Alexander Mackenzie, discoverer of the Mackenzie River and the overland way to the Pacific and now, by the grace of King George III, Sir Alexander Mackenzie, one of the most farseeing and important of the great company's partners, who had been in the Northwest since the time of Peter Pond. He appreciated more fully than any other man of his day the ruinous cost of the long haul from Montreal to the Athabasca fur areas. He had proved that no cheaper route existed over the mountains to the Pacific. There remained only one solution—use of Hudson Bay and Strait, with the Saskatchewan an essential link. When his associates in Montreal stubbornly refused to consider the proposed route, which would, of necessity, curtail the importance of Montreal, and when they would take no steps toward approaching the Hudson's Bay Company to discuss transit rights, Mackenzie had pulled out, temporarily, later to head the XY Company. But his ideas were not forgotten. That short haul to Hudson Bay compared too favorably with the long expensive trip to Montreal.

Mackenzie traveled the Saskatchewan till he knew it as one knows his own street or road. He had paddled up it on his way to spend his first winter in the Northwest—with Peter Pond on the Athabasca. From its waters he branched off to the Mackenzie and across the mountains to the Pacific. He noted the vast silting that is still taking place down toward its mouth, in the vicinity of Cedar Lake.

"The immense quantity of earth and sand brought down by the Saskatchiwine," he wrote in his famous *General History of the Fur Trade*, published in London in 1801, "has filled up this part of it for a circumference whose diameter is at least fifteen or twenty miles . . . it is more than probable that this river will, in course of time, convert the whole of

Cedar Lake into forest." From Cedar Lake he reported that the "Saskatchiwine may be considered as navigable to near its source in the rocky mountains, for canoes, and without a carrying place." Mackenzie clearly did not consider the use of boats on the river.

His opposition to his former associates was worthy of a Nor'wester. Before the year was out scarcely a known fur-bearing area lacked a post of all three companies, and none was pulling any punches. Even the Hudson's Bay Company was becoming belligerent. The XY Company built a post at Fort St. Louis, not far from the Forks. It built one near Carlton House and at Sturgeon River. It occupied the post built by the Forsyth Company at Island Fort the year before, and which became the new company's most important depot on the Saskatchewan. There were three rival posts at the present site of Edmonton. And, in 1800, when Peter Fidler made a move unprecedented in the annals of the Hudson's Bay Company for apparent lack of caution and built a post far up the South Branch on the prairies at the mouth of the Red Deer, the XY followed. The Hudson's Bay people called their South Branch house Chesterfield and hoped it would draw the Blackfeet and Piegans southward and, possibly, the Missouri River Indians north. Neither happened. Even with the older company's comparatively good connections with the natives the location proved unprofitable and the dangers unwarranted. Things were even worse for the XY Company. The stay was brief.

The North Branch remained the fur highway, even though food supplies came mainly from the prairies of the South Branch. They were becoming considerable, too, those supplies of pemmican. For the Saskatchewan was floating more traffic than ever before. Each company, struggling for the fur trade of the Athabasca as well as that of the Upper Saskatchewan, required enormous quantities of pemmican, dried meat, and grease to maintain its northern brigades.

These were traded to the various posts and sent upriver by canoe or, increasingly in the case of the Hudson's Bay Company, by York boat.

Logically if not legitimately pemmican-laden canoes were considered fair game by both Nor'westers and XY men. Trade depended on them. During the summers between 1800 and 1804 frequent skirmishes took place on the river with the sole purpose of delaying or even destroying the other's life line. On the river every bend presented new hazards. Shots were fired on many a canoe. Men fought with their bare hands on shore. Indians were bought off. With probably a thousand men on the river the number of canoes engaged ran into the hundreds. They transported sufficient pemmican to supply each man with some four pounds a day. They took up thousands of gallons of rum. And each spring they carried downstream the real reason for it all—those valuable pelts. While actual loss of life on the Saskatchewan was small as compared with the fierce struggle on the Athabasca, there was ample opportunity for violence to which Mackenzie's XY Company was especially addicted. The conservative Hudson's Bay Company tried to stay clear of the struggle but eventually it too had to resort to brute methods as a means of defense. Alexander Henry the younger summed up the situation in an incident which took place on the Red River, but which was typical of the Saskatchewan. He said:

"Grosse Gueule and myself had a serious dispute; he wanted to give his furs to the XY which I prevented at the risk of my life; he was advised by them to kill me.

"I went to the Upper Tongue River to meet a band of Indians returning from hunting beaver, and fought several battles with the women to get their furs from them. It was most disagreeable. It is true it was all my neighbor's debts," that is, furs for which his competitors had already given the natives goods.

From Island Fort, as elsewhere along the Saskatchewan, men were sent out to smoke with the Indians, thus placing them in their debt, as well as to minimize the dangers of concentration in case of attack. The practice led to almost as much danger from one another as from the natives. Yet with a naïveté almost childish, rival white men traveled together to meet their trading Indians though time after time the journey ended in disagreement. With some three thousand warriors along the Saskatchewan system, any danger from rival white men was preferable to an attack from a band of those fearless, proud fighters. White men at least did not scalp.

So it was that from Island Fort in the winter of 1802 Nor'wester James King set out on an overnight fur-gathering trip with XY Company clerk La Mothe, also on a similar errand. Upper Saskatchewan weather, because it is so far inland and so far north, is given to extremes. "Forty below" is common in winter, often accompanied by a gale so strong as to hurl snow against the traveler like a sand blast. King and La Mothe found it much colder up on the prairie than at the forts down in the protection of the deep river valley. Accompanied by two or three assistant clerks they set out with dog sleds and on snowshoes, an apparently congenial group of young men. As usual they started early in the morning, traveling until about three in the afternoon when they stopped to make camp. A clump of bushes protected them from the wind. Food was such game as they hunted along the way, moose, deer, or buffalo. Tossing hunks of the raw meat to the yelping dogs, tied nearby, they lit a fire and soon the smell of sizzling steak or buffalo hump was so tantalizing that no one could wait until it was fully cooked. Meat was their sole diet, often without salt, but by the time a fur trader had reached the Upper Saskatchewan he had learned to do without bread or biscuit. For drink he melted snow, topping it off with a precious dram of rum. And then after a smoke all slept.

They lay close together, each man sharing his body warmth with his neighbor. The two at the outside suffered most, but if their bed was made of spruce or pine boughs, as it might have been in that location and at that period, even they were comfortable enough. Sleeping snugly together with their clerks on either side King and La Mothe showed no evidence of the violent animosity which characterised the North West and XY companies.

Daytime found them tramping on again, calling to one another, commenting on the weather, noting familiar landmarks. King suggested to La Mothe that they come to an agreement about credits before reaching the tepee village. La Mothe agreed. The journey brought no unpleasant disagreements.

At the Indian encampment each trader and his men slept in tents of natives who had smoked with his company. Next morning, after the usual formalities dear to Indians, King packed up the furs he had collected and then went over to the tent where La Mothe was staying for some pelts due him there. He was told that La Mothe had taken them all. Brusquely King demanded restitution at once.

"You would give them up?" asked La Mothe, coming out of the buffalo-hide tepee.

"I would not!" retorted King.

"Ha! So you do not get these, my friend!"

The two white traders glowered over the bundles of furs while the natives gathered round. Each had forgotten the amiable journey together. Nothing mattered now but to get as many skins as possible. It was one company against the other, and all that implied.

"Be careful," warned La Mothe. "Do not force me!"

King looked at him and reached toward a pile of beaver skins. It was too much. La Mothe fired, killing him. In the heat of the moment he threatened any who might interfere. But his ardor died quickly. Remorsefully he blamed his action on the system under which they worked.

The shooting of King created much excitement. La

Mothe went east to stand trial, only to return when it became apparent that he must spend months in jail while the limits of the jurisdiction of the Canadian courts were settled. One immediate result was the Canada Jurisdiction Act, which provided for civil magistrates and justices of the peace with authority to try offenses committed "within any of the Indian territories or parts of America not within the limits of the Provinces of Upper or Lower Canada or of any civil government of the United States of America." No mention was made of the territory under monopoly to the Hudson's Bay Company. The person charged might be committed to Lower Canada for trial and it would be lawful for "any person or persons whatever to apprehend . . . or cause to be conveyed with all convenient speed . . . any person guilty of any crime, there to be delivered into safe custody for the purpose of being dealt with according to the law."

That first step toward justice in the sparsely populated spaces of the Northwest provided plenty of opportunity for errors of omission and commission. For one thing an unscrupulous trader might arrest his opponent on a false charge and take him all the way to Montreal. The victim could most likely prove his innocence, but in the meantime he had been removed from competition for a season, much to the advantage of his rival. Naturally every opportunity would be taken to work the scheme in reverse the following year. It was extremely handy during the struggle between the Nor'westers and the XY men and the excuse for many a boisterous "arrest" with and without warrants.

Several Nor'westers were named justices of the peace, including Duncan McGillivray and Sir Alexander Mackenzie. No Hudson's Bay Company men were named; the English monopoly left them out of the dispute, where most of its servants preferred to be. Though they were paid whether they got any furs or not, they certainly were not paid enough to want to risk their lives with any bloodthirsty Nor'wester.

It took only a year or two for both Nor'westers and XY people to realize that the competition was rapidly becoming ruinous economically and morally.

During the years 1802, 1803, and 1804, when the total population was about a hundred and twenty thousand, more rum was imported than at any other period during the entire fur trade struggle. The average each year for the North West Company was 14,400 gallons of concentrated high wines, the variety of alcohol that could be adulterated with water by as much as one to nine or ten, making better than a hundred thousand gallons. The XY Company averaged at least five thousand gallons of concentrated liquor a year. Altogether the Hudson's Bay Company had to cope with an annual flow of nearly two hundred thousand gallons of the most potent persuasion ever turned on the Indians. But, while the English company had more than enough difficulties trying to trade with drunken natives, its financial saving as compared with the dual opposition was considerable. That fact had its influence on the Canadians, as well as their natural sickening of the debauchery of red men outside their stockades and red women within. They wanted an end to the mad struggle before it put an end to them.

Few more welcome canoes ever appeared on the Saskatchewan than the express that bore word of the union of the North West and XY companies, the older company to have seventy-five shares in the newly organized North West Company, and the XY to have twenty-five. An interesting clause in the agreement allowed for the possible absorption of the Hudson's Bay Company, evidence that Sir Alexander Mackenzie was influencing the Canadians at last. Now the fur trade struggle was reduced to a two-way opposition between the Nor'westers and the English company.

CHAPTER TEN

Her Ladyship, My Squaw

MOST servants of the Hudson's Bay Company as well as Nor'westers had Indian "wives." As Henry Kelsey and Anthony Henday had discovered in common with many a French voyageur, a man needed a squaw to carry and do for him. Nature demanded a mate. Fortunately Cree women, and, later, Assiniboins and Blackfeet, turned out to be loyal and loving—and extremely useful. Apart from cooking and carrying, sewing and producing a family, they were good at intelligence; a white man with a chief's daughter in his house enjoyed the protection of her tribe; he knew what was going on. He also enjoyed her family's trade.

The relationship was by no means one-sided. Many an Indian girl fell in love with her white man in the best storybook tradition. On the whole white men living in the Northwest were like white men anywhere else; they even fell in love, so much so in some cases that they preferred to remain permanently in the Indian country because they realized that their wives could never be happy in civilization. Some white men made the mistake of taking their squaws back to civilization. Many deserted them and their families in the Indian country without making provision for their care. But whether by book or bell or the gift of a keg of dilute rum to the girl's father, an Indian woman was little more than a slave. There is scarcely a record of a squaw's name. "She" was good enough.

They were comely, though, those Cree girls of the seventeen-seventies who with their tribes waited each year at Peonan Creek or Nipawin for the hunters' return. From the river many a white man looked with eager eyes to the high banks of the Saskatchewan as their indolent native canoemen quickened their paddle pace. There were great reunions in the tepees and much eating and singing and dancing before the tribes finally drifted off toward their hunting grounds. The scenes were much the same as white men pushed farther upstream.

From early times white men were popular with native men as well as women. While an Indian resented another Indian's having an affair with his wife, except with his permission, a child by a white man was usually welcomed. Chiefs vied with one another in presenting their daughters to the traders and their servants, sometimes for a considerable gift and, until spoiled by white men, often attended by traditional ceremony. Indians were not given to monogamy. Though their women were regarded as drudges, they were happy enough. Left alone by white men the natives might have continued long as happy nomads, following buffalo and beaver, enjoying a little warfare attended by a lot of drumming, worshiping their tribal spirits, blissfully ignorant of change and progress.

Some of their customs were familiar to traders coming from the East, especially from New England where bundling was famous. A young Indian, attracted to a maiden, watched her tent until he discovered the location of her sleeping robe. When night came he crept under the tent and, rolled in his own robe, spent the night beside her, slipping out quietly before dawn. If the attraction proved mutual, gifts were arranged and either he went to live in her tent or she came to his. There is no reason to suppose young white men were less observant than young Indians.

They added a lot of interest to the posts on the Saskatchewan, those Cree women. As the trade moved up the river, Assiniboin and Blackfoot squaws came to live within the stockades. The Hudson's Bay Company, on paper at least, preferred not to acknowledge them and their dusky progeny. Nor'westers and the other traders from Canada took a more liberal view. There was a brief time when they ruled that the burden of women and children was too heavy for the forts to maintain, and that they must be kept outside and at the men's own expense. But the ruling was ignored. Indian women were indispensable.

Nor'westers weren't reticent about mentioning them. David Thompson, Alexander Henry the younger, Duncan McGillivray, Daniel Harmon, and Sir Alexander Mackenzie, who abandoned his native wife and family in the Northwest—all paid tacit if not eloquent tribute to their usefulness and, sometimes, to other qualities equally endearing. Useful qualities merited most space. "Women gathering gum for the canoes" . . . "women drying buffalo hides for boats" . . . "women pounding meat for pemmican" . . . "making snowshoes" . . . "gathering and drying berries" . . . "women hauling firewood"—there wasn't much which Indian women did not do for their lords except hunt game and press pelts.

In the great days of the two main companies, about the end of the eighteenth century, posts on the upper river often had as many as seventy or eighty white men. With rare exceptions each had his Indian consort. Occasionally some had more than one; there is at least one record of a voyageur keeping two wives and his children at the expense of the

North West Company. They fought among themselves, both men and women. They died for one another and sometimes killed. They trapped and traded furs. Rum and syphilis took a toll. And when the annual trip had been made to Grand Portage with the furs, there was a great home-coming by way of celebration, never without an all-night ball. It was a fulsome, rugged life.

Indian women quickened the paddles of the great North West Company brigades just as they had done with the few canoes decades earlier on the lower river. As the time of the home-coming approached they prepared great quantities of meat and berries. Each woman waited in her gayest and best finery, while downstream from the post the brigades halted to give the men a chance to shave and put on bright shirts and scarfs. There was no straggling up to the fort after the great trip. No arriving weary and dull. With a rollicking song that echoed and re-echoed from the high banks they announced their coming, paddles keeping time, hearts beating faster as eyes strained for the women on the lookout and ears tensed for the crackle of the welcoming "feu de joie."

It was a wonderful sight, the forts as seen from the river, log houses large and small surrounded by the log palisade, company flag flying from its high pole, gun smoke from the salute blown like pennants from each of the corner bastions. And behind the fort, generally situated on one of the lower shelves of the river, high banks rose up and up to the sky line.

With a flourish and a love song—that is how the returning fur brigades drew up before their fort. The trip upriver had been grueling and long, the rapids dangerous, and the shoals tiresome. Perhaps they had been short of food and restless when they paused for a smoke at nooning. But it was all past now. At hand was plenty of good food, the kegs of rum they had carried over the portages, the music of the fiddle and the bagpipes, and their women who had waited so long. Not a man but had a precious gift tucked away in his dunnage.

Alexander Henry the younger had a home-coming ball at Fort Vermillion when the brigade arrived in September of 1809. His men, in spite of the rigors of their journey, were as alert as though they had rested for a month. Later they could sleep. But first, the ball. There were seventy-two men and thirty-seven women with sixty-five children in the bourgeois's house for that ball, in a room only 22 by 23 feet. The crowding was uncomfortable, the heat of so many bodies oppressive. Yet they danced till daybreak, well sustained by plenty of buffalo meat, wild swans and ducks, and rum. To the voyageurs such good times made up for a lot of hardship.

Alexander Henry had with him "her ladyship, my squaw," who was first lady at the post and a very useful servant as well. Years before, when Henry was at the Red River post, this chief's daughter "took possession" of his room following the New Year's festivities, and refused to leave. Realizing that "the devil could not have got her out," Henry went off buffalo hunting. But "the encumbrance," as he called her, remained. In time she endeared herself to him and he took her with him to the posts on the upper Saskatchewan. She and their family lived with him in the great days when Henry was in charge of Rocky Mountain House, when that outpost was the base for the historic explorations over the Rockies. Apparently, even her ladyship did not merit the recording of her name. In his extensive journal she is "she."

Henry realized that only a native woman could live the life of the frontier, a woman who could have her baby and be running about the fort in an hour or so, one who solved the diaper problem with moss, who carried her baby on her back wherever she went and while doing most of her common tasks.

Daniel Harmon, a contemporary of Henry's with a religious turn of mind, gave long and careful consideration before he took a squaw, perhaps on account of his inherited Yankee caution. Several chiefs' daughters had been offered him before he finally decided to accept an Indian girl of fourteen, admitting that it was customary for all gentlemen who remained long in that part of the world to have a female companion. Harmon was influenced by the fact that the girl was said to have a mild disposition and an even temper, qualities which he considered "very necessary to make an agreeable woman, and an affectionate partner." Fourteen was a popular "marrying" age for Indian girls at that time.

Harmon was extraordinarily happy with "my woman," as he called her when he did not refer to her as "the mother of my children." At first he planned to leave her with some honorable man who would care for her after he left the Indian country. But he came to love her so deeply that he took her back to Vermont with him. Every year or so while he was in the fur trade, a child of theirs was sent down the Saskatchewan to his eastern relatives for schooling. The names of the children are mentioned, but never that of the mother.

One of the first upper river "first ladies" who was not all Indian was Charlotte Small, daughter of an Irishman of good family and an Indian woman, David Thompson's wife. She heralded the era of half-breed wives who, due to their strain of white blood, often were accorded the dignity of a name. Gradually they took the place of full-blooded squaws with white men. But up to the end of the nineteenth century many a fur-trading post provided a warm corner for a Granny Saskatchewan, clawing her blanket about her shriveled old body as she remembered that once a chief factor had been her lover. "She" or "her ladyship"—it mattered little to the old crone so long as she had warmth and tobacco for her pipe and enough food to suck through her toothless gums. She was the symbol, a little warped perhaps, of the gallantry of white men, much happier than she could ever be in the civilization to which her man had returned.

The Hudson's Bay Company, prior to 1820 and its amalgamation with the fortunes and high spirits of the Nor'westers, lacked gaiety. There were fewer men, for one thing. And they were a more sober lot. Only when men bearing the names of the great clans of Scotland flocked to the Saskatchewan along with the Frenchmen from the St. Lawrence did the posts of the English company ring with laughter and song and the tap of eager feet. The English had not the temperament for making merry under the circumstances; their Orkneymen servants were bred to a stern struggle for existence. Endurance was their main characteristic. But when in 1821 union brought the really great days at the upper river posts, especially at Fort Edmonton, Indian and half-breed girls learned a few words of English to mix with their native Cree and Blackfoot and the already acquired French. They learned to dance the reel and the schottische as well as the gavotte. Bagpipes moaning the "Song of the Isles" stirred their blood almost as thrillingly as their native tom-toms drumming a war dance. For Scotsmen and Frenchmen could be nearly as barbaric as Indians on occasion, much to the discomfiture of the reticent English. Yet it was often the departure of a reticent Englishman that taught an Indian woman the depths of heartache.

Though the Hudson's Bay Company had little space in its journals for mentioning events or incidents in the private lives of its servants, the rival Nor'westers generously kept an eye on them. They recorded balls as well as brawls, perhaps because the balls were rare enough to be news. The arrival of the sturdy York boats of the English company at the home post gradually came to mean a dance, at which squaws sported a counterpart of the gifts the Canadians had brought up from Grand Portage or, after 1801, Fort William. There was no cause for jealousy, since goods for the Indian trade all came from England or Scotland, whether they arrived on the Saskatchewan by way of Hudson Bay or Montreal. They were greatly prized, those gaudy beads and garish calicoes, as much as the rare silks and velvets imported after the union.

Most of the presents came to Edmonton, the great center of trade and social life on the river during the fur trade era as it is today. It was John Rowand, son of a Montreal doctor and of Irish ancestry, fearless, strong, respected by the natives, whose regime brought to its peak the social life of squaws at Fort Edmonton. Rowand married his Indian consort eventually.

White men brought about many changes to the lives of Indian women who lived in those great stockaded posts on the upper Saskatchewan. Sometimes the changes meant grief and heartache when the brief tenure ended and the woman had to return to her own people or stay on at the fort without the social and physical support of her lord. Either way it was bad. That taste of security and enough to eat spoiled her for the rigors of the teepee. If she remained at the fort she was still a woman in spite of her slavelike status, vulnerable alike to loneliness and the taunts of other women. The greatest tragedy that could happen was to have to part with her children, to have them sent away to what the white men called school, never to return perhaps. New sicknesses for which neither famous medicine men nor white traders had remedies attacked her, sicknesses such as smallpox and syphilis. In time even that most natural act of having babies became painful and difficult, perhaps because, as many a white man noted, life within the stockade soon rendered squaws fat and lazy and less attractive. The change-over from a hard, nomadic life seems to have cost Indian women their comparatively easy pregnancies. More than once, when there was some question as to whether a woman was a white child who had been kidnaped by Indians, childbirth settled the point: if delivery was easy, she was native; if it was painful and difficult, she was pronounced white.

White men noted other things about Indian women. Too frequently they reported that squaws became horrible and licentious when debauched by alcohol. They were a nuisance and worse when, with men and children, they joined in a disgusting clamor for more and more rum. Duncan McGillivray, well-known wintering partner, was especially shocked by the effects of rum on native women. They would, when drunk, he reports, expose themselves in the most indecent position, "leaving uncovered those parts which nature requires to be concealed—a circumstance which they carefully avoided in their sober moments." Having no furniture, Indians lolled or sat on the floor, if there was a floor. Generally it was a buffalo robe.

McGillivray voiced an opinion which was becoming current among thinking men all along the Saskatchewan. Too much rum, long a spur to force natives to trap beaver and other animals, was a bad thing when it debauched men. It was unbearable when it demoralized the only women in the country, those soft-voiced natives who, through their half-breed sons and daughters, linked together Englishman and Frenchman, Scot, American, and Canadian to make up the people of the fur trade era in the Northwest. Referred to merely as "she," the squaw proved herself worthy of the lightly bestowed "her ladyship" in the part she played in curtailing rum, whether intentional or otherwise. It was not entirely economics that put an end to doping natives with alcohol. Knighthood still blossomed with the prairie rose, the wild crocus, and the tiger lily.

CHAPTER ELEVEN

Grand Rapids Highwaymen

GOVERNOR in Chief William Williams of the Hudson's Bay Company inspected his cannons with satisfaction. He had ordered it hauled right to the foot of the Grand Rapids and mounted on a swivel. It was trained dead on the regular canoe route. Now let any of those Nor'westers try to slip by at their peril. They were in his power, every last man of them. To be doubly sure he had another cannon mounted on a barge a little lower down toward the river's mouth. His detachment of "de Meuron" soldiers was encamped along the north bank. Well armed they were, and well in hand. So, too, were the officers of the Hudson's Bay Company. The governor, a very new governor, rubbed his hands gleefully.

William Williams was an innovation in the English company, a minor Churchill sprung up in their hour of need. Ex-captain of an East Indiaman, he had the reputation of preferring a fight to peace any time provided the fight was likely to lead to a successful decision. The hour had arrived when the chances of a decision were very good. Williams' quick Irish wit saw the grim humor of the situation and liked it. He patted the batch of warrants in his pocket, some secured against the Nor'westers by Lord Selkirk and a few issued by himself as governor. Having inspected his two cannons and his men, having taken another look at the white waters of the rapids foaming between the rocky shores and another deep breath of the invigorating northern air, he repaired to his quarters to await the first canoe.

Things had been happening to the Hudson's Bay Company since its reorganization in 1810, a reorganization forced on it by the unrelenting goading of its opposition, the North West Company. Now Rupertsland was divided into the vast Southern District and the even vaster Saskatchewan District, each having a chief factor under the governor in chief with his headquarters at York Factory. A new day was dawning for its servants. It was not a very bright day, but there was a little sunshine here and there. Profits were to be shared to the extent of a third, between factor, trading officers, and clerks, a step calculated not so much for the betterment of the servants as to right the dividends, which had dropped from the steady 8 per cent of the late eighteenth century to 4 per cent during the first few years of the nineteenth century and then to no dividends at all. Stocks which had been selling at £250 were as low as £50, a situation which had provided certain Nor'westers, notably Sir Alexander Mackenzie, with the hope of getting control of the opposition and the use of the short passage by way of Hudson Strait. But most important of all was the change in personnel.

"No more men from the Orkneys to be sent out but men from the Western Islands and Coast of Scotland, where the people are of a more spirited race than in Orkney" ran the official company bulletin.

It was tough on the reputation of the Orkneymen who

had served on the Saskatchewan dutifully if not brilliantly almost since its discovery. Perhaps their very devotion to duty and lack of brilliance swung the pendulum all the way over to William Williams. That gentleman's sheer love of force and lack of sublety spearheaded the changes. His very presence was enough to back the story current among Nor'westers that the Hudson's Bay Company planned to build a bullet proof barge to blockade the Grand Rapids. But whether because of his lack of sublety or not Williams grasped the situation and he liked the chances.

A few years previously Lord Selkirk had brought a small band of Scottish settlers to the Red River, setting off the Nor'-western charge which resulted in the massacre of Governor Semple of the Hudson's Bay Company and sixteen of his men. The massacre had led to the importation of the de Meuron soldiers. Lord Selkirk had hoped the colony would produce food for the company, but he had a far more important objective. He wanted to stress the company's monopoly. Without resulting to force or civil intervention from London he planned to cut the North West Company's waterway from the St. Lawrence to the rich fur fields of the Athabasca and the Mackenzie. The monopoly of 1670 covered territories drained by rivers flowing into Hudson Bay. If the Nor'westers at long last bowed to the monopoly, the Hudson's Bay Company would secure the entire fur trade of the Northwest. The Nor'-westers had not bowed. They had increased their opposition to the point of violence.

The bitterest strife in the era of violence occurred about the forts of the Athabasca and the Peace. In recent years the Hudson's Bay Company had really pressed its trade, even enlisting two former Nor'westers, Colin Robertson and John Clarke, to engage Canadians from the St. Lawrence to man their canoes. The North West Company, finding that the English company had at last aroused itself to striking heat, used every weapon of opposition it could lay its hands on including pistols, not always for two, starvation, and presenting warrants for arrests under the Canada Jurisdiction Act. And most of it in weather from twenty to forty degrees below zero! There were tough and ruthless bullies on both sides, though the Nor'westers by choice and tradition had the edge on ruthlessness. The Hudson's Bay Company, also by choice and tradition, steered as lawful a course as possible, instructing its servants to "defend like men the Property entrusted to you [but] if any person shall presume to make a forcible attack on you, you have arms in your hands and the Law sanctions you in using them in your defense."

The route from the St. Lawrence to the Mackenzie cuts right across the continent. It links hundreds of thousands of square miles of territory. In the days of canoes all waterways from the east and the north converged at Grand Rapids on the Saskatchewan. It was the bottleneck down which every canoe must shoot or be portaged. Remembering all this Governor Williams rubbed his hands gleefully as he inspected his two cannons, mounted on swivels so that their noses pointed on the very foot of the rapids.

The first canoe carried John Clarke, of the Hudson's Bay Company. Clarke, still smarting from his treatment by the Nor'westers, eagerly fell in with the governor's plan. Clarke had been arrested on a trumped-up excuse and carried north to Great Slave Lake during the height of the previous year's trading season. He and his men swelled the number waiting behind the cannon at the foot of the rapids. They did not have to wait long.

On June 18, 1819, Nor'westers Benjamin Frobisher, son of one of the early fur-trading Frobishers, and John Duncan Campbell arrived at the head of the rapids with their two clerks. The river was swift and swollen with melting ice and snow from the mountains. The gentlemen disembarked in the usual manner, being carried to the shore on the shoulders of voyageurs as other canoemen stood in the current and held the frail craft steady. While the canoe shot the rapids they strolled over the 2-mile portage. The canoes arrived first and at once the men were taken prisoner and lodged in the temporary jail thoughtfully prepared by Williams. Barely suppressing his excitement the governor dispatched a group of de Meuron soldiers to waylay Frobisher and Campbell.

The gentlemen, with their clerks, had just emerged from the path through the woods when one of the soldiers sprang at Campbell, aiming a blow at his head, "with the butt end of his firelock." The other Canadians were quickly surrounded by soldiers, "armed with muskets, fixed bayonets, pistols, swords & c., and whooping and hollowing like so many demons." There was a terrific scuffle. Campbell and Frobisher demanded by what right this highway holdup was perpetrated. How dare Williams treat them in such highhanded manner! Where were the warrants?

"Legal proceedings are all dam' nonsense in the Northwest," Williams retorted. The governor told his fuming captives that, having the advantage, he intended to follow it up and make the most of it. Against his cannons and his soldiers the disarmed Nor'westers were helpless.

Williams, recalling many indignities to which officers and servants of his company had been subjected by the Nor'westers, had no inclination to be soft. During the struggle Benjamin Frobisher received a blow on the head which is said to have contributed to his death six months later. The prisoners were paddled over to a small island in the river, a little "Devil's Island." They were confined in cramped quarters. The heat was intolerable. Mosquitoes, famous on that part of the river in June, boiled about them.

Eventually Frobisher and Campbell, with other Nor'westers taken prisoner during the summer, were sent to York Factory. Frobisher and two voyageurs escaped. But Governor Williams's brutal treatment and the blow on his head had impaired Frobisher's health to such an extent that he was in no condition for the hazardous, 500-mile journey back to the Saskatchewan and a friendly North West Company post. Already it was October. The winds were cold and small streams were frozen over each morning. The three men were scantily clad. Their food was the fish and game they could catch or snare with their hands. When not even a bird was to be had they boiled bits of hide and, eventually, their moccasins and the heels of Frobisher's "European shoes." Frobisher daily became weaker. He died of exposure on the shore of Cedar Lake, only a couple of days' journey from the post toward which he had struggled.

Governor Williams had no shortage of prisoners for his little island jail. Frobisher and Campbell had hardly been disposed of, the operation requiring a little time as their papers were all examined, when another group of Nor'westers reached the head of the rapids, seven laden canoes under a half-breed, Paul, and his son. Williams arrested Paul and his two best steersmen but let the brigade go through. Next day more canoes appeared. At that season canoes daily could be expected to run the rapids on the way down to Fort William. Governor Williams had plenty of warrants and none of the Nor'westers had been allowed to get away to spread a warning. On June 23 there was a fine haul, Angus Shaw, a well-known wintering partner from Fort Augustus on the upper Saskatchewan, and John George McTavish and William McIntosh, from the Peace River. McIntosh, having an acute indisposition, did not stroll across the portage but went down the rapids in his canoe. He was arrested as he reached their foot, being hauled through the water by his collar. In his case Williams did not even bother to present a warrant.

Angus Shaw protested his arrest in fine Nor'western manner. He demanded to know by what right Governor Williams dared to stop him on the king's highway. Did he not know of the proclamation issued by the prince regent ordering all parties to cease from violence?

"I do not care a curse for the proclamation!" exclaimed Governor Williams. "I act upon the charter of the Hudson's Bay Company, and as governor and magistrate in these territories I have sufficient authority and will do as I think proper."

Williams implied that the Canadian colonial secretary, through whom the proclamation was issued, was bribed by North West gold and that he, Williams, would act independently of the rascally government of Canada. He would use every power to "drive out of the country every D . . . North-Wester it contains, or perish in the attempt."

It was a proud boast, well backed by the two cannons. The little island jail could barely hold any more prisoners so complete were the results of the governor's coup. He had all cassettes and packages opened. Important North West Company papers were confiscated. His prisoners had no chance whatever with the de Meuron soldiers, taking them one or two at a time as they strolled, unaware of danger, across the well-worn portage or as their canoes shot the foaming waters of the rapids. Nor were they treated with much consideration, especially after Shaw announced that he "would return in a space of forty days and spread carnage and bloodshed throughout the country."

One of Williams's main hopes in waylaying the Nor'westers was to free Colin Robertson, who had been arrested up on the Athabasca, following an attempt by Nor'westers to drown him. Robertson, inured to the demands of tough defense as well as tough offense, had survived. While being taken east as a prisoner of the Nor'westers he made his escape at Cumberland Lake. He and Williams had a jubilant meeting at Grand Rapids. With Robertson free and most of the warrants used, Williams felt it was high time to retire to York Factory. He did so, lacking one of his prisoners, McIntosh.

McIntosh's acute indisposition, a bad attack of diarrhea, required his frequent retirement. On every opportunity while out of sight of Williams's guards he forced himself to work on a small raft of branches. It was risky work. Eventually, "while his bed and fire were being prepared," according to Governor Williams's official report, McIntosh, using a branch

Spring Break-up on
the Main Saskatchewan

for a paddle, crossed on his frail raft from the island to the south shore of the Saskatchewan. From there, weak from his illness and without food, he trudged over the neck of land to Lake Winnipeg. With great good fortune he was able to hail a passing canoe which took him down to Bas de la Rivière. Before embarking he covered his track by leaving a book in which he had scribbled that he intended to commit suicide.

Governor Williams left for York Factory without firing either of his prized cannons.

The Nor'westers vowed that they would get Williams. They had a warrant issued for his arrest. The governors of the Hudson's Bay Company, not quite prepared for the boldness of their representative in Rupertsland, discussed the situation thoroughly. Characteristically they appointed a *locum tenens* governor, George Simpson, to be prepared for the possible event of Williams's arrest by the Nor'westers and being carried off to Montreal. The caution of a hundred and fifty years was not to be thrown overboard in one big gesture by one servant, no matter how diligent he might be in prosecuting the company's interests.

Colin Robertson, back on the Athabasca, decided that the "Grand Rapids affair," as they came to call it, had been a very good thing for the Hudson's Bay Company.

"Our opponents," he wrote to Governor Williams by the winter express, "have lowered their tone; they talk now of conducting their business on amicable principles . . . The North West Coys servants have the old story of a junction in their heads . . . whatever their prospects may be, there is certainly a great change in their conduct; the affair of the Grand Rapids has not so much as produced a menace."

Yet rumors began to circulate throughout the Northwest. By spring Robertson heard that the Nor'westers were going to assemble a large force at the mouth of the Saskatchewan by way of retaliation. He decided to go down to see Governor Williams. due at that time of year at Cumberland House.

Robertson had a lot to discuss with the governor. His own post had been on such short rations all winter that his men were scarcely fit to make the trip from the Athabasca. Other Hudson's Bay Company posts throughout the fur country north of the Saskatchewan were on short rations. The men were grumbling. Some, he knew, were half starved. Few were in any mood or condition to put up strong opposition to the Nor'westers. The least the governor could do, decided Robertson, was to supply a large force of men, well armed, and sufficient food for those who were manning the trading posts.

What Robertson learned at Cumberland House tallied with his former estimation of the English company, too little, too late, and with excessive caution. Robertson placed more stress on being on good terms with the natives and on the welfare of his men than on the cold, enduring values of a balance sheet. To him supplies and a defense force were more important at that moment than counting the cost. But he had no chance to discuss these points with the governor.

Governor Williams already had left Cumberland House for York Factory, traveling by the Minago River route, quite good when the waters were high in spring. He advised Robertson to do the same, avoiding Grand Rapids! The governor left very little food, no force to cope with a Nor'western attack except the sixty men from the north who had been on short rations for weeks, and the legal opinion of the company's London lawyers concerning the validity of the attack at Grand Rapids the previous year!

"With a perfect knowledge of the designs of our opponents, he joins the saskatchwine boats, gallops off . . . and leaves for our defense the opinions of Messrs. Scarlet and Chitty!" (the London lawyers) exclaimed Robertson. He was so appalled by his governor's lack of follow-up action that he forgot to put a capital on Saskatchewan and even misspelled the familiar word.

Robertson soon discovered that it was too late in the season to find enough water in the "track" recommended. His only way was to "shape his course" for Cedar Lake in the hope of finding some Indians there who would know whether the Nor'westers actually were at Grand Rapids in force. No Indians were at Cedar Lake—a bad sign. Robertson feared the worst. He encamped for the night and made his plans.

After his men were asleep he and his clerk wrapped the company's papers in a piece of "crocus," or yellow oilskin, and hid them in a bag of pemmican. In case he should be arrested Robertson gave his clerk careful directions for Williams's guidance of the northern trade for the coming winter. He was employing resourcefulness characteristic of the North West Company's wintering partners and clerks, who though not always cautious men of finance were incredibly able in the field.

After passing a sleepless night Robertson "descended the current" to the rapids. There he and four of his men disembarked while the clerk went down with the steersman and the canoe. Each of the men carried a piece to lighten the canoe.

All appeared calm and safe. Robertson walked on and on, not a little apprehensive since he had been on the arresting side of last year's coup. Perhaps the rumor had been exaggerated. If so, what a joke on the governor! They had almost reached the end of the portage when he saw a man's fresh track. He knew what that meant. So, too, did his men.

"We can't go back," said Robertson firmly to allay their fears. "We must advance."

Looking about they saw a small group of men behind them. No one was in front. They walked on. The foot of the rapids was in sight. Beside it stood a group of half-breeds, armed. Yet they made no attempt to stop Robertson and his men. He kept his eye on them, though, as he steadily advanced. Then he saw Nor'wester Henry McKenzie. In a moment he was surrounded by armed Canadians. Robertson struck out to defend himself. The Canadians closed in. Someone, from behind, snatched his gun. Robertson demanded the reason for this highwayman treatment. He demanded to see the warrant for his arrest. His captors laughed in his face. Just then his canoe came down the rapids.

Robertson's men, not being held as he was, at once rushed into the water and leapt aboard. Robertson urged the steersman to push on before the Nor'westers could seize the craft. The steersman, with the canoe, made his escape. In no time, too, Robertson was on his way, but not to York Factory as he had intended. The Nor'westers were taking him down to Fort William, a prisoner.

The North West Company had made a strong protest to the British government concerning Williams's treatment of the previous year. A copy of their instructions to the wintering partners also had been sent to the colonial secretary. Characteristically they followed up with action. A group of partners, including John George McTavish and J. D. Campbell, still smarting under their arrest of the past summer, had journeyed to Grand Rapids. They had sixty or seventy men and placed themselves in two competent squads where they could closely guard the descent. Every Hudson's Bay Company canoe that came down was halted. Every officer who crossed by the portage faced investigation. Most were arrested. It was a glorious month for the Nor'westers in spite of the mosquitoes and the almost unbearable heat common at the end of June. Once again the natives had cause to ponder the incredible ways of white men.

Tit for tat! Last summer the Hudson's Bay Company had carried off the leading Nor'westers and some of their best guides to Hudson Bay and eventually to England, greatly disorganizing their affairs. Now Robertson and various other Hudson's Bay Company men were placed out of reach of their company's business. John Duncan Campbell, gleeful at the undertaking, escorted Colin Robertson personally.

Campbell considerately told his prisoner that not all the wintering partners approved the current reign of violence at Grand Rapids. He even told Robertson that his colleagues realized that the Indians were laughing at the white men, and that union between the two companies was at hand. Robertson did not know how close to union they really were. Quicker communication could have changed a lot of plans if not reshaped the course of the two companies.

Robertson regretted Williams's lack of follow-up whether it was the result of his own ineptitude or the company's many-sided caution. Personally, though he was allowed to escape, the arrest put him in a bad light with the committee in London.

So far as the eventual outcome of the main struggle was concerned the highwayman tactics at Grand Rapids were a mere stumbling block to the inevitable march of events. The Nor'westers could not continue with the long haul from the St. Lawrence. The English firm, due to the force of its slow, dogged accumulation of strength, its belated reorganization, and the infusion of competent North West Company personnel, was in a much better position. The two companies united in 1821, retaining the proud Hudson's Bay Company name, the monopoly, and some of the best men and traditions of the Canadian company.

Union of the two great forces brought about something much greater than the sum of the separate parts. The vigor, independence, and resourcefulness of the Canadians, men who were the best canoemen in the world and who could live off the country, coupled with the cautious, solid security of the English company, resulted in a new era for the fur trade in the Northwest. Without the proud Nor'westers the Hudson's Bay Company might not now be the oldest company in the world. It might have folded up a century ago, unable to stand the unaccustomed excitement of such an unprecedented coup as that of Governor in Chief William Williams.

The governor apparently had tried a traditional North West Company tactic without the traditional Nor'western ability to back it to the limit. He served for a year as cogovernor with George Simpson, and then was relegated to the less important Southern District as chief factor. The New Saskatchewan District of the Hudson's Bay Company was ready to welcome its outstanding chief factor, John Rowand, a Nor'wester brought up in the Nor'west tradition.

CHAPTER TWELVE

"John Rowand, They Say . . ."

THEY still talk about him along the Saskatchewan. Some say he was a just man and liked. Others claim his temper was so violent that it killed him, and just what he deserved. Edmonton proudly recalls Rowand's Folly, the enormous house he built for the Hudson's Bay Company—and himself—within the biggest stockade beside the most dangerous Indian tribe of the plains, the Blackfeet. They say he had great power over the natives, who called him "Big Mountain." The yarns about what happened to his bones sound as though they had improved with every telling, yet none is taller than the truth. And then, of course, there was the romantic affair with the Indian girl. Only the dry Hudson's Bay Company reports of the enormous trade he secured are unembellished.

As the son of an assistant surgeon at Montreal General Hospital young John Rowand easily secured a clerkship with the Nor'westers. In 1802 he was with John MacDonald of Garth. He was still on the river when he died in 1854, in his shoes and in one of his famous rages, on the dock at Fort Pitt. No one knew the Saskatchewan better or loved it more. His fifty-odd years on or beside it were a record for a man in his position in an era when gentlemen in the fur trade usually retired to the St. Lawrence or England, if not to the growing colony at the Red River. But then John Rowand stayed with his Indian girl. The Saskatchewan was home. He was one of the earlier squaw men to realize that an Indian could not possibly be happy in civilized society while a white man could enjoy primitive living, especially if he had enough authority. It was probably about 1810 when "she" came into his life.

Irish ancestry and French-Canadian upbringing were ideal for the Indian country. Rowand soon learned native dialects. He mastered the intricacies of the fur trade and the importance of such little details as impressing the chiefs by boiling water without fire but with some of his father's Seidlitz powders. After the union he was the right man to rule the vast territory from Cumberland House to the Rockies. He did so with the dash of an emperor and the drive of a modern business magnate. Everyone knew his eyes of blue steel, especially a brown-skinned, black-eyed girl who shared some of his qualities—and some of his life.

One morning she watched Rowand ride out of the gate of the Fort des Prairies, off buffalo hunting. Perhaps he had never noticed her. She was young; Indian girls in those days and under their primitive living condition matured startlingly fast. But it was different with her. The young man rode a superb horse, sitting his native saddle with that fine, arrogant Irish way of his. She couldn't help seeing him. She was watching for his return later in the day.

Her eyes narrowed when at last she saw his horse trotting back to the familiar gate, riderless. Her heart filled with apprehension. Well she knew what that might mean. Instinctively she ran to her pony and was galloping across the dry prairie grass while the white men were discussing what to do. Knowing which way to go, she had the edge on them. It led her right to Rowand lying in great pain where his horse had thrown him. His leg was broken. He had been unable to remount or to walk. Doubtless "she" was young and pretty and fresh, but she looked like an angel to Rowand, that brown-skinned girl who already had the eyes of a woman.

She set his leg, binding the splint with some of her own leather garments, doing her best to heed his voluble directions. She nursed him and saved his life. The limp he had for the rest of his days gave him something to boast about, since every fur trader worthy of the name had a few scars to season his yarns. Sir Henry Le Froy, who visited Fort Edmonton and met them thirty years later, reports that Rowand married his Indian girl, though it is likely they lived "according to the customs of the country" until the first priest came up the Saskatchewan.

She must have done much to make him comfortable and happy. No doubt, with her, the first tiny crocus on a southern slope was more thrilling, the music of frogs croaking in a slough sweeter, sunsets and Northern Lights and a great swan hovering over the river at twilight more breathtaking. Into his strong, masculine life of hunting and trading she brought sweet docility and usefulness and at least six half-breed sons and daughters.

It is one of the best Rowand stories, that of the Indian girl riding out to save his life. No one bothers to explain it by propinquity or any of the other silly excuses for love. They like the good, old-fashioned romance, the real thing. They like to recall that the eldest son of John Rowand and his Indian girl, John Rowand Jr., became a chief trader. The second son, Alexander, was graduated from Edinburgh University as a doctor and as surgeon accompanied Sir George Simpson and John Rowand on the trip to the Sandwich

Islands and Honolulu. Later he practiced medicine in Quebec City. There were four daughters: Nancy, who became the wife of chief factor Harriott, probably with a real wedding because there was a priest and church at the fort by that time; and Sophie, Peggy, and Adelaide. They all married well and were the apple of their father's eye. Their names are all recorded. Only the name of Rowand's wife is missing.

Perhaps Madame Rowand had a given name to represent her birthplace, such as Angeline Meadows. She might even have been Susan Pas de Nom, as happened in another case. To the many visitors at Rowand's Folly—another legend, that! —she was the first lady on the Saskatchewan. Her son, when he went to the new and important pemmican center at Fort Pitt, above the Battle River confluence, was known as "Mr. Jack." But the mother of a doctor and a chief trader, the Granny Saskatchewan of a lot of respected and important Canadians was, like many another Indian wife, merely "she."

Horses and buffalo hunting were a passion with Rowand. That was another link with the natives who had introduced horses to the Saskatchewan less than a hundred years before, trading or stealing them up the range routes still in use from the Rio Grande to the great foothills ranches of Alberta. In later years he kept a fine stable at Fort Edmonton and more than one visitor rode his 16-hand chestnut hunter round the level, 2-mile race track. There were always horses where Rowand was, good horses. And dogs. The horses helped provide fresh meat for the fort and some fine sport in the invigorating air of Edmonton's 2,000-foot altitude.

Rowand lived the traditions of the lords of the lakes and rivers. As a young gentleman in the fur trade he had cut his teeth on the arrogant struggle with the XY Company. During two seasons on the Red River he had acquired firsthand knowledge of the fervor with which the Nor'westers opposed the Selkirk settlement. The plan to secure passage to Hudson

Bay was to his liking, along with the fight implied. He was already a wintering partner and a man of some influence when the struggle ended in 1821.

With Rowand there was no thought of leaving the Saskatchewan after union. His loyalty was to the fur trade. His judgment was sound enough to see that union was the only means of survival. Colin Robertson suggested that due attention be paid to his opinions. Governor George Simpson saw in him a man on whom he could rely. In fact Simpson must have welcomed Rowand's good-fellowship at that amazing banquet at York Factory when the bitter enemies of the two former companies met following the amalgamation. They went to that banquet from all over Rupertsland, the gentlemen of the two companies. It is said that no group of greater enemies ever sat down as one company in any dining hall anywhere. They had fought one another with their hands, with weapons, and even by starvation but a short time previous, those proud French and Scottish Nor'westers and the men of the English company. On their bodies, and most certainly in their hearts, they bore many scars of their hard strife. Rowand liked such a situation. That was one reason he was entrusted with the affairs of the Hudson's Bay Company in the important Saskatchewan department.

The officers of the newly organized, revitalized Hudson's Bay Company of 1821 were chosen by deed poll, John Rowand becoming a chief trader. It was probably the best way out of a difficult situation. In fact, in spite of much ineptness and dangerous hatred the change-over on the Saskatchewan was accomplished with a lot of good sense. The Nor'westers lost their identity but they retained the name of their great fort at Rocky Mountain House, the post associated with so much of their enterprise and exploration. With that and with John Rowand in charge no one could take too extreme objection to retaining the name and site of Edmonton in place of Augustus. When it became evident, a couple of years later, that Edmonton rather than Rocky

Mountain House was to become the big center of trade and transport, time had healed some of the old sores. With Rowand in charge—he was transferred in 1823—and his Indian wife and half-breed family within the stockades, the past was soon forgotten. Rowand became chief factor in 1825 and a member of the council of Rupertsland a few years later. Fort Edmonton was the strategic center for the vast Saskatchewan District reaching from Cumberland House to the Rockies. It was the trading center for seven great Indian tribes, the Assiniboins and Crees, who lived nearby all the time, and the Blackfeet, Sarcees, Gros Ventres, Piegans and Bloods, who came twice a year. They all brought dried buffalo meat and fat for making pemmican as well as furs, pemmican being made at Fort Edmonton for many of the big depots of the north as well as for downriver consumption.

There was still much beaver on the river. Governor Simpson reported that, given five years' rest, it would be as rich a source as ever, in spite of being hunted over so ruthlessly in recent decades. Conservation was part of the new policy. There were, as there have been since, years when the river was very low. Recurrent periods of drought are not new to the Saskatchewan country.

Two things brought about the importance of Edmonton, apart from its geographical significance. The one which must have brought most heartache to most people was the passing of the transport canoe. True, the York boat, which took its place, except for express or mail and those canoes used by Governor Simpson on his swift inspection trips, carried more goods and required less personnel, thus increasing the dividends of the Honorable Company. But few of those who took their dividends remembered with a catch in their breath, or ever knew, the clean beauty of a brigade of canoes, the ease with which individual canoes could be carried over a portage or tracked up fast currents, the kind of men they bred. For the canoe had a soul. The York boat had none. No one made up songs to the York boat. There is no counterpart of "The

Song My Paddle Sings." No one loved it and thought of it as being almost immortal. No one was even superstitious about it. Only the wind in its square sails gave it a passing beauty. It was utilitarian, heavy, and safe. It was an instrument of big business, devoid of romance. But it made Fort Edmonton important.

The other contribution to the fort's early importance was the decision of Governor Simpson that the Saskatchewan should be the main highway from York Factory, now in use almost entirely as the port of the fur trade, and the increasingly important Pacific district of Columbia. John Rowand had much to do with that decision.

For some time the hostility of the Indians had driven the brigades to Methye, or as it came to be known, La Loche Portage, and the Pacific north by way of Cumberland Lake and the Beaver River. Rowand showed that much better time could be made by way of the Saskatchewan to Edmonton, even traveling with the heavy, slow York boat brigade. A comparatively large brigade could protect itself from Indian attack, though the presence of John Rowand was generally enough protection from that evil. From Edmonton pack horses and, later, carts could transport the goods overland the fifty miles or so to Fort Assiniboine on the Athabasca from where they were taken up to the Great Divide and on to the Columbia. That was the first pack-horse route in the Northwest. It meant more men to look after more horses at Fort Edmonton, more supplies for the men, more Indian or half-breed women, and their children, more visitors. But the extra men employed at the fort would be Indians and so cheap labor.

The Saskatchewan route saved the company more than a thousand pounds a year, and required less than a third as many voyageurs or boatmen. That was a big consideration when dividends had to be built up after the recent strain. Hardheaded businessman that he was, John Rowand knew, almost as well as did Simpson, that only the constant and painstaking care of every penny, for which the Hudson's Bay Company was often ridiculed, had enabled it to remain solvent and absorb all its opposition. Yet there was his Irish ancestry, his French-Canadian upbringing, and his knowledge of the Indians. He thought much of the prestige of Fort Edmonton, which would entertain many distinguished visitors, for all who journeyed to the Pacific stopped there, from boatmen to governor. Rowand decided that Fort Edmonton must have a suitable house. That house became Rowand's Folly, so called, perhaps, with a tinge of envy. There was nothing like it west of York Factory. Not even York Factory could equal some of its distinctions.

The site itself was imposing, that of "old" Fort Edmonton, high on the river's 200-foot ramparts, on one of the numberless curves so that the river flowed halfway around it. Behind stretched the prairie to its far horizon. Across the great valley that the Saskatchewan had cut through soft cretaceous rock, more prairies bent away to the south. Below, barley and hay, potatoes and turnips grew well on land often enriched by the silt of springtime floods.

Leather teepees, bright with tribal insignia, dotted the benches below the hexagonal palisade, 300 by 200 feet. The palisade was built of logs, 20 feet high, hand hewn and hand split, hauled in place by manpower. The split logs were set in deep trenches filled with earth and secured with horizontal timbers. A sentinel's gallery ran all around, a few feet below the top of the palisade. There were peak-roofed bastions at each corner from which protruded cannons. Massive riveted gates opened to the riverside and to the north, those overslung gates which are still typical of the foothills country. In the center of the imposing palisade rose Rowand's even more imposing new house.

It was of the traditional French-Canadian "poteaux sur sole" type, with squared horizontal logs slid into the grooves of squared uprights, mortised into the foundation sill. Though this type requires less laborious lifting than the log cabin with the round logs notched together at the corners, Rowand had comparatively few white men for the job. The big house was indicative of his ability to get things done. Flogging was still in vogue. Rowand may have used it. Yet it is more likely that he employed more persuasive diplomacy. Since the union rum had been discontinued for the men, even for voyageurs, with whom prohibition must have gone hard. But gentlemen supplied their own. Well enough John Rowand knew the value of a keg or two.

Rowand's Folly had three stories with a gallery running the length of the building and opening off the second floor. That gallery was the favorite place for the governor's kilted piper, Colin Fraser, to walk his slow measured tread as he skirled the Highland airs that never fail to curl the emotions of listeners regardless of the color of their skin. The Indians had never seen or heard anything like it; they supposed Fraser to be related to the Manitou, or Great Spirit. And either because the gallery pleased Fraser or because the kilted Highlander pleased the chief factor, he later became post manager.

Off the gallery was a wide hall with the gentlemen's mess on one side and the ballroom on the other. The Rowand family lived at the rear of these rooms. Upstairs, in the high pitched roof, were offices and bedrooms. Downstairs was the steward's room, armory, storeroom, and cellars. Built just fifty years later, it was a vast improvement on Samuel Hearne's first Hudson's Bay Company house down the Saskatchewan at Cumberland Lake.

They say there were hundreds of small-paned windows in the house, that over two hundred were broken in one hailstorm alone. All the other buildings of the time at Fort Edmonton had parchment windows. There were several cabins for the men. There was the bachelors' hall, the gentlemen's quarters, men's quarters, and the interpreter's house. There were warehouses and some stables and the blacksmith's smithy, his forge burning coal dug out of the riverbanks.

There was that extremely important structure, the glacière, or ice pit, a deep square hole, "paved with blocks of ice from the river," cemented together with water frozen to make a tight compartment. In it were placed quarters of buffalo, hides still on, as they were brought in, seven or eight hundred of them, enough to keep the people of the fort in fresh meat all the next summer. It was topped with a thick layer of straw and protected by a shed. But nothing impressed the natives more effectively than the big house, the *okimaw wikumik,* or chief's house.

Within the palisades and without, women were occupied making clothes and snowshoes, leather for thongs and harness. And pemmican. Hundreds of 90-pound leather bags of pemmican were made each year. The *thup bup, thup bup* of wooden pestles pounding dried meat in a hollow log within the palisade was the undertone for the rhythmic *swish thud, swish thud* of wooden flails beating out fibers of meat on buffalo robes thrown on the ground beside the tepees. The pemmican made within the stockade was much superior to that made on the prairie, where the high wind swept bits of dirt and small stones into it and where the women were less careful than those working under the watchful eyes of the *okimaw* house. Some say it was delicious, especially when made with berries. Others, probably too familiar with the variety made on a none-too-clean buffalo hide, echo the distaste of the man who said of it:

"Take scrapings from the dirtiest outside corner of a very stale piece of cold roast beef, add to it lumps of tallowy, rancid fat . . . than garnish all with human hairs . . . and short hairs of dogs and oxen, and you have pemmican."

Next to the fur and pemmican trade boatbuilding was the big activity at Fort Edmonton. Because there was much more downstream transportation than up, many boats were never returned. It was cheaper to build new ones than to maintain men while they toiled upriver with the old ones. Edmonton had a good supply of suitable timber nearby. In winter the boatbuilders selected and marked the logs, which were floated down in spring. Betweentimes they searched for the right cedar roots needed for making the all-important bow and stern pieces. Cutting boards in the sawpit and boat-building kept men completely busy all winter. In fact, no one stayed long on Hudson's Bay Company's careful payroll and under the direction of Chief Factor Rowand who wasted any of the hours of daylight.

The York boats built at Edmonton were a modified Orkney boat, as might be expected, so many men in the old company having come from the Scottish Isles. They were almost direct descendants of the Viking galleys of the Norsemen, modified and without figureheads and colored sail. Those built on the Saskatchewan were 28 feet long by 6 feet wide. When they were not hauled or, briefly, under sail they were propelled by long sweeps so heavy that the boatman had to rise to his feet with every pull and sit down to complete the swing. It is easily understood why they disappeared so quickly as soon as cheap gasoline marine engines were available. By the nineteen-thirties a search had to be made to find one in good condition for the Hudson's Bay Company museum at Lower Fort Garry.

Perhaps the sight of York boats on the Saskatchewan made the governor's canoe especially welcome along the river, at Cumberland House, at Carlton, at the new pemmican center of Fort Pitt, and at Edmonton. Everything was in order and everyone doubly busy when Sir George Simpson was due to arrive. John Rowand, having traveled with him, knew exactly what would be happening in the governor's canoe, downstream. There would be the usual pause while the men donned clean shirts and their bright scarves. The governor's top hat and cloak and gaiters would get a good brushing by his man. The piper would be in his best kilt. And a few Scottish airs would echo back from the high banks while the piper tuned up. But when the head canoe rounded the bend before the fort not a Scottish lament but a gay French chanson announced their coming. The voyageurs' families loved to hear those songs almost as much as the men liked to sing them. On landing Piper Colin Fraser stepped ahead. With great ceremony he preceded the governor, walking a proper distance before him, keeping his stately tread over the rough ground and climbing the winding path to the fort without missing a bar or losing his breath. Behind the governor billowed his cloak. Carefully he pressed his tall hat firmly on his head, aware of what a strong gust of wind could mean to his dignity.

Up at the fort the wind stretched out the flag, the great Hudson's Bay Company standard with the letters H.B.C., by many irreligiously dubbed "Here Before Christ." From the bastions cannon boomed. Along the banks crackled the musketry feu de joie. Dogs barked and dusky children swarmed all over the place while their elders watched the proceedings with impassive faces.

There was always a lot of business to transact at Fort Edmonton. Inspections had to be made. To that post went as many as five hundred pieces annually, as much as to any other in Rupertsland. At Rowand's Folly Governor Simpson saw Indian chiefs and held court. Probably several couples were married, the governor having authority to perform a marriage ceremony. The business for the entire Saskatchewan District was arranged and many a discussion took place concerning districts far afield and the details of forthcoming outfits. On one occasion Simpson wrote:

"Found Mr. Rowand up to his ears in business as usual and without exception he is the most active and best qualified person for the troublesome charge he has got of any man in the Indian country."

They got along well together, those two. Rowand admired the governor's drive. The governor had reason to admire Rowand's contribution to the company's gradually increasing dividends. Apart from being "up to his ears," Simpson noted in his carefully guarded Character Book that Rowand was "warm hearted and friendly to an extraordinary degree where he takes a liking, but on the contrary his prejudices exceedingly strong. Of a fiery disposition and strong as a lion. An excellent trader who has the peculiar talent of attracting the fiercest Indians to him while he rules them with a rod of iron . . . has by his superior management realized more Money for the concern than any three of his colleagues since the coalition . . . Will not tell a lie publick is very uncommon in this Country but has sufficient address to evade the truth when it suits his person . . ."

Governor Simpson had many a fine meal in the gentlemen's mess hall, of which artist Paul Kane wrote later: "The walls and ceilings are boarded as no limestone for plastering is found within reach. But these boards are painted in a stile of the most barbaric gaudiness, and the ceiling filled with centerpieces of fantastic gilt scrolls, making altogether a saloon which no white man would enter for the first time without a start and which Indians always looked upon with awe and wonder."

The governor usually "gave the people a danse," which he, too, enjoyed. It is said of Simpson that the population did not decrease as a result of his coming, an honor duly appreciated by the native chiefs. One of them mentioned their approval, subtly, in a toast to Sir George. He said:

"May your horses always be swift, the buffalo instantly abound, and your women live long and always look young."

The toast was apt. Simpson enjoyed a buffalo hunt, though the arduous nature of his duties left him little time for such sport. He liked a good horse, and he insisted that his men provide for their children and even for their women. Some of his own "bits of brown" were given an education but they all learned that they must expect no special favors on account of their paternity.

Most people who traveled the Saskatchewan in the three

decades after union did so in company with John Rowand. In spring he went down to York Factory with the fur brigades. In late summer he returned with trading and other supplies and a few passengers. At Grand Rapids, in 1852, Rowand was joined by one of the early missionaries to the upper Saskatchewan, Father Lacombe, known later as the black-robed voyageur, an oblate of the Order of St. Mary Immaculate.

Father Lacombe was a voyageur in spirit, gay, droll, enterprising, untiring, fearless, content to live on what the country could provide, a man whose very presence clashed with the fur trade traditions of the time, as chief factor Rowand very well knew. Their conflict of spirits intrigued each of them and offered a challenge.

The first few days of the journey up from Grand Rapids delighted the young priest. In late August most of the agony of mosquitoes and black flies was past. The days were warm and pleasant, the nights not too cool for sleeping in a blanket. Their brigade of ten York boats with a crew of eighty men hoisted the great square sails and, catching a breeze, swept across Cedar Lake. On the river they sailed or used the long sweeps past the new Wesleyan Mission at The Pas, on to Cumberland. Father Lacombe had come from the St. Lawrence and knew the voyageur's routine, sleeping à la belle étoile, up by 3:00 A.M., weather permitting; tents packed and canoes pushed off with a song; traveling till breakfast at eight. Then the hardier gentlemen shaved while the pemmican was being boiled or fried. Dinner was at two, when no fire was lit, a mere stop of twenty minutes. In the long daylight of August north of the 53rd parallel, the brigade often traveled until nine o'clock or later. Supper was more pemmican. With no rum for a regale, the men doubly enjoyed their pipes during their brief rest spells. In fact, they came to use their pipes to designate time, as "row for one pipe," or for distance, as a lake "two pipes across." Only six hours were allowed for rest. But, reflected the priest, it was the way of the voyageur. The men were strong and young with their passions still high. Honest toil they must have.

Father Lacombe felt different about the trip after they passed Cumberland. Soon the men put on tracking harness, thrusting their arms through the leather straps with the bands across the chest. They fastened their harness to the long hauling lines and commenced the grueling toil of pulling the boats upstream.

> Imagine, if you please [wrote the priest] after resting for a few hours on the bare earth, to hear at three o'clock the cry, "*Leve! Leve!*" Et puis—hurrah—to pull and pull the lines drawing the heavy boat up against the current, walking in the mud, the rocks, the swamps, along cliffs and sometimes in water to their armpits—and this under a burning sun or beating rain from early morning until darkness fell about nine o'clock. Without having seen it one can form no idea of the hardships, the cruel fatigues of these boatmen.

Father Lacombe was reminded of "slaves in darkest Africa." His heart ached for the dashing young men who had so blithely signed on at Montreal. Yet many returned year after year; no other life suited the boatmen so well, even without a regale of rum. Not often were they surly or bad tempered. It took something really serious, such as a towline breaking and throwing them sprawling on their faces, to rouse them to bitter oaths. Mild, colorful oaths were as numerous as sand bars in the river.

The men accepted the struggles as part of their day. So, too, did Rowand. Neither they nor the chief factor expected any better lot for them, not even when a man was ill, as happened one day on Father Lacombe's journey. As the poor fellow struggled on, slithering about in the mud, the priest begged that he be allowed to rest. The request amazed Rowand. It brought nothing except permission for the priest to share his slightly better food with the man and the sharp retort:

"Any man who is not dead with three days' illness is not sick at all!"

A ripple of excitement passed through the brigade as the party left palisaded Fort Carlton. It increased as they embarked on leaving Fort Pitt, where Rowand's son was chief trader. Soon the long journey would be over. They were almost home. On the last day, as the brigade neared Edmonton, every man sprang eagerly from his blanket on the bare earth and donned a treasured gay shirt with "fresh kerchiefs binding their heads and knotted tartanwise over their left shoulder." They sang gaily as they passed the sand bar below the fort.

"En roulant me boule . . . Hon! Hon! Hon!"

Perhaps their Gallic natures were so deeply touched at being home again, perhaps it was their mood, perhaps because it was in their blood that some sang the sweet Algonquin canoe chant of their mothers:

"*Moniang nind onjiba*
Mondaminek niji kasowin . . ."

The flag flew at the prow of the chief factor's boat. Guns boomed from the bastions. Half-breeds and Indians fired their muskets into the air. On the landing stage everyone crowded dangerously close to the swift waters, eager and excited. Among them were Rowand's Indian wife and perhaps his daughters. Every man tried to be the first to land and greet his family. It was a marvelous scene to greet the eyes of a priest.

Rowand loved his home-coming. The pelts had been delivered and the goods brought back safely. He liked plodding up the path to the fort in the slanting evening sun. He would take pride in showing this priest about his domain.

Father Lacombe was given a small shack for his headquarters and took his meals in the gentlemen's mess. But he acknowledged no obligation which would interfere with his duty.

John Rowand he admired. More than once he wrote of him in his diary: "He was a grand man!" Yet one day when Rowand came to him with a painful felon on his finger he remembered the sick voyageur. He dressed the finger. Then looking the chief factor in the eye he said:

"You are not sick, Rowand!"

Three days later when the felon was still very painful the priest went to the fur trader. He said:

"You will understand what I mean, my friend, when I say that you are not sick. Three days have passed now, and you are not dead."

For a moment he thought Rowand was going to strike him, the chief factor was in such a fury, such a "can of powder." Probably the priest's steady eyes saved him.

Rowand won the next round.

The winter was bitterly cold. Up at the little settlement at St. Annes north of Edmonton Father Lacombe found some muskrat skins taken out of season. He asked one of the squaws to make them into a collar and cuffs for his coat. When Rowand saw the collar and cuffs his face purpled with rage and his eyes flashed. He did not even greet the priest.

"What," he yelled, "you priest, you! You say you have come here to preach what is right . . . Who gave you the right to wear that fur?"

Father Lacombe did not stop to explain that the skins had been taken out of season. At once he ripped them off and flung them in the chief factor's face. It was too true, then. The company would allow no white man to trap furs or get them in trade for any purpose except the company's benefit! The company came before everything! Father Lacombe understood without hearing Rowand roar as he slammed the door:

"We know only two powers—God and the company!"

Father Lacombe's quizzical good humor stood him in good stead many a time. He knew that while Rowand was of his faith most of the gentlemen of the company were not. Yet the company was always hospitable to the clergy of any denomination. It aided them in their hard and difficult journeys. It was a fact that without the company's co-operation they could not have survived. But there must be no interfering with business. That was a delicate point at times.

Father Lacombe finally brought the greatest bully at the fort into his fold, an enormous half-breed voyageur named Paulet Paul. It was an occasion for great rejoicing on the priest's part even after word came that Paul's new Christianity was making poor bargains for the company. Well the black-robed voyageur knew how the chief factor would take that news. Rowand spoke to Father Lacombe about Paul.

"That man of yours, that Paulet you baptized last year and recommended as a good man, he's made a damn fool of himself!"

"Oh, ho!" The priest went out to meet Paul as he approached the fort with his toboggan and dog. He must think up something.

"Paulet," he instructed him, recalling a custom common among half-breeds, or métis, on important occasions, "you must go to Rowand and right away ask his blessing as your godfather."

Father Lacombe hurried back to the big house so as to be there when the half-breed arrived. At once Paul went to the factor and fell on one knee before him.

"My godfather," he begged, "give me your blessing."

Rowand was amazed. He did not know what to say. Such an important custom must not be treated lightly. He advised Paul to ask the priest's blessing.

"Non, non. This is not my affair," said Father Lacombe, not a little amused. "He is not my godchild. Give him your blessing."

Rowand knew when to give an inch. He liked a man

with finesse. Muttering some sort of blessing he turned and strode across the room to the cupboard he always kept locked. He unlocked it and then there was a gurgling sound. Rowand was pouring a glass of rum—for Paulet!

So they parried together, Rowand and Father Lacombe, of diverging interests and tastes amazingly similar. Once, when they were traveling on the prairie together and had paused for nooning, a band of some two hundred Blackfeet rode down upon them, shouting their war whoops. Quick as a flash Rowand jumped up and limped to meet them, waving his arms and roaring:

"Stop, you villains!"

The Blackfeet were most apologetic. Some of them even cried with vexation. They begged to be allowed to tent near Rowand and the priest, though any other white man likely would have been scalped. Rowand's influence with the natives smoothed many a situation for Father Lacombe.

In time a little log church was built within the palisade and Mass was said on Sundays and fete days. Christmas was especially momentous, though only in the little church was more emphasis placed on the religious significance of the day than on feasting. Artist Paul Kane spent Christmas of 1847 there, on his return from a trip to the Pacific with the Hudson's Bay brigades.

The entire post was in a gala mood that Christmas Day. From each chimney a plume of white smoke rose in the frosty air. There were fragrant smells from every house. And in the *okimaw* house, at two o'clock, the gentlemen sat down to dinner. There were no ladies present. At that time, military discipline was the order at Rowand's Folly and Indian and half-breed women did not eat with gentlemen. Huge fires blazed in the fireplaces. In fact, there were almost always fires burning in the mess hall, and often in the ballroom. Upwards of eight hundred cords of wood were used each winter at Fort Edmonton, a fact which may account for the steady clearing of the banks. The table was candlelit. Well-scrubbed tin plates reflected cheery faces. The furniture was large and suitable and comfortable. But the menu—that is what is recalled, a menu in no way comparable to the first meager Christmas dinner eaten by Samuel Hearne and his men down at Cumberland House in 1774.

There were bowls of potatoes and turnips and piles of bread, all delicacies on the Saskatchewan in 1847. Only fifty years before Daniel Harmon, on his way to the Northwest, had written: "I have this day eaten no bread or bisket for the first time." There was a large, boiled buffalo hump before the chief factor. At the foot of the table was a boiled buffalo calf, taken by Caesarean operation before it was fully developed, a dish worthy of an epicure. Paul Kane helped a dish of mouffle, dried moose nose. The priest served buffalo tongue. There was a white fish, delicately browned in buffalo marrow; beaver tail and a roast wild goose. By this time salt was common and added much to the palatability of all meats and fish. There were no desserts.

No alcohol had been allowed the people on the Saskatchewan since union. The gentlemen brought in their own. And they had tea and sugar. After dinner there was the ball.

Indians came with their faces painted. Voyageurs wore their gayest scarves and shirts. Half-breeds put on every ornament they could find. All talked in their own tongues, Cree, French, half-breed patois, and a little English among the gentlemen, the only ones present who could talk that language. There was a fiddler, keeping eager time with his restless toe as couples pranced about the floor. Even in the large ballroom at Rowand's Folly the dancers had to keep to the middle of the room to avoid the circle of squaws and babies and old men squatting on the floor. There were chairs or benches for the gentlemen only.

Everyone who could, danced. The white men wore off the effects of their enormous dinner with Indian girls who jumped up and down, up and down, quite rhythmically and lightly, keeping their feet together. Everyone joined in the

Chasse aux Lièvres, the round dance in which either a man or a girl is put in the center and danced about, till there is a pause when someone must be kissed, generally "with great decorum," while another sings

> "De ma main droite
> Je tiens Rosalie,
> Belle Rosalie!
>
> Qui porte la fleur
> Dans le mois de mai,
> Belle Rosalie!
>
> Embrassez qui vous voudrez
> Car j'aurai la moite."

French and Scottish tunes were played over and over until the gentlemen were more than ready to retire. Everyone went to bed hearing the *slip-slap, slip-slap* of moccasined feet and the lilt of the violin. Through their dreams persisted the "Red River Jig," "McLeod's Reel," or some haunting Gallic melody.

Like Father Lacombe and many others, Paul Kane had made his trip up the Saskatchewan with John Rowand. That summer the brigade carried the special consignment of otter skins for Russia, five thousand prime pelts carefully selected and carefully packed. Most of them had come from the Mackenzie by the Churchill to York Factory and were being transported to the Pacific. The otter skins were packed in seventy pieces and were the Hudson's Bay Company's payment to the government of Russia for trading privileges in what was then Russian territory. They made up an entire boatload and caused a lot of heavy carrying for the men at the portages.

Paul Kane's sketches, some of which were for paintings

commissioned by the Hudson's Bay Company and some which have been collected in the Royal Ontario Museum at Toronto, caused no little excitement among the natives. One half-breed girl, Cun-ne-wa-bum, or "One that looks at the stars," and with whom Kane danced at the Christmas ball, sat for him with great patience. Generally it required a lot of patience on his part to persuade natives to sit. One young girl's mother was afraid having her likeness made would shorten her life. The chieftain father of another maiden was not too sure of the artist's intentions. With an important native, such as a medicine man, it often helped if someone whom the native knew and trusted assured him that Kane, too, was a very great medicine man. When the Indians understood what it meant they all wanted their likenesses made, in great detail, even to including scars on parts of their bodies generally considered unpaintable.

Late in May, in 1854, Chief Factor John Rowand led the spring brigade downstream from Edmonton, his boats laden with pemmican and furs from the vast region north to the arctic and west to the mountains. At Fort Pitt his son, Chief Trader Mr. Jack, was to join them with the pelts from that depot. Together they would go on to York Factory, picking up the boats from the various posts as they went. Rowand was always relieved to get under way. No one but himself knew the work and worry involved in organizing the brigade to maintain its tight schedule with only an express canoe for communication. The journey itself was not without worry. At every stop he could expect trouble from his young voyageurs with spring in their blood and spoiling for a fight. He determined to flog the hide off the first one that got into a fight on this trip.

Rowand was in his son's house at Fort Pitt when he heard the noise on the floating platform that served as a dock. He rushed down to see what was happening. Baptiste Paul, one of the Edmonton voyageurs, was already in a fight with one of the Fort Pitt men. This was no time for the fellow to get himself injured or even killed with the long journey ahead and a valuable cargo! Rowand roared at him to stop. In his fury he cursed Paul. They say the chief factor was even foaming at the mouth in his excitement. Suddenly he dropped down on the dock. When they reached him he was dead.

Because the river was in flood and the brigade must keep its schedule, they buried John Rowand at Fort Pitt. But that is not the end of his story.

His son swore that he would kill Paul for bringing about his father's death. Those who still talk about Rowand say that one of Mr. Jack's men actually followed and shot the man with the excuse that he thought he was a bear in a thicket, and that Mr. Jack paid him to do the shooting.

The chief factor had told his son that he wished to be buried beside his father, in the East. On the Saskatchewan they say it was typical of Governor Sir George Simpson that he would honor such a request though there are those who insist that Rowand, like the governor, had been a hard, driving man and that he deserved no honors. But the stories continue. Next year Simpson had the body disinterred. An old Indian was instructed to boil the bones and, so runs the yarn, the women of the fort used the fat for making soap. They say the old Indian was drunk all the time he was at his gruesome task, one of the gentlemen having provided a little rum.

"The old race of officers is extinct. Mr. Rowand has been . . . the most influential white man among the wild tribes on the plains," said Governor Sir George Simpson, giving explicit directions concerning disposal of the bones of the good servant of the Hudson's Bay Company. They were to be placed in a keg of rum and taken in the governor's own canoe to Lake Winnipeg. Some claim the keg was marked "Salt Pork," Simpson understanding the superstitious natures of the voyageurs. When a gale rose and the shallow waters of the lake threatened to swamp the canoe everything that might be annoying the spirits was thrown overboard, including the funeral keg. Only after the gale had subsided was it recovered, and to avoid further risk, the governor had it shipped to York Factory, and from there to England. In England someone discovered that the rum had been replaced by water!

On the dockside, in England, proper tribute was paid. There was a band with muffled drums and a funeral service befitting an officer of the Hudson's Bay Company. Rowand would have enjoyed it all very much had he been there instead of his bones. In due course the bones were sent back across the Atlantic. This time they were taken to the St. Lawrence, eventually to rest in peace, it is hoped, where he wished them to be.

CHAPTER THIRTEEN

South Branch

THE great South Branch, left fork of the Saskatchewan as one travels upstream, had beckoned many a traveler during the fifty years since La Vérendrye discovered it. But few had explored it for more than a few miles. Winterers had gone out with the natives, bringing back stories of the great river and the vast plains that were the home of the buffalo. Far out on the prairies, right to the Rocky Mountains, roamed the fierce Blackfeet, given to establishing their social position by the number of scalp locks strung on their belts or hung at the flaps of their tepees. It was not good beaver country. The fur traders did not consider it worth the risk of a sortie, especially with little wood to build a house and stockade and, probably, only buffalo chips for fuel.

Strategy rather than possible profits had prompted Peter Fidler to build a Hudson's Bay Company post far up the South Branch at its confluence with the Red Deer, a daring move even for the company traditionally on good terms with the natives. That was in 1800, about the time John Rowand arrived as a young clerk, when the struggle between the XY Company, the Nor'westers, and the Hudson's Bay Company was at its bitterest. Fidler expected few pelts except those which might come from the upper Red Deer. But he did hope to draw the Blackfeet and Piegans southward, away from the important North Branch posts. The XY Company followed and built nearby. Next year the North West Company arrived. No location was left for long to be exploited by any one group and the two latter companies also wanted to rid themselves of Plains Indians about their well-stocked northern posts. The site of Chesterfield House was never a comfortable one. Those lithe, well-mounted, well-fed Blackfeet braves were too unpredictable. Their favorite activities were war and horse stealing. The confluence of the two rivers was a natural meeting place. The combination made life harrowing for the rival white men in their tiny, vulnerable posts.

John MacDonald of Garth, in charge for the North West Company, was a man as fearless as the natives and one of those inquiring individuals to whom an undiscovered river is a torment. He was one of the first white men to paddle up the South Branch and the trip was a delight. MacDonald referred often to the "grand old Saskatchewan." He thought of it as his river, since he considered himself entitled to the best. In the preface to his biography he wrote:

> It is asserted in the Highlands of Scotland that the MacDonalds are coeval with the family of Noah & c., and that they had a boat of their own on Loch Lomond, independent of the ark, by which the chiefs of the clan saved as many as the boat could safely hold, of course the finest and fairest of both sexes. Hence the superiority of that race above all others ever since.

Born in the Highlands of Scotland in 1774 of gentle blood, he never hesitated to claim descent from the Lord of the Isles. He was grandnephew to General Small and had been apprenticed to the North West Company in 1791. A withered arm may have accounted for his pugnacious nature and his fondness for the fine art of using pistols, especially defensively. He never underestimated his own prowess with them, either. But he was frank and generous. Generally he contrived to have his own way. In 1804 he secured permission to winter far up the South Branch. With four canoes and twenty-four men he set out. Perhaps that boat on Loch Lomond accounted for his fondness for canoe travel. On the exciting trip southward each new bend in the unknown river stirred his blood. Rounding one bend they came upon a band of Plains Crees, their faces blackened for war.

"I did not hesitate to jump among them," boasted John MacDonald of Garth. "After some parley I gave them a bit of tobacco and a glass of liquor and left them."

That spring the "grand" prairies abounded with so much fine game that the little party could scarcely believe their eyes. Eagerly the men scanned the brush on either side. From their four small canoes they looked up at the high banks of the wide valley, too excited with all they saw to remember that seldom had even four canoes traveled this great South Branch. Never had they seen such game. Coming from the hungry halls along the main river, this seemed a paradise of good food. So large were the herds of buffalo and antelope that huge fires had to be kept blazing at night and shots fired for protection. It was the rutting season and the animals were so numerous that the force of those behind often crowded the ones in front over the steep banks like an avalanche.

MacDonald did a little exploring at the Elbow, the glorious site of the one-time outflow into what is now the Qu'Appelle River. Climbing the high, tortuous banks he looked down on the cross valley and marveled at the remains of so many campfires. Here Indians had come in search of buffalo from time immemorial. The protection of the valley, the fine supply of wood and water, and that breath-catching beauty of rolling hills appealed to the Scot so easily pleased with the best. Had the Qu'Appelle River, sometimes called the Arm, actually linked another stream with the South Saskatchewan, MacDonald would doubtless have decided to build his new post there. But he had to content himself with camping where so many had camped before, where, in the years to come, sportsmen and explorers and surveyors would build their campfires, and where settlers, traveling laboriously overland with oxen or horses, would pause for a much-needed rest on their trip to the farming communities farther north.

The Elbow was approximately halfway from the Forks to the mouth of the Red Deer. Each day's paddling the riverbanks seemed higher. Great cross coulees cut down from the prairies on either side, and in them grew poplars and shrubs. While his men built a campfire near the site of the present Saskatchewan Landing, MacDonald looked about as he had done at the Elbow. Strange, spike-leaved plants drew his attention. Cactus. Nowhere along the river had he seen them before. They seemed part of the drier country through which he was traveling. Looking up he realized that the shoulders of the coulees were covered with a different kind of grass. They looked like gray carpets with furrows of green where the spring runoff had provided ample moisture.

At the Red Deer the banks were gorge-like. MacDonald would have liked to travel on, up that still-beckoning South Branch or up the Red Deer. But he had a house and stockade to build. The men must cut poplar sticks. Pemmican and dried meat could be traded; already there were many tents of Indians nearby. When he put up the large military marquee that was to serve as Indian Hall, over a hundred teepees were pitched beside him. MacDonald gave the chiefs tea to drink, which they called medicine water. They would much rather have rum, they told him. Over his campfire the Scot grilled buffalo and antelope steaks, seasoned with a little salt. The chiefs had never tasted such good meat. They wanted more and more. MacDonald found steaks popular and, with natives who had no pelts to trade, much more economical than even very dilute rum.

During the winter, every war party on the prairies, it seemed, clashed at the confluence of the South Branch and the Red Deer. Braves dashed up on horseback from the "Mississouri." They galloped down from the foothills country. There were so many green scalp locks to be seen that the little party of white men and half-breeds could never relax. Trading was almost at a standstill, except for pemmican. As spring approached, MacDonald knew that he would have to think up some means of getting his remaining trading goods away unnoticed. If the natives knew he had tobacco, rum, and ammunition he would be mobbed. His interpreter suggested a workable plan.

Within the stockade walls, out of sight of Indian eyes, the interpreter made a huge kite. One clear spring night, when the river was in full flood and the stars so bright they lit the prairies, he flew it. The lovely, strange bird shimmered in the sky. The natives were as amazed as MacDonald and his interpreter had hoped they would be. They called all the other Indians to see it. Everyone watched, spellbound, until the kite finally disappeared on the slow night breeze. Then they all started to talk. What medicine was this? What ill fortune did it foretell? MacDonald was ready with an explanation.

He called the chiefs to the Indian Hall. There the interpreter "showed them a pretended letter with some marks on it, and told them that it was from the Master of Life ordering them off in three days to a stated point, and bidding them not to return for several days, else they would meet a numerous army of Crees and Assiniboins who were in search for them."

John MacDonald of Garth got away with his trading goods, but he kept close watch at night for fear of treachery. It didn't occur to him that he invited treachery. He often boasted that he was lucky. Probably he was. He never expected to live until he was eighty-six and then to die in his bed beside the St. Lawrence.

The South Branch posts were soon abandoned. Without furs to be had in trade the risk was too great considering the number of Blackfeet who continued to disturb the forts along the North Branch. The prairie stream never became a highway. In 1858 Captain Palliser traveled on it in his survey for the British government. Palliser had little that was good to say about the country through which it has cut its deep valley. British sportsmen and explorers crossed it from time to time, scenting the presence of water in a dry land almost as quickly as did their horses. Butler wrote about the prairies as the "Great Lone Land." None saw much future for the South Branch, often on old maps including the present Bow River. Little to interest people in its favor was written until surveyor John Macoun published his packed-with-fact-and-information book, *Manitoba and the Great North West*, in 1882. Macoun explained that "frequent demands upon my time and patience for information regarding the North West have compelled me to put in book form the gleanings of the past ten years . . . a portion of the magnificent heritage of which my countrymen know so little."

Soon after that the world came to know much about the country through which the South Saskatchewan flows. In 1885 the first railway bridge was thrown across it by the Canadian Pacific Railway at Medicine Hat, only a little upstream from the fur-trading posts built by Peter Fidler and John MacDonald of Garth. Strange bubbles in the river water along that stretch led to the discovery of enormous underground lakes of natural gas. Coal was found and good brick clay. The land of the buffalo and the antelope became the home of wheat farmers and ranchers. When that had occurred, in the eighteen-eighties, even the North Branch had ceased to be a highway. The settlement hiatus had commenced.

II

Hiatus

CHAPTER FOURTEEN

Settlers

By 1870 a new sound had made itself heard along the Saskatchewan. Little groups of men and women listened to it at Fort Carlton, Fort Pitt, and Edmonton. Echoes reached the remotest settlements, disturbing echoes. It was an alien sound. Well they knew the sound of men's voices along the river, in song as they swept downstream, cursing and groaning as they hauled heavy York boats against the current. The thunder of thousands of buffalo hoofs was music in every ear. Even the absence of that thunder, ominous as it could be, was known and in a sense understood.

Many and pleasant were the familiar sounds—a lark, high and sweet in the morning; wild geese overhead in spring and autumn; wild ice crunching on the river in the April breakup or cracking with the report of a shotgun in the cold of winter; the monotonous, exciting drumming of the war dance; the music of the very word "Saskatchewan" as some folks said it, the word for home. They were right sounds and understood. This new noise, though it became increasingly familiar, was suspect. Unless there was a mirage it could be heard long before it could be seen, the eerie creak-creak of ungreased Red River cart wheels, the Saskatchewan's first overland contact with the outside world.

They were two-wheeled and all wood, those horse- or ox-drawn carts which made the 1,000 mile journey from the Red River. Ten or twelve years before there had been only a few. Now they were so numerous as to make up a train. Some men along the Saskatchewan, perhaps a hundred, had made the trip to and from the Red River until there was actually a trail. They called it the Touchwood Trail because it came by the beautiful Touchwood Hills to the east of the South Branch. Fording rivers, crossing buffalo trails, getting stuck in mud, enduring blizzards and subzero weather in winter, knowing that their horses might be stolen while they slept—this was all part of the journey. It was taken for granted as much as the cowbirds traveling with the train and settling on the horses' rumps when there were no bushes along the way or, in July, picking off each troublesome bulldog, or gadfly. Historian John Macoun used to say that the cowbird, the whisky-jack, and the Indian were equally sociable, congregating for food wherever white men camped.

Those who traveled from Fort Carlton to the Red River knew all about the trips. Because most were employed by the Hudson's Bay Company, they had horses and their horses had some oats to supplement the prairie grass. At night horses were hobbled, and a man could be cozy in a robe of woven rabbit skins, incredibly light, often made of as many as two hundred unsplit skins fastened head-to-tail, and some eight feet square. There were skin or canvas tops on many of the lurching carts, though the true covered wagon or Conestoga did not appear in this part of the continent. The carts carried flour, tea and sugar, and varieties of trading goods. A few, drawn by oxen and making a one-way trip northwest, brought the first settlers and their effects. None of these things disturbed the people along the river very much, not even the first few settlers. What worried them did not appear on any bill of lading. What caused fear and panic was that intangible and most powerful commodity—news. Every Red River cart brought news. Each raucous turn of a cart wheel was a rumor.

No one was free of anxiety. Factor and chief trader and clerks of the Hudson's Bay Company shared it with métis and English-speaking half-breeds at the posts and in the older communities where a little farming was done, at Nipawin, Cumberland House, and The Pas. (Of these only Nipawin has developed a comparatively valuable agricultural crop, coarse cereals, and peas which are shipped to Quebec for making the famous habitant soup, a nice return of courtesies from the Saskatchewan to the St. Lawrence.)

The newer communities were either predominantly French or English speaking. St. Albert, near Edmonton, named for Father Lacombe, had nearly nine hundred métis in 1869. Bishop Grandin had recently come there to live, the first bishop on the Saskatchewan; the nuns had a convent, a school, and an orphanage. Two very much smaller French settlements had grown up at Lac La Biche and Lac Ste. Anne, not far from Edmonton. Two small English settlements at Victoria and Fish Lake had Wesleyan missions, with the Rev. John McDougall in charge, and the homes of a handful of settlers and a few former Hudson's Bay Company servants. Then there was Prince Albert.

Prince Albert, named for Queen Victoria's beloved consort and founded by a Presbyterian missionary, James Nisbet, in 1866, was an important community thirty-five miles above the Forks. The Hudson's Bay Company had a small store and a large farm. There were a few rough buildings and some hardy, resourceful people who were already dreaming of a sound agricultural future. By 1878 Prince Albert had 831 inhatitants.

Orkneymen, Highlanders, English and French ex-fur

traders, and settlers from the outside, on the entire Saskatchewan they numbered not more than a couple of thousand whites and half-breeds when Red River cart wheels brought the news. With thousands of Indians they wanted to know what it all meant. How would it affect Saskatchewan people? Was it true that their very existence was threatened?

Now they began to piece together certain facts. As far back as 1857 Captain Palliser had come from England with Dr. (later Sir James) Hector and Lieutenant Blakison to survey Rupertsland. Palliser and his associates had stayed at each post along the river. They had paid men to hunt for them and to be their guides. The depths of the water and ice in the river had been measured. Altitudes and temperatures had been studied and recorded right up to the headwaters of the Saskatchewan and the Bow and out across the buffalo plains. The simpler métis and Indians blamed the scarcity of buffalo following this visit on the bad medicine of the white man from across the bitter water.

There had been other visitors. The Earl of Southesk, a fine gentleman, considerate of the men he engaged in the country, and a keen sport, was given to making many entries in his journal beside the evening campfire, just as Captain Palliser had done. Two more young Englishmen, Lord Milton and Dr. Cheadle, arrived with letters of introduction from Governor Sir George Simpson. The young gentlemen hunted and traveled and also made notes. They left a few beaver worth of English pounds in the territory, English currency being in use until 1870. And now, this year, Lieutenant Butler had come up from the Red River to investigate the present smallpox scourge and incidentally gather material for his book, *The Great Lone Land.*

Butler was welcomed warmly when the people learned that he had brought a large supply of smallpox medicine and disinfectant. He took care, good soldier that he was, not to broadcast the shocking discovery that more than half the bottles and vials of medicine had burst in the 30-below weather of his overland journey, spoiling most of the paper packages of powders. That winter smallpox caused panic comparable to the uncertain news. Indians and half-breeds and whites died of it. Often those who were well fled in terror from those who were afflicted, fearful even of burying the dead.

Butler had a second commission to the Saskatchewan River people. At Fort Garry, at the site of the present city of Winnipeg, down on the Red River, he had been sworn a justice of the peace and commissioned to confer a similar authority on the chief factor of the Hudson's Bay Company at Edmonton. From Butler's point of view the jurisdiction of a justice of the peace in the Northwest was comparable to the title "Czar of all the Russias" or "Khan of Mongolia." Actually there was no means of enforcing the authority beyond the company's traditional attitude of justice. Even while it was being conferred various crimes from horse theft to murder were uninvestigated and, of course, unpunished. The Blackfeet certainly did not consider the fine sport of horse thieving a crime. Everything depended on the point of view. Butler, a British soldier with a British soldier's sense of duty, regarded the appointment of a justice of the peace as being as important as the distributon of smallpox medicine. People living along the Saskatchewan viewed it differently. To them it confirmed the worst rumors.

Until 1872 the Hudson's Bay Company continued to use Fort York as the port of entry for official news as well as goods. The port being open only a few months of each year, a lot of news reached the Saskatchewan from the Red River settlements long before official messages came from London. The railway to St. Paul brought news to the Northwest with a speed undreamed of in the days of canoes. Now events occurring at Ottawa, capital of the new Dominion of Canada, were being discussed at Fort Carlton in a matter of weeks. And what events there were to discuss at Forts Carlton and Pitt, at Edmonton, and in the half-bred settlements!

The Hudson's Bay Company had sold out. That was the most incredible news of all. Only slightly less credible was the rumor that Canada had acquired Rupertsland. Like a prairie fire before a strong wind rumors sped along the river.

It was true, said some. Did the Hudson's Bay Company care what happened to its servants so long as the shareholders got their dividends? Of course not! It was all business. And if this old company should care so little as to sell its people along with the land, why should the Dominion of Canada hesitate to buy them? Half-breeds whose fathers had been born in the country saw themselves and their Indian relatives about to be dispossessed. They recalled stories of how Governor Ramsey of Minnesota had bought a tract of land from the Sioux in the vicinity of Pembina without consideration of the claims of residents. Like the people at Pembina, those who held a little land along the Saskatchewan did so by right of tenure, using all the arguments of squatters in a new land. Even the arguments of loyal Hudson's Bay men lacked the ring of conviction. For, much as officers of the company wanted to believe the best, the rumors disturbed them too. There was every reason to believe that the Dominion of Canada had bought the Northwest. They all talked about it, at the company trading posts and by their evening fires. All eyes were on the Red River settlements.

Louis Riel! That was the name that peppered their talk. Scotsmen and Englishmen denounced his assumption of authority at Fort Garry. Half-breeds, French and English speaking, rallied to his views. Everyone talked about Riel, the fiery young métis, Riel, eager to lead his people in defense of their lands. Yet people living along the Red River were as ignorant of facts as were those along the Saskatchewan. No authority, neither the Hudson's Bay Company, the British government, nor the new Dominion of Canada, had bothered to tell them of their changed status. When surveyors had arrived at the Red River settlement, only one course was open for men of courage who believed in justice and liberty.

Riel, accompanied by his followers, had ridden out to meet the surveyors from Canada, placed his foot on the chain and ordered them to go no farther. Métis on the Saskatchewan sided with métis on the Red River. Riel was a hero! His provisional government was a good thing. Many approved his "Memorial and Petition of the people of Rupertsland and the Northwest Territories, British America, to His Excellency U. S. Grant, President of the United States" protesting their treatment at the hands of a foreign power. Along the northern river they cheered when word came that Riel's provisional government had taken over Fort Garry, the great inland center of the Hudson's Bay Company a thousand miles away.

Old company men, brought up in a tradition of unswerving loyalty, loathed the thought of rebellion. Several had been present on the Red River when ex-company servants protested the refusal of the Hudson's Bay Company to permit them to trade with the Indians; they recalled the case won by the men and the cries of "Vive la Liberté" and "Trade is free!" which accompanied celebrating volleys.

Never had there been so much to talk about. Rumor had it that one of the terms of the acquisition of the Northwest by Canada was a railway linking Canada with the Pacific coast. Some actually believed that the railway would come north from St. Paul to Fort Garry. There was talk of a gold rush, since "wash" gold had been discovered along the upper Saskatchewan. The old days, the young people said, were tame when compared with all that was happening now. But, argued the older men, there was more security then. Now even the buffalo were failing.

Settlers from the outside brought ideas disturbing to the traditional order enjoyed under the Hudson's Bay Company monopoly since union. One day a settler came to Fort Carlton trading post. When he had warmed himself by the fire and bought his supplies he sat down on a pork barrel for a chat with the chief trader and his clerk and interpreter. While the company men were busy valuing muskrat pelts for a young métis, the settler looked about the post. Everything in the country was new and interesting. Squaws, such as the métis's young wife with her child on her back, still intrigued him. Moving his position so as to try to avoid the stench from the pile of hides in the corner, he ran his eyes over the trading goods. Strings of beads and thong hung from the rafters. There were old muskets and newer rifles, rolls of bright calico, blankets and kegs of shot. And no one, thought the settler, with a tinge of bitterness, dared trade with the Indians but these Hudson's Bay Company people! His thought exploded when the chief trader came over and sat in his chair by the fire.

"It's high time the Hudson's Bay Company was forced to give up its monopoly!" the settler cried. "What this country needs now is free trade and free land!"

"But what use is this country for farming?" parried the chief trader quietly. "Sir George Simpson himself satisfied the special commission that it was useless for settlement. He saw more of it than most of us!"

The dark-skinned trapper did not know the English language. He pushed back the hood of his capot. In French he asked the clerks what the settler and the trader were saying. As he listened to the interpretation his eyes flashed. He took the calumet from between his lips.

"Ah," he exclaimed, "the same as the good Archbishop Taché. How did his Grace say it?" he asked the chief trader.

The Englishman laughed indulgently. He quoted the official statement of Archbishop Taché in French, and then in English for the benefit of the settler:

"Because there are extremely great difficulties in the way of colonizing the few points in this vast territory capable of cultivation I would prefer to see the country remain as it is than to see the changes that would likely take place."

The settler jumped from the pork barrel.

"But this is good land!" he exclaimed. "There was millions of acres of good land all along the way from the Red River. I saw it myself . . . You can't keep people out when there's land and they need it. Besides"—he looked at the clerks and the chief trader—"what's going to become of you when your fine company tells you you're sold along with the territory?"

"That's what I want to know!" agreed one of the clerks before the chief trader could comment. "D'you think they care a damn for us over in London?"

"Not bloody likely!" The interpreter's tone was bitter. "Buy their trading goods cheap and sell 'em dear, and give us a pittance. Get valuable otter and beaver skins for a few tawdry beads and some colored calico and old guns, and make a huge profit. Then they sell us out like a lot of cattle!"

That was too much for the chief trader, trained to discipline and a horror of insubordination. Eyes blazing he leaped from his chair and faced the clerk.

"You fool!" he exclaimed, his voice low and ringing with authority. "What if the company does charge high? Hasn't it had to do so to survive? And hasn't it bent every effort to maintain law and order and keep bloodshed at a minimum? Hasn't it fed the Indians, and half-breeds, when they would have starved? And cared for them when they were sick with smallpox and even clap? Now let the government of Canada take over, if that's what the company has arranged. But be loyal, man. For God's sake, be loyal—especially when we aren't alone!" Turning to the métis with his wife and children behind him, the chief trader spoke in French, assuring him that all would be well if he trapped assiduously. Yet, as though he wanted to convince himself, too, that all would be well, he cut off a few inches of twist tobacco and gave it to the man. The squaw grinned and the young métis pulled on his hood and led the way outside.

At last the news brought by the Red River carts was confirmed. Canada wanted the territory that Governor Sir

George Simpson and Archbishop Taché had claimed as useless for settlement. The dominion government, doubtless on information of such men as Captain Palliser and Professor Hind of the University of Toronto, who had been sent out to make a special survey, were willing to pay the sum of £300,000 sterling, or $1,500,000, for the region. There were those who claimed the price was unconscionably high, especially when the terms of the mammoth real estate deal became known. Again its governors proved the sound business acumen that had made the Hudson's Bay Company the oldest in the world. Apart from the $1,500,000, they were to retain one-twentieth of the territory involved, thousands of acres of which were soon put up for sale as excellent farm land. The fur trade would remain practically unchanged.

Things turned out better than expected for the company's servants. Over half the sum received was set aside to buy out the rights of the wintering partners, direct descendants of the men who had opened the Northwest to white domination. Land surrounding each fort or post was retained so that the business of the fur trade north of the Saskatchewan would go on as usual. Wintering partners, factors, chief traders, and clerks as well as outsiders had reason to appreciate the wise choice of the Honorable Company between sentiment and security when the slow process of 1870 communication unfolded most of the details. Only free traders suffered.

Who was to know that in sixty years the small Hudson's Bay Company trading posts would become great, modern department stores in cities such as Edmonton and Calgary? Who could imagine stores where imported fruits and nylon stockings and the latest hair tints would be available to great-granddaughters of Blackfoot and Cree women? Who, indeed, could even dream of a day when prosperous trappers would have their own "cats" for winter hauling and that planes would land on the broad Saskatchewan with cargoes of furs? And if anyone could glance through the veil of the future would he credit all these changes and see them side by side with the old ways, the dog teams and the snowshoes, the canoe and the carrying place?

Yet that is what has happened. Not far from the handsome, modern Hudson's Bay Company store in Edmonton dog teams race over the glittering snow of winter and lonely trappers remember the old Chipewyan legend as they bend back their heads to see the zenith of the Northern Lights, the legend that sees in the twinkling stars the souls of the departed. Today people living at Edmonton and Prince Albert and The Pas watch planes taking off from Mother Saskatchewan, winging northward to meet distant trappers. The new ways of caterpillar tracks and planes with landing gear for both water and ground strip are a great improvement over the old laborious tracking of sixty years ago. The impact of change was too swift for Métis Ba'tiste and Scottish half-breed Angus. And though the old squaw might marvel at the sight of the great iron horse, a lifetime was too short for her to become part of its ways.

In 1870 there was no apparent security for half-breeds and Indians living along the Saskatchewan. Resentment and misunderstanding were rife. If the Red River carts had been able to bring a little more news, the natives could have relaxed and fitted into the new order. Trouble and bloodshed might have been avoided. If the Canadian government had shown evidence of realizing that there were men and women and children who had rights to their narrow farms patterned on old Quebec, there would have been less apprehension. Lacking that assurance, inclusion in the Dominion of Canada looked much more like the end of an era than the dawn of a new day.

Ottawa and the old highway of the Northwest were a continent apart in more ways than one. Yet it was so little the simple métis or English half-breed needed to avert panic —a clear title to his land and assurance that there would be no taxes which he could not meet. Few cared or had reason to care for the Great White Mother—Queen Victoria.

There were some who took the changes philosophically, making the most of them—or the least. They were the true frontiersmen who could balance one whisky bottle hourglass-wise on another and drink "till the sands run out," or even repeat the process. They were usually bachelors or grass widowers. Family men were interested in the Land Act of 1872 whether in favor, as new settlers, or from fear, as ignorant métis.

It greatly increased the length of the Red River cart trains, that Land Act. Louder and longer the raucous creak-crawk of ungreased wheels echoed across parkland and prairie. Up from the Red River and the Assiniboine they came, past the Touchwood Hills, fording the South Branch near the present site of the city of Saskatoon, peopling the narrow wedge of land between the two branches.

By the Land Act any man who was head of a family or who had reached the age of twenty-one could apply for a quarter section (160 acres) and could obtain title at the end of three years provided he had cultivated part of the land and done some building. The cost was ten dollars and the prospect was alluring.

Only a few settlers came at first, working their land with oxen because oxen needed no oats and could live off the land, and the precious Prairie Queen plow. A tent did for a time and then the sod or log house, built with the help of neighbors if any neighbors were near. Wheat and oats—cabbage, cauliflower, and peas—potatoes and turnips—that was what was coming with the sound of cart wheels, that and everything for which it stood. Yet just across the river stood the fur trade post, operating much as such posts had operated for over a hundred years, stocking ever more and more varied goods, mediating between the old regime and the new.

The narrow angle of land between the North and the South Branch of the Saskatchewan acquired new importance.

More settlers arrived. Soon the surveyors would come, said the native half-breeds apprehensively. The Indians grew increasingly alarmed. That angle above the Forks came to be more than the meeting place of white- and red-skinned men. There, logically, one ideology or the other must become supreme.

The raucous creak-crawk of ungreased Red River cart wheels was a sound made by white men. The Indians had no medicine with which to stop it.

CHAPTER FIFTEEN

"While the Sun Shines and the Waters Run"

THE winds still blew across the prairies, the sun shone, the grasses grew, and the river ran strong. But the buffalo were going. The time had come when the great tribes of the upper Saskatchewan must treat with white men.

Already their brother chiefs on the lower river had marked the X that gave them $25 for each chief, $15 for each headman, and $5 for every ordinary man, woman, and child. Each year they were to receive the same amount of money with a promise of tools and farming equipment if they desired to take up agriculture. A square mile of land would be reserved for each family of five. There was a gift of clothes, too, and a medal for the chiefs with a Union Jack to display on ceremonial occasions. To make the agreement perfectly legal, to extinguish all claims to the land, there was a present of $12 a person. Twelve dollars looked like a lot of money to people accustomed to the simple barter of the beaver regime. Down in the swampy country where game was often scarce and existence a struggle everyone was happy about it, even the government of Canada, whose officials envisaged a near boom in agriculture.

But the lower river is not the upper river. At the angle between the two branches, above the Forks, it meanders across the rich park belt, at the edge of the prairies of which nostalgic Westerners still sing:

> Oh give me a home where the buffalo roam,
> Where the deer and the antelope play,
> Where seldom is heard a discouraging word
> And the skies are not cloudy all day.

Word of the treaty had come to the Upper River tribes, the better-fed, more independent nomads. Land travel had made their territory more easily accessible to white men. The Indians were resentful. Fear motivated their councils. Silently scouts, breechcloth clad in summer or in blankets and moccasins in winter, had watched the coming of the talking wires; already there was an advance party of workmen at the mouth of the Battle River. Survey parties were measuring the land and marking it for white settlers. Now, said the chiefs and medicine men, was the time to treat, before many white settlers arrived.

Sweet Grass, chief over all the chiefs, from the Edmonton country; Big Child, a small man for an Indian in that territory; Big Bear and Poundmaker and Red Pheasant—they all met about the council fires. There had been great bitterness among the natives when the government had ignored every request for treaty. Apprehension increased as buffalo decreased. For long the braves had wanted to "dance," the traditional means by which they worked themselves up to war pitch.

At last the government had signified its willingness to meet with the "Indian children of the Great White Mother." Older and wiser chiefs advised negotiation. Some chiefs, like Big Bear, demanded war. Big Bear was not popular with the white people, who called him a troublemaker. He wanted to do what the white people would do if their country was invaded. He wanted to fight for the land that had always belonged to the Indian. Had there not always been buffalo until the government people came? Could the young men no longer fight? Were they not better off having the Hudson's Bay Company to supply them with goods in exchange for their furs? The challenge was worthy of a brave chief.

Chief Factors Christie of Edmonton and Clarke of Fort Carlton, priests and missionaries, and the large native McKay family told those chiefs who would listen of the strength of the British Army. They reminded them of the courage of the new North West Mounted Police, whose tunics were red because red was the color of authority to the Indians; of the Great White Mother who loved her Indian children as she loved her white children. The older chiefs thanked their friends for their "good medicine," for the honor of becoming children of the White Mother of whom they had heard so much since their country became a part of Canada. They promised to welcome the representative of Queen Victoria when he came to Fort Carlton for the treaty making.

In spite of the avowed willingness to treat, white people and some half-breeds were nervous. Their feelings were summed up in a letter from Chief Factor Christie to the Indian commissioner:

> The buffalo will soon be exterminated and when starvation comes these Plains Indian tribes will fall back on Hudson's Bay Forts and settlements for relief and assistance. If not complied with, or no steps taken to make some provision for them, they will most assuredly help themselves; and there being no force or any law up there to protect the settlers, they must either quietly submit to be

pillaged or lose their lives in defense of their families and property, against such fearful odds as will leave no hope for their aid.

All the panoply and dignity of the Victorian British Empire were concentrated in the treaty-signing ceremonies of the Canadian Northwest. It was the era devoted to what was popularly known as "carrying the white man's burden," the incomparable mixture of duty and kindly arrogance, of devotion to the caste system and an almost fanatical avowal of individual liberty.

The stage was set on a grassy knoll on the Carlton side of the North Saskatchewan. Poplar bluffs doted the meadows. Two hundred teepees clustered in nicely spaced groups. The official tent was pitched on the top of the knoll, with the required piece of red carpet and a folding table and camp chair for the lieutenant governor of Manitoba and the Northwest Territories, Alexander Morris. On the appointed day, August 18, 1876, the governor arrived to preside at the treaty making. The Union Jack flew proudly in the prairie wind. Red-coated Mounties took up their stiff, silent positons. Beside the governor were his clerk and interpreter and the chief factors of the Hudson's Bay Company.

This was the sort of thing the Indians loved. With their muskets and a few new repeating rifles they fired a salute. They beat their tom-toms and danced and sang. Then, majestically and with their horsemen in the lead, they advanced on the treaty tent in a wide half circle. The governor went to meet their chiefs, resplendent in his uniform, and flanked by his official party. The pipe stem, that precious symbol upon which no woman must ever look, was pointed solemnly to north and to south, to east and to west. Proudly the leading chief presented the pipe stem to the governor. Solemnly the governor stroked it. Then the Indians sat down on the grass, satisfied that proper friendship had been shown the Cree people. It was time for the representative of the queen to open the procedings with a speech.

Those treaty speeches by representatives of the queen were masterly examples of diplomacy and florid rhetoric. Native apprehension must be quieted, and the good intentions of the government made clear. The new era must dawn on the natives gradually but firmly. They were told that the time had come when gardens must be planted and farms tilled, that big game was becoming scarce. They were reminded of the bounty of the Great White Mother in allowing them a little of the land that had been theirs from time immemorial, and of the largess of the government in paying for it and granting them the protection of the new North West Mounted Police.

The Indians and their chiefs listened to the speeches with the polite attention customary among them. They considered each point carefully. Then the chief spokesman addressed Governor Morris. The Indians, he said, expected much more than had been promised. Terms which satisfied the Swampy Crees were not good enough for the Plains Crees. He did not agree with Big Bear, who had said: "We want none of the queen's presents."

Poundmaker wanted extra assistance if they must settle on the land. Under the terms offered he did not see how he could clothe his children and feed them as long as the sun shines and the waters run. With the other chiefs he asked for a horse and harness and a wagon for each chief, with a grant of $1,000 for provisions for those who settled on the land. They would like a cooking stove and free medicine. They wanted a hand mill for each band and aid in time of pestilence or general famine. General Morris, on behalf of the Dominion of Canada, agreed to most of their demands. As a gesture of great good will he presented each chief with a suit of clothes, a medal, and a flag.

Actually the Indians had little with which to negotiate. Their claims were picayune when compared with what they must relinquish. As is always the case under such circumstances, the terms granted were those which the weaker group would accept without resistance. The monetary allowance was less than that given Indians by the United States government and the reserve acreage smaller. A treaty Indian has no franchise and an Indian woman marrying a white man loses both her own and her children's treaty rights.

The ceremony at Fort Carlton lasted for several days. The chiefs had to consider the terms with their traditional slow ceremony. The governor was prepared to be patient though countenancing no nonsense. When the signing was formally accomplished he made another speech and told them he was much gratified with the manner in which they had behaved throughout the treaty making. He hoped the Indians would do much to help themselves. He prayed that the Almighty would give them wisdom and prosper them. The terms, he said, especially the horse and wagon and the stove and aid in time of pestilence and famine were extremely generous. The Indians could not possibly understand the implication of it all. They gave three cheers, white man fashion, for the queen, for the governor, the police, and the factors.

Next day they appeared at Fort Carlton to say good-bye. They wore their new clothes adorned by such items of native attire as each Indian cherished. The chiefs wore their medals and the Union Jacks showed which way the wind blew. They were an enormous group of delighted children showing off. The governor was a proud Victorian papa beaming on his family.

Not all the Indians in the big angle between the branches of the Saskatchewan signed the treaty. Some were away hunting. Every opportunity was given them to sign, not so much for the good of the Indians as for the peace of mind of the government and the settlers. Some chiefs flatly refused to sign, or, like Big Bear, who eventually led nontreaty and insurgent Indians, put it off till next year. Big Bear was a natural leader of the die-hard Crees who did not want to sign away the territorial rights of their forefathers for a few promises which, to them, seemed inadequate. He had many reasons for refusing to sign, most unusual of all being the refusal of the government's commissioner to promise him immunity from hanging. Big Bear argued that an Indian did not like the thought of a rope about his neck.

On the whole the treaty making was a peaceful victory for the white invaders. Today the names of the great chiefs of 1876 and 1877 are remembered in the names of the reserves they selected, Sweet Grass, Poundmaker, Red Pheasant, Mistawasi, Strike-Him-on-the-Back, Thunderchild, and many others equally descriptive.

In 1877 the powerful Blackfeet signed at a gravel bar in the Bow River which was long known as Blackfoot Crossing, the bridge under the water. Chief Crowfoot proved himself worthy of his high rank when he spoke to Colonel McLeod (Stamixotokon) of the North West Mounted Police before signing the treaty. He said:

"We all see that the day is coming when the buffalo will be all killed and we shall have nothing to live on, and then you will come into our camp and see the poor Blackfeet starving and I know the heart of the white soldiers will be sorry for us, and they will tell the Great Mother, who will not let her children starve." Later he said, "I will be the last to sign and I will be the last to break my bond."

Crowfoot was proud of the medal given him. He wore it all the time and added to it, later, the framed pass given him by the Canadian Pacific Railway for his good offices in preventing trouble when his braves resented the approach of the railway. His tall, gaunt figure and clear-cut profile were liked by the Mounties and the first ranchers and settlers of the foothills country. Crowfoot accepted the new ways philosophically. He welcomed the embargo on firewater. With an understanding far beyond the average native of his day he saw the need for the white man's law and order. There was little trouble where he was.

Being fed when they were hungry was understood by the natives. Agreeing to settle on land reserved for them was another matter. It did not mean that they were ready to build houses and plow land and generally become self-supporting at agriculture. To stay in one place after countless generations of roaming was more than they could bear. A show of authority had to be made to round them up.

The difference between white and Indian cultures led to inevitable misunderstanding. The Crees had no written language until 1853–1854 when the Rev. E. A. Watkins invented a phonetic system, and put their words into writing. White people, even those coming to minister to them in various ways, were ill prepared and, from their point of view, ignorant. What could the Church of England missionary John Hines know of Indian customs? Mr. Hines had come directly from England to the Woods Crees of the North Saskatchewan. He couldn't speak their language. His Christian philosophy had no basis of understanding with the pagan beliefs of the Indian. Yet, eventually, he served his people well, teaching them and advising them and building schools and churches.

Mr. Hines faced the usual difficulties in introducing the Indians to the ways of civilization. The evil he called bigamy was good sound Indian economics. A hunter and warrior with two or more wives, and their children, was well off. Other hunters and warriors envied him and even, on occasion, made off with an especially useful wife. Wives hewed and carried and made clothes and pemmican and shelters. Many sons were potential hunters and warriors; daughters might bring good sons-in-law to the band. If a man tired of a wife or wanted to get rid of her for some other reason, it was good sense to do so. Now all that was to change. Even getting rid of a wife presented a problem hitherto unknown.

Baptism was behind it all. The priests and missionaries, according to the tribes with which they worked, urged the red-skinned people to be baptized. But they would baptize no man who had more than one wife. Without abundance of buffalo and other game many an Indian began to see a lot of sense in the words of the man of God. Much as he cared for his family, and he did care for them usually after the manner dictated by the circumstances of his way of living, it was obvious that he could not feed and clothe many children under the new regime.

Good old Father Time often came to the Indian's aid. The older wives who could no longer work went to live with their grown-up daughters, politely avoiding all direct speech with their sons-in-law according to good Indian manners. Some died. Others married again. But there were occasions when there was no place for the extra wife or wives to go, no daughters, no husband because they were too old. Death did not come soon enough. To complicate matters the clergy frowned on some of the good old ways of getting rid of a wife.

What could an Indian desirous of accepting the white man's religion do with a surplus old and unwanted wife? The choice between wives and the decision as to how to solve his dilemma remained his and not that of the priest or missionary. Carefully one Indian weighed the merits of both his wives. The older one was good at making pemmican. She set up a teepee quicker than any other squaw in the band. But she was getting old. Soon she would not be able to do much work. The younger wife still had children needing her care. She was also good at the trap lines.

The Indian took his older wife fishing in his canoe. Later he returned, alone. Next day he went to receive the drops of holy water. He had complied with the missionary's teaching!

In the days after signing the treaties hard times came upon the Plains Indians. By the eighteen-eighties there were no buffalo to be hunted. The police distributed such food as they could spare. The government began to question the Treaty Clause, which required it to feed the natives in time of scarcity; it might be setting a precedent which they would try to make a habit. Farming fell far short of the glowing

The Foothills Country,
Farm and Rangeland

hopes of the treaty-making governor. Thousands of restless braves tutored in the ancient Indian devotion to the war dance longed for excitement. Indeed, some of them did enjoy a brief, sweet orgy.

Some tribes have made good on their reserves. Perhaps most successful of all is the group living near Gleichen, on the Bow River in Alberta. When their treaty was signed they represented remnants of Blackfoot, Blood, Sarcee, and Stony tribes. Their land was valuable. There was coal. The Canadian Pacific Railway offered to buy rights. The Canadian Land and Irrigation Company wanted right of way. On the advice of the reserve's Indian agent various deals were arranged which have set up the Blackfeet in perpetuity. The group, numbering less than a thousand people, is said to be worth well over two million dollars. They have good homes and hospitals. They work their coal mine. Most significant of all, they are good ranchers. The tribesmen who were the proud owners of the first horses in the Northwest and the best buffalo hunters are today successfully raising horses and cattle. Though they pay no taxes or rent and though by a special arrangement they are assured a pound of meat and a pound of bread a day, those Indians are still proud and independent and earn their living.

On some of the reserves in the valuable territory about Battleford farming is successful and the Indians are comfortably situated. In the woods country most make a small living by hunting, trapping, and fishing. They have never been agriculturally inclined like the natives in eastern Canada and parts of the United States. Many bands need the help of the provincial and federal governments, financial help as well as leadership in better methods of fishing, trapping, and farming and in marketing their products. They have schools and hospitals and churches. Many on the lower Saskatchewan have outboard motors. A few have been graduated from universities. Some have played an important role in national defense in spite of the treaty term that excuses them from such service. Yet the Indians of the swampy and wooded areas of the lower river are indolent and lacking in initiative, much as their fathers were in the days of the fur trade. These Bush Indians, as they are currently called, are not like the proud Indians seen along the upper river or in the foothills.

What is the difference? Why do the Indians of the swampy river territory differ from their brothers? Why did the fur traders and explorers so often write of them:

"You can never fill an Indian!"

Fur traders and explorers did not always realize how often, along the lower Saskatchewan, an Indian stomach was empty nor how necessity had taught him to eat all he could hold when he could get it against the day when he must chew his moccasins to ease the pains of hunger. But that often repeated comment is the key to his lack of initiative.

Scientific tests have proved that the diet of the Bush Indian is and always has been deficient. He did not get enough or the right kind of food. Shades of Alexander Henry and Peter Pond! The Bush Indian will still eat all he can get when food is available.

Today, if he lives near a trading post, he buys too much white flour and white sugar and white lard, and fails to get a balancing amount of good meat or fish. His squaw has copied white man's ways and cleans what game there is too well. She throws away valuable organs which, with the flour and sugar and lard, might go a long way toward balancing the family's diet.

It looks as though the main difference between the Bush Indians and the Indians of the plains has mainly to do with food. Buffalo meat gave the Blackfeet and the Plains Crees energy to hunt and wage war and indulge in the strenuous sport of horse stealing; buffalo marrow and fine pemmican fed their young children when they were weaned at the age of two or three or even four years.

The passing of the buffalo, whether from extermination or from disease, paralleled the passing of the regime of the

Indian. Herds which had literally darkened large tracts of prairie during their regular spring and autumn migration treks disappeared, almost within a season. The North West Mounted Police on their famous the-law-marches-west trek of 1874 saw as many as fifty thousand at a time. Ten years later the last buffalo hunt took place.

The same was true in Montana, the Saskatchewan herd customarily roaming down into the States each year. There an astute Montana rancher who had some free range saved them from complete extinction. He bought the last ten or twelve, and after the manner of buffalo his herd increased rapidly. But even this token herd was threatened. The United States government at the time was far more interested in finding land for settlers than in keeping it for buffalo. So the buffalo were offered to Canada. Owing to the foresight of the Hon. Frank Oliver, one of the early settlers of Edmonton, $250 a head was offered and accepted. A herd was established at Wainwright, Alberta. During World War II the Wainwright herd was destroyed, but not before drafts of buffalo had been moved to Wood Buffalo Park, far north of the North Saskatchewan. In Banff National Park a small herd attracts tourists from behind high, strong wire fences.

There are no red Indians along the Saskatchewan. Most fur traders and explorers wrote in their journals the adjective "swarthy" or "dusky" or "brown." Governor of the Hudson's Bay Company Sir George Simpson coined an unforgettable phrase when he ruled that white men must provide for their "bits of brown" born of Indian mothers. Today from Rocky Mountain House to Grand Rapids not an Indian with red skin will be seen. There may be, of course, a few with red hair, like the group who gave their name to the Tete Jaune Cache on the Fraser River a hundred years ago. But that is as easily explained as an occasional pair of blue eyes in a brown face—or black eyes in a pale face!

Strangely Governor Morris, in his official report on

Treaty No. 6 at Fort Carlton, referred to "red" Indians. His interpreters may be to blame for the fact that the chiefs are said to have referred to themselves as such. While modern lecturers and the popular press are addicted to using the adjective "red," artists refute it, early artists such as Paul Kane and modern artists such as Grandmaison and the late Arthur Heming. The artist sees a northern Indian's skin as it really is, at reddest a warm copper tint, usually a dark nut brown, a flesh color to excite his enthusiasm.

Few Indians are seen in the large cities along the Saskatchewan. But on the reserves, in the smaller towns, and far into the northland they link the past of the Northwest with its present. Still in use are the canoe and the snowshoe, the two Indian contributions that hastened the discovery of the territory and its opening to settlement. Side by side they appear with the plane that can land on water or land and the caterpillar track, the beloved "cat" of the country of rivers and lakes and woods.

Today most have houses or shacks for winter use. Those who continue to live as nomads have canvas tents in place of the skin tepees of the past. They remain a marvel of utility, those teepees of buffalo hide or deerskin. No finer movable dwelling has been developed by man. Easily pitched, easily taken down, easily carried on horse- or dog-drawn travaille, or by a sturdy squaw, they were warm in winter and could be cool in summer. The sturdy squaw was adept at lashing together the three or four long poles for the frame, and putting up the cover with its typical tribal decoration. Settlers coming to the Saskatchewan country as recently as the beginning of the twentieth century came across the circles of stones that had surrounded these tepees. Sometimes the circles were comparatively small, the site of a 14-skin teepee which might house six or eight people. Occasionally they had surrounded a large 40-skin dwelling. If the weather was cold and the wind bitter, a coulee or a protecting bluff was sought. In hot weather the lower part could be rolled up. When mosquitoes were a torment, a knoll or hill which caught the breeze assured comfort. But they were always smoky, in spite of smoke vents. Crouching over the fire during a lifetime of cooking, the common name for an ancient squaw was the obvious and descriptive "Old Smoky."

They were objects of pride, those nomadic homes. On the lower part the story of the tribe was drawn and colored. In front, especially of that of a Plains chief or headman, hung the scalp locks that denoted his rank; perhaps a rude tripod held the sacred pipe stem. Scalps were reluctantly parted with no later than the momentous eighteen-seventies. The war dance has been banned during the nineteen-forties.

Probably the treaties were as fair a way of dealing with the Indians as any at the time and under the conditions when they took place. But if ever a people had cause to pine for the good old days it was those Crees who signed the treaty at Fort Carlton. With no longer any real authority over their people, the chiefs lost heart. With no hunting and no war parties, life lapsed into getting enough to eat. No longer did the chiefs and headmen hold their ancient authority or exert their ancient wisdom. Treaties stated that the Indian must obey the white man's laws. He must be tried before the white man's courts of justice. Indian agents regulated his affairs. It was a heartbreaking, morale-breaking business for once-proud, respected chieftains.

No longer to have any meaning behind the ancient war dance. No longer to roam the wide prairies. No longer to hunt the buffalo. What was there for the young men to look forward to except what the white people regarded as insurrection? Had it not been for that small force of five hundred young men who made up the North West Mounted Police, there might have been more serious fighting. Had the Mounties been men of a different stamp, the Saskatchewan might have had another story to tell. But there was some bond of understanding between the nomadic, red-coated riders of the plains and the people whose freedom they had, in a sense, usurped. The young men of the police force understood, to some extent, what the young men of the Indian tribes had lost.

Life changed for Indian women too, though not so grievously as for the men. There was still wood to collect and food to cook, and that was a woman's work. There were still babies to bear and tend, though gradually most Indian women gave up the ancient custom of putting up her own small tent and periodically living alone. Now, when she is old, when the young girls and the blades refer to her as Granny Saskatchewan, she shares with the old men the duty of keeping alive the long-drawn-out tales of her tribe. Happy with a little tobacco for the pipe she clamps between her toothless gums, her old face wrinkled and tanned by wood smoke to a soft, rich leather, she is often happy and beautiful as only an old woman can be beautiful.

They are long and ingenious, those tales the old Indians and squaws delight to tell. They will go on as long as there is an appreciative audience with a little tobacco to proffer or until the Indian is tired. A blind storyteller, and there are several to be found due to the combined effects of snow glare and nutritional deficiencies, invariably wants to clutch a hearer's hand as if afraid of losing the all-important listener, like an actor putting everything into holding his audience.

And the stories themselves? They explain everything—the origin of man and of the wavy goose, why the whisky-jack is clumsy and how the moon was made. Sex plays an important part, generally quite proper from a primitive point of view. There are few climaxes or highlights, just a simple narrative of events simple and touching the supernatural. One Wesakaychak or Wisahketchahk plays an important role in tales of both the present-day Bush Indians and the tribes at the confluence of the Battle River with the Saskatchewan.

They are a highly poetic people, the Indians of the Saskatchewan. Perhaps if and when they all get enough of the right food, year in and year out, they may dispute the lightly made taunt that the Indian never contributed anything of enduring worth to the territory over which he hunted. They may remind their white brothers that without their contributions the territory might even yet be a frontier. If that day ever comes, it will likely be from the angle between the branches and the country immediately to the west along the North Branch. There the métis made their stand against settlement in what history books refer to as the Rebellion of 1885.

CHAPTER SIXTEEN

Rebellion, 1885

"Let us send for Riel!" cried the métis living in the angle between the north and south branches of the Saskatchewan.

Ever since the Northwest had been transferred to Canada they had been appealing to Ottawa for recognition of their rights. For fifteen years they had addressed petitions to the government through their priests and Chief Factor Lawrence Clarke of the Hudson's Bay Company post at Prince Albert. Assisted by their Scottish and English half-breed neighbors, several times they had scraped together enough money to send a delegate to plead for scrip. Always the result was the same. Every appeal had been ignored or answered as though there were no half-breed grievance at all.

"Let us send for Riel!" they cried, desperate and bitter.

Riel had led the métis at the Red River in 1869. Again his fiery patriotism was needed. Natives of the Saskatchewan and those who had trekked from the Red River to escape inroads of white civilization held meetings during the early months of 1884. At the new schoolhouses and in trading posts in each parish they vowed that their aboriginal rights must be met. No longer would they live in fear of losing their homes to white settlers or land agents. They would have a title to their land—or fight.

Now white settlers were bringing their intolerant and superior civilization to the Saskatchewan. Along the South Branch surveyors were measuring the land into great squares instead of the traditional narrow strips facing on the river. One promoter—it was the promoters they distrusted most—had a grant for land including the métis settlements of Gabriel's Crossing, Batoche, and St. Laurent, a grant which cut across the farms of a few chains' width and possibly two miles' depth with no consideration for homes and stables or hard-tilled fields. Already farms of men whose land had been chosen by their fathers before them were marked by the surveyors' four holes and wooden posts at the northeast corner of each square mile. So far no changes had been made along the North Branch. None would be made, it was rumored. But who knew? Who could feel safe with no title to his land? On both sides of the angle between the branches, some twenty miles wide, the surveyor's chain became a feared and hated symbol.

Others living along the Saskatchewan shared their grievances. Native Scottish and English half-breeds wanted scrip and the security it implied. One English-speaking group complained that it had forwarded five petitions to the federal government without result. The white communities on the North Branch were roused, Prince Albert and Battleford, from where the seat of territorial government had recently been moved to Regina, and the village of Saskatoon.

The white settlers and townspeople had been sending their own petitions to Ottawa. Times were bad. Hard frost had ruined crops and prices were low. The changed route of the railway from the valley of the Saskatchewan as originally proposed to a line some two hundred miles to the south had resulted in a serious depression of the land boom of 1881 and 1882. The métis' meetings became popular even among white citizens who did not generally fraternize with them. The Prince Albert *Times*, but a few years old, took up the cause. Its editor wrote:

We presume that the descendants of men who wrested from the hands of a grasping monarch the safe-guards of their rights and liberties contained in the Magna Carta, Bill of Rights, Grand Remonstrance, Habeas Corpus and Act of Settlement, must be fully alive to what their constitutional rights consist of . . . the people of the Northwest have for a long time past been struggling by every legitimate means in their power to impress upon the Eastern Provinces the fact that they have been treated with deliberate and gross injustice, and that however anxious they may be to avoid extreme measures, they will not shrink . . . from taking any steps absolutely necessary for the vindication of their rights . . . The Dominion Government . . . occupies the contemptible position of a greedy, grasping, overbearing bully who has . . . totally misjudged the fighting power of the subject it has chosen to oppress.

Everyone in the Northwest Territories was aware of the Indian problems. Many were due to the inexorable progress of a civilization to which the Indian could not easily adapt himself. The tepee, the crackling wood fire, and the endless trails were in his blood. He needed a few generations of wise and understanding guidance to merge his independent, nomadic spirit with the ways of white men. Instead, he had been pushed onto reserves. Why, he asked, should his friends, the North West Mounted Police, arrest a young man who had knocked down an Indian Department official with an ax? It would be better to let the Hudson's Bay people deal with him. Racial antagonism was mounting. Along the banks of the Saskatchewan the *tom-tom, tom-tom, tom-tom, tom-tom* rose and fell about the campfires.

Sitting Bull's bands had brought tales of terror and depredation at the hands of white men in Dakota. Sioux tribesmen carried north the story of Indian successes at the Little Big Horn. There was talk of an uprising against the whites. Poundmaker, tall, handsome chief of the Plains Crees, though advising restraint, had tried to hold a council in 1883 and was forcibly prevented by the police. In 1884 Big Bear succeeded and the tribes from Fort La Corne to above Fort Pitt met to discuss their grievances. It was a great council for Big Bear. To it came all the chiefs and headmen. The Indians complained that the government talked with the forked tongue. Big Bear himself spoke for those who had not gone on the reserves. He said:

"As I see they are not going to be honest I am afraid to take a reserve."

But the great complaint of the Indians was that they had come to realize what white men had meant when they asked the natives to sell their land. To the Indian selling actually meant lending. Had not Governor Morris called upon the Great Spirit and the queen when making the treaty? Had he not said that the white people came "to borrow the country, to keep it for you"? Now they knew the truth.

At the conclusion of the council the chiefs stated that "they were glad that the young men had not resorted to violent measures . . . it is almost too hard for them to bear the treatment at the hands of the government after its sweet promises." The implied threat was tempered for the time by the wisdom of Indian Agent J. A. McRae at Fort Carlton. Twice during the council the chiefs had sent to him for food. They were all hungry. McRae's generous allowance of provisions and the chance to talk over their grievances quieted the Indians for a time. They would "wait until next summer to see if this council has the desired effect," failing which they would "take measures to get what they desire."

As dry as tinder lay the prairie and parkland along the Saskatchewan when the métis decided to send for Riel. His very name was a potential spark. To many of the white people he was a firebrand and a dangerous visionary, a man lacking good judgment. Upon hearing the decision the Prince Albert *Times* withdrew its support from the métis and did a complete volte-face. At Battleford, the *Saskatchewan Herald* protested against Riel while it acknowledged every grievance voiced in the declaration prepared to send to him. The Edmonton *Bulletin*, published by Frank Oliver, regarded Riel as political dynamite; certainly he was not the man to lead the Northwest in its struggle with Parliament. The clergy, especially those of the Roman Catholic faith to which the métis patriot adhered, would have nothing to do with his works.

Several white people attended a meeting which drafted the call to Riel. The four-man party dispatched to the Sun River in Montana, where Riel had become an American citizen and where he had been teaching school since the troubles of 1869, consisted of one English half-breed and three métis. They took with them the resolution:

> We, the French and English natives of the North West, knowing that Louis Riel has made a bargain with the Government of Canada, in 1870, which said bargain is contained mostly in what is known as the "Manitoba Act," and this meeting not knowing the contents of said "Manitoba Act," we have thought it advisable that a delegation be sent to said Louis Riel, and have his assistance to bring all of the matters referred to in the above resolutions in a proper shape and form before the Government of Canada, so that our just demands be granted.

They were but a few thousand uneducated half-breeds, men born along the Saskatchewan, married into Indian families or born of Indian mothers. They were ill equipped for a struggle against a British government. Actually they were as averse to armed rebellion as the Canadian patriots of 1837, or any group of British people who finally had to resort to that step in the empire's long fight for freedom. They hoped a show of force would be sufficient. But if necessary they had a weapon. They could instigate all the terrors of a general Indian uprising.

Louis Riel arrived on the Saskatchewan, and on July 11, 1884, began his task of co-ordinating white, half-breed, and Indian discontent. Riel was not much of a soldier himself. But he could stir his own people to fight. His fiery magnetism had a tremendous power over them. Better educated than average métis, he seemed to them a prophet and a great leader. Had he enjoyed better mental health he might indeed have been a great leader. The fits of gloom and exaltation that punctuated his life handicapped his judgment; he had, indeed, spent two periods in what were then called insane asylums in Quebec. Yet from the time he led his people at the Red River in 1869 until the end he remained stanch to the cause of the métis. To them he was always a patriot no matter how often the rest of Canada called him rebel.

Father Pierre André, who had long ministered to the métis in the angle, wrote a letter of protest to Lieutenant-Governor Dewdney at Regina. In turn Governor Dewdney wrote to Prime Minister Sir John A. MacDonald at Ottawa. Several prominent white citizens also protested the presence of Riel in the community. Without Riel, they said, everything would quiet down.

Meetings continued during the winter of 1884–85. Riel and his followers drew up a Bill of Rights, a reasonable statement of which all terms eventually were recognized by the government. There was much talk about land rights and provincial autonomy; even the British connection should be tolerated only so long as it was advantageous. One meeting was referred to as a "war whoop which it was determined would be heard in Ottawa." As a result the North West Mounted Police, of which there were five hundred in all the Northwest, increased its complement of men at Battleford and Prince Albert and stationed a detachment at Fort Carlton. But no one expected much real trouble. Father André and

D. H. MacDowall, member for the Territorial Council, were of the opinion that a settlement of from $3,000 to $5,000 "would cart the entire Riel family across the border" and peace would descend upon the angle between the branches of the Saskatchewan.

Ottawa ignored the suggestion that Riel be bought off. It ignored petitions for negotiation. Desperate and in one of his periods of extreme exaltation, the métis leader decided to form the provisional government for the Saskatchewan. The new government would take possession of the country and the terms of entry into confederation would be changed. It was a madman's scheme. Perhaps it was the direct result of the last petition to Ottawa.

For days the half-breeds had waited at Clarke's Crossing for the return of their latest ambassador to Ottawa. When at last his horses appeared along the well-worn, snow-covered trail from the south they rushed to meet him. Perhaps the man was tired from his long trip. Perhaps he, too, had lost heart. With very poor judgment he blurted out the curt statement:

"The government will answer you with bullets!"

Instead of more liberal treatment for the Indians, instead of scrip for the half-breeds, responsible government, vote by ballot—they were offered bullets! To Riel it was a sign from heaven. Now as never before he was called to defend his people.

The English settlers who had originally backed him turned against Riel. The clergy declared him *non compos mentis* and not to be allowed the sacrament. Fired with an unreasoning zeal to protect his people, Riel armed his métis under Gabriel Dumont and on March 18 arrested several men from the next settlement, including the Indian agent and farm instructor from One-Arrow and Beardy's reserves. He took over the Roman Catholic church at Batoche as his headquarters. The success of 1869 would be repeated, he assured his simple followers. To impress them he resorted to the tactics of the magician. "God would draw his hand over the face of the sun," he told them, "if the future movements of the métis were to be courted with success." Having an almanac, of which most of his followers had never heard, Louis Riel successfully predicted an eclipse. After that they were more devoted to him than ever. The spark was struck that ignited the tinder.

Superintendent Crozier of the police at Prince Albert telegraphed headquarters for help, urging "immedate action." He received word that Inspector Irvine had been dispatched from Regina with reinforcements. He notified Governor Dewdney at Regina, and appealed to Ottawa. Father André also addressed appeals to the government. And all the time most of the métis, the people most closely concerned, were scarcely aware of what was happening. At Batoche and St. Laurent, at Duck Lake and other settlements they were busy with their simple duties, plans for spring work and chores and going to Mass. Few appreciated that Riel's band of four or five hundred crack buffalo hunters meant war in spite of their generally poor arms and limited ammunition. The women and children, being largely Indian, left such things to men. They had little to fear from rumors that natives at Fort Pitt were buying all the ammunition obtainable. The increasing *tom-tom*, *tom-tom*, *tom-tom*, *tom-tom* of Poundmaker and Big Bear's warriors was old music to them. Gabriel Dumont's wife, like many another, merely added more meat to the huge pot of venison stew on the fire.

It was different at Prince Albert. Mounted horsemen dashed south to the telegraph crossing. Messages flew like arrows. Crozier organized volunteers and the first Prince Albert Company commenced drill. Plans were made to defend white women and children—"in case there should be trouble," they kept adding. The villagers of Saskatoon looked to their defenses. Battleford Police Division urged that reinforcements be sent at once. Riel's men raided a store for supplies. The fire blazed fitfully for a moment.

Inspector Crozier tried to put it out. Like other leading citizens, he appreciated the reality of half-breed grievances and hoped they could be met by peaceful means. But Riel's excitement was spreading to his followers. Hilliard Mitchell, storekeeper at Duck Lake, made several attempts to mediate between the police and the métis. But Riel was in no state of mind for mediation. He demanded that the police give themselves up to his provisional government.

By then a strong wind was fanning the tiny flame. Riel's men, captained by Gabriel Dumont, tried to provoke the police into firing on them. They held up a detachment sent under Thomas McKay and a sergeant to Mitchell's store for supplies, and, possibly, on reconnaissance, forcing the detachment to return without their beef and oats. Seldom if ever in their short and already famous career had the North West Mounted Police had to admit even minor defeat. It was too much for Crozier, now at Fort Carlton with forty or fifty Prince Albert volunteers. The volunteers demanded that they go out in force to defend the fort before "the rebels" attacked it. Crozier would have preferred to await the arrival of Inspector Irvine and his reinforcements, but he knew the tactical value of preventing the métis and their Indian allies from getting the upper hand. His volunteer force urged him to get on with the "picnic." On March 26 he ordered the "boots and saddles."

To assert the authority of the 18-year-old Dominion of Canada, Crozier had Inspector Howe, Surgeon Miller, fifty-three Police, forty-one Prince Albert volunteers—and one 7-inch gun. They traveled in sleighs and on horseback. Because the snow was so deep they had to keep to the packed and rutted trail with spring's warm sun to mute the glare of endless miles of rolling whiteness and temper the bitter wind. Leaving the North Branch behind, the column hurried toward the South Branch and Duck Lake, five miles from Batoche. Six mounted police under a sergeant made up the advance guard, traveling a little too close to the main column to allow sufficient time for proper disposition in case of attack. But then who really expected the métis to attack? The mere presence of the North West Mounted Police would be sufficient to keep order. No shots had been fired. Horses' harness jangled. Men tossed quips to one another. They would soon show Mr. Riel which was the properly constituted government—and police—in the Northwest! It was a fine, bright day for a drive, a fine, bright day . . . and Inspector Crozier kept to himself any misgivings he had.

Gabriel Dumont and Riel were enjoying their first round of success when a scout rushed into the house where they were staying at Duck Lake.

"Voilà la police!"

Dumont gave a few crisp orders. He and such of his men as had horses leapt to their saddles. Others followed on foot. Opposite a small bluff of willow brush, beside a couple of log shacks, the two forces met. A métis waved a white blanket and Crozier with Constable "Gentleman Joe" McKay, his interpreter, and another man went forward to parley. Dumont's unmounted men raced for the shelter of the shacks while the police force drew up their sleighs in a barricade across the road and led their horses to the rear. Their gun was well to the front.

Dumont used the brief parley time to get his men in position. In the no man's land between the two forces one métis grappled with McKay while another, falling to his knee, covered him with his gun. Seeing there was no likelihood of a real parley, Crozier snapped out an order. As he turned, an Indian grabbed his shoulder. Gentleman Joe McKay whipped out his pistol and shot the man covering him. It was the first shot fired in what became known as the Rebellion of 1885.

Volleys followed that first shot. From the cover of their sleighs the police and volunteers fired on the métis and Indians. But the natives had the advantage of good cover. From the protection of the shacks they directed a deadly fire. Only the 7-pounder remained silent. It was up close to the front, within range of rifle fire. The gunner in his excitement had rammed in the shell before the shot. For the next fifty or sixty years he was reminded as often of that incident as Gentleman Joe boasted of having fired the first shot.

The métis and Indians had the advantage of position and numbers. Most were expert marksmen. They shot twelve of the police and volunteers—practically all through the head. Eleven others were wounded. Five transport horses were killed. In less than forty minutes Crozier gave the order to retire. With the greatest difficulty he extricated his men and sleighs and made for Fort Carlton. The men and horses behaved with coolness and discipline. But the situation was hopeless. The métis had always had to make every shot count when shooting buffalo or antelope. They lost only five men killed, though Gabriel Dumont had his scalp furrowed by a stray bullet cutting between chinks in the log shack where he was directing operations, a bad omen in Riel's opinion. Riel himself, armed only with a crucifix, watched the swift engagement. When his men would have annihilated the retreating column he cried:

"Pour l'amour de Dieu de ne plus en tuer . . . il y a deja trop de sang répandu."

Twelve good men dead, eleven wounded and—defeat at the hands of men who were their neighbors! Inspector Crozier was acutely aware of the propaganda use Riel would make of the métis' success. No longer would the métis respect the North West Mounted Police. Throughout the Saskatchewan country Indians who had often thought of rising but had been deterred by fear of the redcoats would now have nothing to restrain them.

Colonel Irvine made the forced march from Regina to Prince Albert over heavily crusted snow in seven days. The distance was two hundred and ninety miles. Each morning reveille sounded at 3:30. The cold was bitter. Men and horses alike suffered from ice cutting their feet. The detachment had had little time to rest at Prince Albert when a haggard rider who had been in the saddle all night galloped into camp. Gentleman Joe McKay brought word of the Duck Lake battle, fought but a few hours before. Irvine at once issued orders to go to the relief of Fort Carlton while the people of Prince Albert looked to their meager defenses with fearful hearts. The little blaze was a roaring prairie fire, fanned by the strong wind of racial animosity.

At Fort Carlton a grim council was held. The fort, built for the fur trade many years before and stockaded, was no longer defensible against repeating rifles. There were not enough men available to garrison it and at the same time protect the people of Prince Albert. There was only one course—abandon Fort Carlton and retire in force to Prince Albert.

At night, by lamplight, the snow was shoveled away, graves dug, and the dead buried. Such supplies as could be transported were loaded on sleighs and the balance destroyed so that they might not fall into the hands of métis or Indians. As the column headed toward Prince Albert in the cold morning of March 28 fire broke out and old Fort Carlton was practically destroyed; for its loss the Hudson's Bay Company claimed and won $52,540.78.

Men ran beside the sleighs to keep themselves warm. Every effort was made to make the wounded as comfortable as possible and to keep them from freezing. With the good luck that often attended both sides during the haphazard campaign the trip was accomplished without attack. At Prince Albert the Presbyterian manse was stockaded with cordwood. The church bell was to be rung to warn the people and in case of an attack or siege women and children were to be taken to the church. But the preparations proved to be unnecessary. Only rumors and enforced inertia marked the Prince Albert part of the rebellion. Riel's headquarters at

Batoche were between the town and the telegraph line. Crozier and his men having seen the first action had to remain idle for the remainder of the campaign.

The day following, Duck Lake Indian runners were at Battleford with the news, urging the métis of the Battle River and Fort Pitt to rouse the natives and to do all they could to embarrass the police. Next day word reached Frog Lake, more than two hundred miles away.

The town of Battleford, south of the Battle River, was in a frenzy. Its 500-odd population heard that Chiefs Poundmaker, Little Pine, and Strike-Him-on-the-Back and their braves were on the way to make demands of the Indian agent. Though the local magistrate still considered it all a bit of "political bluster," many of the settlers abandoned their homes to seek the protection of the police barracks on the high land across the Battle and south of the North Saskatchewan. Soon the Indians began to arrive. When it was learned that they brought with them only enough squaws to do camp drudgery, the remaining white population moved to the stockade. Indians without women and children meant one thing—war.

Poundmaker and Little Pine were armed and in war paint. They told William McKay, in charge of the Hudson's Bay Company store, that they needed food and clothing. If they were given necessities with some sugar, tobacco, powder, and shot they would return to their reserves. The experienced Hudson's Bay man sized up the situation quickly. He at once telegraphed to Regina to Governor Dewdney for authority to meet their request. The governor wired back, but his message backing McKay arrived too late. The Indians broke into stores and helped themselves.

At night the citizens, from across the Battle River, saw their houses and stores being burned, not in one grand conflagration, but a few at a time so that the Indians could prolong their sport as long as possible. Fearful news trickled through to the crowded 200-yard square stockade. Now everyone realized that the Indians were in no mood for conciliation.

Up at Frog Lake, to the west, the Indian agent had advised the small detachment of police to leave; they were too few to hold out against a determined Indian attack and their presence was disturbing. Yet no sooner had the police started on their unhappy journey downriver than Big Bear's Indians, hungry and short of clothing, arrived to make their demands on Indian Agent Quinn. The agent and the little group of nine white men and the white wives of two of them soon saw that Big Bear had lost control over his band. His young warriors were bent on pillage. During the night his son Imasees tried to murder Quinn. Next day the Indians took possession of the small village. They ordered the white people to proceed to their camp as prisoners. Agent Quinn refused. One of Big Bear's warriors, Wandering Spirit, repeated the order. When Quinn again refused, the Indian shot him. In vain Big Bear came running from his tent shouting "Stop! Stop!" Racial hatred, never more than a smoldering, fitful ember between the white people of the Canadian Northwest and the Indians, suddenly flared into a blaze. The farm instructor, two priests, and five other white men were shot at once. The two women were taken prisoner, receiving the protection of half-breed friends. One white man, William Bleasdell Cameron, managed to escape.

Word soon reached Fort Pitt, a little downriver. Like everyone else, Inspector Dickens, son of novelist Charles Dickens, had been inclined to take a mild view of the unrest along the Saskatchewan. The massacre at Frog Lake shocked him into action. His fort was four hundred yards from its water supply. In his command he had only twenty-four police, including the small Frog Lake group, and about forty civilians. Even with sufficient food his ammunition supply was inadequate for a long Indian siege. Dickens decided to evacuate for Battleford on learnng that the Indians would attack if the police remained. It took him and his men several days to build a scow large enough to transport them all. On April 15 they destroyed such ammunition as they could not carry and embarked in their leaky scow. It was another of those incredible trips down the Saskatchewan which took place during the days following the ice breakup of 1885. That particular journey took a week, traveling night and day.

The Saskatchewan was its accustomed unco-operative, cold, dangerous worst that spring. One by one small boats, isolated and far apart, were pushed out amidst its crunching cakes of ice by refugee settlers, traders, and missionaries. About them its swirling, muddy waters tossed an icy spray. The river was wide. Its banks made excellent cover for lurking Indians. Any moment boats might be crushed. Often they were lifted out of the water, tipping crazily among blocks of crunching ice. The refugees were short of food. They dare not risk struggling to shore to make a fire to warm their shivering and numbed bodies. To survive long enough to reach Battleford was their only hope. Fired on from time to time, lacking all conveniences, and without shelter, they huddled together while the racing Saskatchewan carried them on to Battleford. The high sentinel trees in front of the North West Mounted Police barracks must have looked like heaven to the police from Fort Pitt, to the family of McKays, and all the other white refugees. Later romance entered the scene and one of the McKay daughters became the bride to Gentleman Joe McKay, no relationship before the event.

Word of Duck Lake had electrified eastern Canada. At once Ottawa became aware that it had a territory in the northwest. People read their papers with shocked indignation. Riel was a rebel, they cried in Ontario. He was a patriot, said the people of Quebec. The result of the belated excitement was one of the quickest bits of action Canada had ever shown. A militia force was recruited and in two weeks the not-quite-completed Canadian Pacific Railway, an aroused government, and a wildly patriotic people had a field force at

Qu'Appelle, prepared to march to Batoche, two hundred miles north. The troops were under command of General Fred Middleton, a British officer, Canada at that time being considered much too colonial to provide a commanding officer. General Middleton's plan was to take one column to Batoche himself, and to send a second column under General Strange north from the railway at Calgary to Edmonton and then down the North Saskatchewan to Fort Pitt.

His command consisted of the five hundred North West Mounted Police, some two thousand men from western Canada, and over three thousand from the East. There were two batteries of artillery, A and B, the entire regular army. Last, but by no means least in potential value, was the surveyors' corps, fifty men who proudly claimed to be rough-tough-and-dirty and who knew the country. One of them discovered a novel and effective means of delousing shirts. The formula consisted of placing the affected shirt on the prairie on a sunny day and letting the ants do the job. It was never mentioned officially, possibly because the general found the surveyors too addicted to ignoring red tape.

Middleton was a fearless soldier handicapped by the snobbery to which his military caste was bred. He had an undying affection for the British regular, contempt for the militia, and mistrust of the North West Mounted Police. His unwillingness to accept the advice of men familiar with the country caused bitterness and serious delay, especially to the citizens of Battleford. Informed of the danger to the five hundred people cooped up within the small stockade at Battleford, General Middleton insisted that the situation was greatly exaggerated. Only under the greatest pressure from Governor Dewdney and local citizens did he decide to make even a token of relief. He commanded Colonel Herchmer of the North West Mounted Police at Regina to proceed to Battleford with fifty men!

Herchmer received General Middleton's command the same day as he received word of the massacre of nine white civilians at Frog Lake. He did something almost unheard of in police annals. He refused to go. Herchmer knew the territory between Regina and Battleford, over two hundred miles. He knew the difficulty of transporting food and fodder and that only half of his men were mounted. The South Saskatchewan, swollen with spring waters, had to be forded without boat or ferry. Anywhere along the way Poundmaker's Indians could annihilate them before they had a chance to relieve Battleford.

General Middleton was forced to revise his plan. He divided the Edmonton column, so that one detachment could travel to Swift Current by train, from there going north to Saskatchewan Landing on the South Branch, crossing the river, and then marching to Battleford. The other went on to Calgary.

Leaving a rear guard of Quebec Cavalry and the Governor General's Bodyguard at Qu'Appelle, Middleton made his own march by way of the Qu'Appelle valley, the Touchwood Trail, and Humboldt to the South Saskatchewan. He had nine guns and two machine guns and a large wagon train of supplies.

The Canadian government secured assurance from Washington that no arms or ammunition would be permitted to cross the border to aid "the rebels." That assurance greatly relieved Middleton's rear. The arrival of the troops persuaded the métis and Indians of the Qu'Appelle valley to remain quiet. But by far the most effective ally Middleton had in the south was the government's belated shipment of two hundred carloads of flour and fifteen thousand pounds of bacon, with extra rations for all Indians who would work. The extra rations included tea and tobacco. It was a wise move. More than once before, trouble had been averted when police or Hudson's Bay men handed out food to half-starving natives. Also, after ignoring all petitions for years, the government on April 6 authorized the issue of scrip. Scrip and food localized the métis' rising to the territory of St. Laurent on the South Branch. Much of Riel's authority was dissipated by the fulfillment of so many of his demands.

While General Middleton made his majestic way north from Qu'Appelle to Batoche, the Battleford relief column commanded by Colonel Otter and augmented by the fifty policemen whom Herchmer had refused to squander awaited the arrival of the steamer *Northcote* at Saskatchewan Landing. The *Northcote* had been ordered down from Medicine Hat, with a cargo of supplies and to ferry the troops across the river.

Already the Battleford column felt that it had been making more geography than history. The 30-mile march from the handful of buildings and tents that made up Swift Current had given them some idea of the prairie's wide horizons and bitter early-April winds. Coming upon the great valley of the South Saskatchewan with its treed coulees was a welcome surprise. There they had plenty of fuel for fires. There was protection from the wind. Water was good and few sentries expected "red Indians" to leap out at them from the bushes at night. It was the fate of the five hundred civilians at Battleford that kept their eyes turned upriver.

The *Northcote* took a week to make the trip from Medicine Hat, a distance which can be traveled by modern trains in about three hours. The rush of mountain waters had not yet raised the water level. Drawing twenty-six inches of water, the stern-wheeler often had less than twenty. Shoals delayed her progress. Literally she hauled herself almost the entire distance. A great cheer went up from the troops at the Landing when they saw her eventually round a bend and promptly get stuck on another shoal. A cable and winch and a tree on the shore got her going again. She had arrived to ferry the five hundred men, two hundred wagons, and horses across the river.

The column climbed laboriously out of the deep valley to the endless vista of prairie beyond. The grass was not yet green. Everywhere it was sprinkled with the white bones of buffalo, later gathered up and shipped to American sugar factories. Here and there a few early crocuses gave a hint of the riot of wild flowers that would soon bloom everywhere. Gophers sat like pickets by their holes. Overhead in the clear blue sky meadow larks sang to greet the morning and the troops alike, though the troops were soon too preoccupied to appreciate the song. They were engrossed in making geography on painful feet, in drinking tea made from bitter alkali water, and grumbling about hardtack. The hardtack was referred to by General Middleton as "capital biscuit." The general had not had occasion to share his men's avowal that the "capital biscuit" was especially nourishing when it was "inhabited."

The *Northcote* carried one extremely important passenger when she continued her trip downstream, Captain Howard, of the U.S. Army. In the valuable cargo being sent by river to the relief of General Middleton's columns, though it could have been transported much quicker overland, was a precious Gatling gun. Captain Howard, very soon nicknamed "Gatling," was in charge of the gun and was to instruct the Canadian troops in its use. Having seen service in the western states for some years, Gatling Howard soon found the snail's pace of the *Northcote* more than he could bear, so he took to land. He did a little antelope shooting with the boys of the surveyors corps who were engaged in patrolling the enormous territory from Swift Current to a spot somewhere below Clarke's Crossing, with their headquarters at the Elbow. The Elbow provided plenty of wood for fuel. It was a pleasant bivouac. Indians who wanted to elude the corps had plenty of space in which to do so and none seemed inclined to attack.

Teamsters making their slow way between Middleton's forces and Moose Jaw halted at the Elbow. Settlers, nervous about the rebellion, went that way, bringing word to Captain Howard and the surveyors that General Middleton had had a brush with the métis at Fish Creek, near Clarke's Crossing, and that the General had lost eight men killed and forty wounded. Captain Howard and the surveyors felt they could be employed better than traveling slowly down the scenic South Branch by boat or guarding the trail against cattle and settlers. Howard decided to travel overland and the surveyors followed to join the general's forces.

Fish Creek was another victory for the métis. Again they had the advantage of position. From coulees and depressions of the rolling, bush-dotted country they kept the troops against the sky line. On at least one occasion they resorted to the old Indian tactic of setting the prairie on fire. The Saskatchewan River natives were doing their best to defend their homeland. But though they delayed Middleton's forces, steady rifle fire discouraged many of them. Though some métis deserted at the end of the day, they still held their coulee and once more, as at Duck Lake, one of them confessed: "We prayed all day, and I think prayer did more than bullets."

April 24, the day of the Fish Creek battle, was a great day for the beleaguered white people at Battleford. For almost a month they had existed within the small police stockade on the high angle between the Battle River and the North Saskatchewan. As in the case of the besieged at Lucknow, it was the sound of band music that brought them the first hope of relief. Far away they could hear it, in spite of the strong wind that almost always blows on the prairie, loud and then fading away so that they thought it was imagined. But at last there could be no doubt. Colonel Otter's men had tramped all the way from the Landing, footsore, annoyed because some of their provisions had been taken over by Poundmaker's Indians, but proud to be the first outsiders to reach the people of Battleford.

At the town south of the Battle River they saw plenty of evidence of how the Indians had brightened their nights by burning houses and stores, a few at a time to wage a war of nerves on the owners as well as to prolong their own excitement. The shouts of welcome from the people as the troops marched up to the stockade was worth all the geography and hardtack they had endured.

Riel's runners soon had word at Battleford of their success at Fish Creek. Poundmaker and Big Bear received messages urging them to send warriors at once to drive the invaders out of the Saskatchewan country forever. Colonel Otter faced a serious problem. General Middleton had ordered him to remain at Battleford. But delay might be disastrous. The Indians, like the métis, were wild with success. If they were allowed to meet up with Riel's forces, the war might be prolonged indefinitely. Otter wired to Governor Dewdney instead of to General Middleton, hoping to get a go-ahead signal even at the cost of a breach of military etiquette.

Fortunately for the white people, Chiefs Poundmaker and Big Bear were having trouble with their bands. The Stonies wanted to go at once to Riel's aid. Poundmaker, having been assured that Riel could carry all before him, wanted to know why there should be a call for help. Big Bear could not unite the Woods Crees, who were satisfied with the food they had secured and a little fighting, with the Plains Crees, who were traditional warriors. Colonel Otter wanted to punish Poundmaker for looting his supplies and the town of Battleford and, at the same time, prevent the union with Riel. With defection within the Indian tribes the time seemed ripe. Receipt of a telegram from Governor Dewdney advising action and pointing out that Colonel Herchmer knew the country well, decided Otter. The Battle of Cut Knife Creek resulted.

Otter's men moved forward at night to attack the Indians camped at Cut Knife Creek on the morning of May 2. Because an Indian village never sleeps, the troops were discovered at daybreak. At once both sides raced for the hill around which the creek flows, the Indians adopting tactics similar to those used at Fish Creek. Taking advantage of depressed positions, they were able to pour a cross fire upon the exposed soldiers. Otter's men soon discovered that their guns were almost useless. Under a fresh coat of paint the gun carriages were rotten. No sooner were the guns fired than the trails gave way. After seven hours Otter managed to extricate his men and the bitterly disappointing guns. That the loss of life among the troops was not greater was due, as at Duck Lake, to the intervention of a "rebel" leader. When his exultant warriors would have pursued the fleeing troops to the woods Poundmaker held them back. Eight of the troops were killed and fourteen wounded. The Indians lost five killed.

On May 14 Poundmaker had further success. He captured twenty prisoners and a large supply train on the way to Battleford. Not only had he a good supply of provisions, but the troops and white citizens were short. On every hand there was news of Indian success. The métis were gathering forces, eager to unite with the Indians following Otter's defeat at Cut Knife. From Fort Pitt to Battleford and down the South Branch to Batoche the Saskatchewan was in the grip of civil war. Nothing seemed to be done to stem the tide. General Middleton had retired after the Battle of Fish Creek. Nearly two weeks lapsed without further attack. Rumors were rife. They said he had sent for regulars, distrusting the militia and police. They claimed he was awaiting the arrival of the *Northcote* with Captain Howard and the Gatling gun. Bitterly they denounced calling up the surveyors and leaving the Governor General's Bodyguard and Quebec Cavalry in idleness at Qu'Appelle. Middleton refused to be hurried. He spent two weeks seeing to his defenses, planning an offense, and caring for his wounded men. Some wounded men were sent to the temporary dressing station at Saskatoon. More serious cases traveled the rough buckboard journey to the hospital improvised by the Sisters of St. John the Divine at Moose Jaw.

On May 9 Middleton moved toward the métis headquarters at Batoche with about eight hundred and fifty men.

He was escorted by the *Northcote*, arrived at last and with her decks hastily fortified with plank and piles of sacks of oats and boxes of meat. She had two heavily laden barges in tow. A combined attack was set for 8:00 P.M. But somehow the boat was a little early and the troops a little late. The rebel fire on the *Northcote* was heavy. Just as the stern-wheeler came abreast of the ferry cable there was a shuddering crash on the afterdeck. Too busy to see what had happened, the troops returned the fire from both shores. Not until that had slackened and the boat was a couple of miles downstream below Batoche did they discover that the enterprising métis had dropped the cable, slicing off the funnel and whistle. The loss of the funnels was bad—there was the danger of fire—but without the whistle there was no means of sending the planned signal. That had to be repaired. It was the first thing the belated troops and their irate general heard as they approached the scene of the battle—the fading whistle of the *Northcote* now well out of range of métis shots.

Batoche was a small village on the right bank of the South Saskatchewan, seven miles above Gabriel's Crossing. Near Batoche's house, from which it took its name, was the ferry with several houses to the north. To the south of the ferry stood the Roman Catholic church, the priest's house, and, just above the river, a cemetery. The métis camp and an Indian village were situated in a coulee just beyond the crossing. Well-constructed rifle pits with breastworks of earth and logs and having openings for rifle fire guarded the approach. A wooded height running parallel to the river protected the eastern flank. For three days the métis held back the soldiers with no loss to themselves.

Again the mètis used the tactics that had stood them in such good stead at Fish Creek. When Middleton's troops attacked the church they had to do so in full view of the protected métis. Being on land lower than the troops the métis always had them against the sky line. It was ideal strategy in the rolling country where the half-breeds knew every bush and slough. It made the most of their carefully hoarded ammunition, pitifully inadequate for any kind of campaign. By the second day of battle Middleton's surgeon reported that the métis were using slugs and duck shot. Next day some were reduced to small stones and nails. They had no chance against the superior ammunition, machine guns, and steadiness of trained troops.

At the same time Middleton's men were indignant over rumors that British regulars were being sent for. They fumed at his lack of speed. When the battle was resumed on the third morning they all longed for real action. That day the general planned to silence the rifle pits to the east of Batoche, using the Gatling gun and a small force of men. Orders were that the main body of troops would attack from the south when they heard Middleton's fire. But prairie winds are strong. Blowing across the angle between the branches there was almost a gale. Not a sound of Middleton's fire was heard to the south. Irate at their apparent lack of co-operation the general galloped back on his white horse. In no time the Midlanders under Colonel Williams and the Grenadiers under Colonel Grassett were charging down the hill.

Their red and black tunics were excellent targets. Puffs of white smoke burst in the air, like bits of cloud. The *sk-r-r-r* of the Gatling mingled with the cheers of troops in action at last. When no attack from the south had followed the fire from the east Dumont had decided that the main charge would come from the east. The wildly cheering, eager troops caught the métis off guard as well as without ammunition. The first line of pits fell quickly. Soon they were dislodged from their positions in the houses. The coulee was cleared and firing from across the river ceased. The Battle of Batoche was over. General Middleton had lived up to the British tradition of losing every battle but the last. The only difference with Batoche was that rather than Middleton's winning that battle, the métis lost it, a nice point for history.

The general and his staff came to look over the field

while detachments of troops cleared up. A couple of métis brought a letter from Riel, who had scribbled on the envelope "I don't like war."

There was a lot of celebration among the troops, much sadness among the métis and their families. With the pomp of a Victorian general Middleton rescued the prisoners and hostages. He was amazed at the "excellence of the construction of the rifle pits" dug by the métis. General Middleton did not seem to realize that the French half-breeds whose "judiciously placed" pits amazed him were inspired to make their best effort to defend their homeland. He did not understand their lonely, leaderless position when Riel surrendered next day.

Middleton dispatched telegrams to Ottawa. Ottawa telegraphed back congratulations. And then the general spent most of two days questioning the depressed and unhappy Riel.

"I found him," wrote Middleton, "a mild spoken and mild looking man, with a short beard and an uneasy frightened look about his eyes, which gradualy disappeared as I talked to him."

But General Middleton decided that Riel was "sane enough in general everyday subjects" to stand trial, and sent him off to Regina under close guard, aboard the *Northcote*. Gabriel Dumont, Riel's deputy, escaped over the border to Montana.

While the *Northcote* was preparing to steam upriver to Medicine Hat the SS *Baroness* arrived from the south. The SS *Marquis*, one of the largest boats to travel on the Saskatchewan, was below Batoche undergoing a few repairs during the time of battle. Middleton dispatched both to Prince Albert to await his arrival. Meanwhile he mounted his white horse, assembled his forces, and marched to Prince Albert to receive the congratulations of the thankful populace, which had suffered only the rumors of war. That accomplished, he set out for Battleford aboard the *Marquis* with strong detachments of troops and guns. The remaining troops went by land.

On May 23 the river was rising from the rush of mountain streams. The banks were green. Young leaves made a lovely mist against the sky. The tawny Saskatchewan swirled past the stern-wheelers as they churned its strong current. Near Battleford a canoe shot out from the shore. Middleton gave orders to slow down, and Indian Agent Jefferson, who had been a prisoner of the natives, handed up a letter from Poundmaker. The Cree chief wanted the terms of surrender in writing "so that we may be under no misunderstanding, from which so much trouble arises." The letter contained greetings and was signed by Poundmaker's mark.

Middleton ignored the greetings. He sent word that he had utterly defeated the half-breeds and Indians at Batoche. He had made no terms with them, nor would he make terms with Poundmaker.

"I have men enough to destroy you and your people," wrote the victorious white general to the vanquished Indian chief, "or at least to drive you away to starve and will do so unless you bring in the teams you took and yourself and councillors with your arms, to meet me at Battleford on Monday, the 26th."

The picture of General Middleton receiving the surrender of Poundmaker at Battleford does not shine brightly in the pages of Canadian history. All along Poundmaker, his people hungry and bereft of their liberty, had used his influence to prevent bloodshed. The powwow was set for one o'clock. "It was rather an interesting sight," wrote Middleton. "Poundmaker opened the ball by making a long oration."

The general sat on a chair with his interpreter nearby and his officers in a half circle behind him. Poundmaker, tall, proud, carrying himself like the great chief he was, came forward prepared to shake hands. General Middleton refused. Those who were there say that of the two the aborigine was the greater man and the commander in chief a sorry figure.

The pipe of peace was placed on the grass. Poundmaker sat down with the other chiefs behind him. General Middleton said:

"Poundmaker, you are accused of high treason. What have you to say?"

The interpreter endeavored to make the accusation clear to Poundmaker. But there is no such phrase as "high treason" in the Cree language. The interpreter had to make the best explanation possible. He said:

"You are accused of throwing sticks at the queen and trying to knock her bonnet off."

Poundmaker insisted that he had not fired first at Cut Knife Creek, that he had tried in vain to secure food for his people. The general was only mildly interested. He waved Poundmaker aside and demanded the surrender of the Indians who had murdered certain white officials. They were brought forward. At that moment an old squaw, mother of Breaking-Through-the-Ice, interrupted. She wanted to speak. The general said that, like the Indians, he did not listen to women in councils of war.

The old woman was quick with her retort.

"Were not the white people ruled by a woman—the Great White Mother?" she demanded as she was hustled away, her request unheard.

Her confusion was typical of her people. That May day, at the season when the grass grew green, Poundmaker and four of his warriors were taken away to Regina, charged with treason and murder, when they considered they had been defending their people as courageously as ever the white people had defended theirs. Though General Middleton had said to the interpreter, "Tell Poundmaker I'll mention that he treated his prisoners well," the Cree chief was given a prison sentence. Public opinion intervened and he was freed the next year, but imprisonment was too much for his nomadic spirit. Within a few months he died of tuberculosis.

The rebellion was over, though Big Bear had not yet been captured. He had fled to the woods and lake country to the north. With nothing more to do after the surrender of Riel and Poundmaker, General Middleton himself headed one of the three columns in an undignified search for Big Bear and his white prisoners from Frog Lake and Fort Pitt. Over almost indecipherable trails, across muskeg and clear shimmering lakes, through woods where mosquitoes drove horses and men mad, the pursuit continued through the hot days of June. Middleton gave up, doubtless wishing he had accepted the offer of the North West Mounted Police to find the Indian chief. Toward the end of June the white prisoners were released. On July 2 Big Bear, alone except for his 8-year-old son, surrendered to the police at the ruins of Fort Carlton.

The Northwest Rebellion cost the Dominion of Canada more than five million dollars. The expenditure of a few thousand on food might have prevented it. The total number of lives lost by troops in action and white citizens shot by natives was about sixty. Métis and Indian losses were at least twice as heavy. There were many wounded. Several chiefs escaped across the border. Eleven Indians were hanged for murder. Louis Riel, after a trial and several dramatic reprieves, was hanged at Regina on November 16, 1885.

Riel's death and the fight for minority rights that he had led strained confederation to the utmost. Yet irrationally led and ineptly subdued though it was, the struggle formed a keystone of Canada's nationhood. In common with most struggles for peoples' rights "a lot of good came of it." As a result of the autocratic, bungling methods of the fearless British General Middleton, Canadian troops were placed under command of a colonial, a Canadian, whose ability never surprised Canadians though it may have disturbed a few old soldiers in the empire capital. Soon "God Save the Queen" echoed lustily along the Saskatchewan.

Many a white man who came from the East and from Winnipeg to fight "The Rebellion" remained to make his home along the Saskatchewan, variously described in letters to wives or sweethearts back home as being "glorious," "wonderful," "majestic," "grand." Settlers flocked to the vast parkland and prairie confident at last that there was no longer a danger of "wild, red Indians." They came as a direct result of the disturbance, fired to enthusiasm by the space that had been devoted to the Northwest—the last, best west—in the press of the East and elsewhere.

CHAPTER SEVENTEEN

God Save the Queen

THERE is a story which claims that the Fathers of Confederation thought so much of the North West Territories that they sent out the very table on which they had signed the confederation pact. It is a pleasant story. Doubtless statesmen of the young Dominion of Canada could neither foresee the effort involved nor hear the curses inspired by freighting that sturdy oak table, 15 feet 6 inches long by 6 feet wide, all the way from Ottawa to the Saskatchewan. The last thousand miles from the Red River to Battleford was made by ox cart. Edgar Dewdney, second lieutenant-governor of the territories, in accepting the table probably thought more of the sentimental value of the connection than of the difficulties involved. At the time he could scarcely have known that Charlottetown, P.E.I. proudly claimed that it had the confederation table—and chairs—and that not only were they arranged in the manner in which they had been used at the historic conference but that the table had been in Charlottetown ever since it was imported from England in 1848!

Just which capital possessed the Confederation table caused a fair bit of local argument, some of it sizzling, until it was finally established that there were two tables, one oak and the other mahogany, and that, as might be expected, one was used for the preliminary discussions leading to the British North America Act and the other for the actual signing. Evidence suggests that the latter, oak and so heavier, caused all the groans and curses heard that day in the late eighteen-seventies when a gang of men hauled it up to the new legislative building at Battleford, then capital of the Northwest Territories. Fortunately time relieves sore muscles, and the sentiment remained.

Then everything was hauled overland from Winnipeg by those long, raucous Red River cart trains, drawn by horses or oxen. Cargoes were heavy, varied, and occasionally as cumbersome as the oak table. Transported on carts lurching through sloughs and mudholes, careening down riverbanks and crossing precariously by ford or ferry, fine furniture had to be well crated. Yet at least one Steinway grand piano withstood the rigors of Red River cart transportation, including a dip in the muddy waters of the South Saskatchewan, and needed only a tuning to put it back into good condition. Lumber, nails, furniture, storm windows and office supplies for over twenty government buildings reached Battleford by the same laborious, noisy transport as the Confederation table and the piano. The first printing press in the territories was hauled by oxen from Winnipeg, set up in a log shack in Battleford, and printed the pioneer newspaper, the *Saskatchewan Herald*. Even the first governor, David Laird, and his family traveled by cart, though they had horses. The fare was $70 each, the party providing their own food!

For a couple of years after 1875 when the Dominion of

Canada passed the Northwest Territories Act, the territories were governed from Fort Livingstone, North West Mounted Police depot on the Swan River. But Swan River was out of the line of new development. In 1877 the lieutenant governor and his council of "not more than five persons appointed by the Governor General in Council and invested with both executive and legislative powers" moved to Battleford. All foresaw a great future for the new capital. Lawmaking accompanied the erection of parliament buildings, governor's residence, land title office, judge and registrar's house, and many humbler shacks. At Battleford laws were made to govern the vast territory lying between Manitoba and British Columbia and from the international boundary to the Arctic. And while they were being enacted many a leading citizen occupied a rough, temporary shack with mud fireplace, packing-case furniture, and windows and doors of thin rawhide. First things first was the rule as territorials developed their complex civilization amid the primitive culture of the Indian.

The great oak table formed a link, intangible but strong, between the new territory and the slightly older provinces of Canada. It bore mute and reminding evidence of the constitutional struggles that had preceded confederation. Many a pioneer legislator thumped his fist on its sturdy surface. Slowly and laboriously the first laws governing the territory were evolved, laws which dealt with purely local matters such as civil and property rights, administration of justice, local taxation, and the requirements of police, roads, highways, bridges, and health. They were the only laws the governor general in council then had authority to make for the Northwest Territories. Resentfully and frequently the pioneer legislators fumed over limitations placed on it by the dominion government. Why shouldn't they have complete control of their finances? they demanded, time and again.

Control of the public purse was an issue which occupied territorial legislators for thirty years before the dominion government finally granted rights such as the other provinces enjoyed. During the regime at Battleford the revenue from issuing marriage licenses was a matter of great importance, so limited was the Council's taxing authority. Paternally the dominion government collected taxes, but the grants it made to the territories were never considered adequate by men who saw so many pressing needs for money.

Local problems facing the first legislators were varied and sometimes delicate. Settlers and squatters, who had built their log shacks and stores wherever the location suited, resented the arrival of surveyors. Roads and streets laid out according to plan cut through not only homes and gardens but through the feelings of individualistic people who had never seen a street before. Settling those problems was almost as difficult as finding a substitute for the fast disappearing buffalo.

The site of the present city of North Battleford was a ranch where many North West Mounted Police remounts were grazed. That ranch and the few others far to the southwest near McLeod brought about legislation to regulate the use by ranchers of registered brands. On the statute books it was known as "An Ordinance Respecting the Marking of Stock." Passed at the second session of the Territorial Council on August 2, 1878, the law was to play a vital part in the enormous ranching industry developed within the next few years.

Everything was new at the capital. Life was gay, primitive, enterprising, and a little raw. But British justice followed its slow, steady course, backed by the authority of the stockaded North West Mounted Police division on the high promontory between the Battle and the North Saskatchewan River. It was truly a Victorian British frontier community. The Union Jack flew before the barracks and the governor's house. When the Council met, when the courts had to be summoned, when there was a ball and the few ladies of Battleford donned their best frocks, the event was preceded by the playing or singing, or both, of "God Save the Queen."

"God Save the Queen" meant little to the natives. They preferred to watch a North West Mounted policeman stride toward the flagpole, run up the Union Jack, step back smartly and salute. Most Indians welcomed and respected the justice for which both the flag and the police were symbols. Their respect was always heightened by colorful pageantry.

Compared with the native population the white was a small minority in 1877. One of the more ingenious sections of the Northwest Territories Act provided that when the lieutenant-governor was satisfied that any part of the territories not more than a thousand miles square contained at least a thousand "adult white persons entitled to the franchise," that area would become an electoral district which might elect a member to the Council. When the number of elected members reached twenty-one the Council would cease and the elected members would become the Legislative Assembly. By 1884 the elected members outnumbered the five appointed members, so quickly was the territory increasing. In 1888 the territories elected twenty-two members, who formed the first Legislative Council with an appointed advisory body.

By that time the Canadian Pacific Railway, which originally had been planned to pass through Battleford, had been constructed some two hundred miles south. The confedeation table had been packed up again and hauled overland to "Pile O' Bones," or Regina, the new capital. A couple of decades later six feet were lopped off the table's length, the remainder being used for repairs and not, as might be supposed from its sentimental origin, made into gavels or other souvenirs. By that time the territories had autonomy, the ties with the older provinces were strengthened, and people along the Saskatchewan were singing "God Save the King"—Edward VII—instead of "God Save the Queen."

There had been constitutional struggles comparable with the best British tradition. The new Legislative Council had had to fight for the right to charter railways, borrow money for development and to free the territories from dependence on the dominion government for most of its revenue. The struggle, like most struggles for the people's rights, proved that the territories had able citizens willing to devote their energies and abilities to principles which they considered necessary to their way of life. Many were young men with dash and genius and foresight. Among them they numbered two outstanding young lawyers, R. B. Bennett, who became prime minister of Canada and eventually Lord Bennett, and F. W. G. (later Sir Frederick) Haultain. Haultain held an office similar to that of premier during the critical days of the territorial government's struggle for provincial autonomy, though he never became premier. He had urged, among other things, one great province for the Northwest Territories. When the two provinces of Saskatchewan and Alberta were inaugurated, Walter Scott, an able newspaperman, headed the former's first government, with A. C. Rutherford installed at the new capital of Alberta, Edmonton. Mr. Haultain became chief justice of the province and chancellor of the University of Saskatchewan.

Along the river they have changed the lettering on public buildings from VR, Victoria Regina, to ER, Edward (VII) Rex; from George V to Edward VIII and then to George VI. In that time there has been a wide variety of legislation, much of it social, some of it definitely experimental. Citizens rather boastfully claim that the altitude, invigorating climate, and high winds of the Saskatchewan River country make them enterprising politically. Co-operatives have gained popularity and made much progress. Complete socialized medicine, with airplane pickup service, is a fact in some communities. Some legislation has turned out to be more experimental than social. In Alberta thousands of people fell for a political platform which promised everyone $25 a month. The province of Saskatchewan may prove to the rest of the world, though unintentionally, that socialized industry will not pay if it must meet the charges of normal taxation and provide "rainy-day" reserves generally required of industry. A wealth of zest has gone into the experiment.

Yet, on the whole, people on the prairies and along the parkland to the north probably were never better off. Less than half of British stock, an average population of some six persons to the square mile, Saskatchewan River Canadians of Scotch, English, French, Ukrainian, Polish, German, Chinese, and many other racial origins apart from the native Indian have sought, and found, a way of life as good as there is anywhere. Regardless of background, most have adopted the British attitude of grumbling about the government, that useful psychological outlet which usually wins its point short of bloody revolution. The altitude, invigorating climate, and high winds combine with space and a common dependence on "the crops" to make a people quick to spot a fault and equally quick to see and to try to remedy a need. That quickness is implied in the manner in which they have tried to handle the making and management of their laws since "God Save the Queen" was first heard along the banks of the river. The characteristic may be as much a curse as a blessing, but it makes for a mighty nice, often interesting people.

CHAPTER EIGHTEEN

Steamboat on a Shoal

THE railway arrived in the Saskatchewan country about the same time as the steamboat. Those who can recall steamboats on the river will tell you that it was the railway that put the boats out of business.

"If it hadn't been for the trains . . ." they opine regretfully.

"If it hadn't been for the Saskatchewan . . ." they ought to say, the unco-operative, beautiful, high, low, meandering, lovable Saskatchewan. The damned Saskatchewan. But old-timers don't blame the river. They remember the boats. Like the odor of jack-pine smoke that lay along the valley hours after a boat had passed, the brief, exciting era lingers in their memory. Five or six decades have merely bestowed a patina of romance.

The real story of steamboating on the tawny river runs something like this: "SS *Marquis* beached at Prince Albert,

1886" . . . SS *Northwest*, wrecked by high water at Edmonton 1903" . . . "*Northcote*, run ashore at Cumberland" . . . on a meadow opposite the Pas River" . . . "*Medicine Hat*, keeled over at Saskatoon" . . . "*Lilly* sank below Medicine Hat" . . . And so on. And on.

The SS *Lilly* lasted for six years. The *Manitoba* five. The *Northcote* was venerable when she was beached after thirteen seasons. Largest boat ever afloat on the Saskatchewan, the 202-foot *Marquis* was built in 1882. Her reign as proud queen ended in 1886, when she, too, joined the long list of hulks that lie buried or half-buried in the mud and sand that settles about them each spring.

They were all stern-wheelers, those steamboats which were built with such high hopes at the end of the nineteenth century. Proudly their owners launched them. Optimistically their captains navigated them against odds of almost comic-opera proportions. For a brief season each summer their shrill whistles created excitement at little settlements from Grand Rapids to Edmonton and up the South Branch to Medicine Hat. For a decade or two they carried pioneer families and all their worldly goods. But they never kept anything approximating a close schedule. Even during the urgent days of the métis uprising General Middleton wrote of the *Northcote*:

> On the 5th of May the long expected steamer arrived after a tedious journey, most of which seems to have been made on land. All the steamers on this river are sternwheelers, and have four strong spars fastened, two on each side of the bow, by a sort of hinge. These spars are kept triced up until the vessel runs on a shoal or sand bank—which are many and shifting—when they are lowered and the vessel is forced over the obstacle, made to walk over as it were.

Shoals, sand bars, ice, and floods—the words pepper all accounts of Saskatchewan River steamboating. The only difference between the bigger craft and York boats was that York boats, being smaller, could be hauled farther up on shore when low water and ice brought the season to a close. Not a boat of any kind made the trip from Grand Rapids to Edmonton without a mile or two of hauling. Captains and caretakers, it was often one and the same man, never could trust their ships to the river, summer or winter. During the winter of 1884-85 Captain Dogle of the SS *Marquis* lived in a shack on the north shore of the North Branch at the mouth of the Sturgeon, or as it is known today, the Shell River. Stern-wheelers were always wintered out of the main channel if possible. Sometimes, except at the safe depths of Cumberland Lake, there was barely enough water in the fall to float a big boat out of the main channel. In spring no one could predict where the ice would pile up, nor how high. He merely guessed. So Captain Dogle was on hand in March when Louis Riel's métis uprising promised a busy boat season.

The boats were commandeered for transport. A gang of men was sent up from Prince Albert, six miles below, to get the *Marquis* ready for the spring breakup and to salvage the remains of the *Manitoba*, beached nearby. Both were frozen to the river bottom. All that could be done till the ice went out was to clear away the winter's debris, close the holds and hatches, and get the boilers ready. After that was accomplished Captain Dogle sent the crew back to Prince Albert for the protection of their families momentarily expecting an attack from Riel's forces. With Archie Ballantine to keep him company, he waited in his little shack. Waited and watched.

One morning when they wakened in the little shack there was the sound of rushing water. During the night the river had risen four feet, almost to the top of the hull of the *Marquis*. There was still ice in the middle of the river, with water on either side. Captain Dogle and Ballantine saw the stern-wheeler move and raise herself a little before she settled back to her rudders, still gripped in the ice. The *Manitoba* was full of water.

The flood threatened the little shack. The two men raced to get their belongings and food up to higher and drier land. Soon the swirling, shifting ice was piled twenty feet high, completely covering the *Manitoba*'s hulk. Nothing could be done until the ice went out, except cut wood.

The big day that year was April 10. The crews came up from Prince Albert to get the *Marquis* afloat. The water level dropped. The navigation season of 1885 was about to open.

Captain Dogle and Archie Ballantine moved back to their shack, cleared out the silt deposited by the river, put dry wood in the stove and soon had a fire going. The captain, a first-rate cook, poured the water off the pot of baked beans he had left in the oven and heated them. Beans never tasted better, the men vowed. Soon they were ready for work.

It was hard work and called for ingenuity. The *Marquis* lay at an angle of 45 degrees. Her rudders were frozen in the mud; all her hog chains and one big clevis broke when she finally let go from the river bottom. Getting the broken clevis out to be repaired was a difficult job undertaken by Archie Ballantine, one of those enterprising, handy men who were largely responsible for keeping Saskatchewan boats afloat. Ballantine went into the bitterly cold water. Two and a half hours later he had a chain around the clevis, had managed to windlass it out, and was drying his soaking clothes, still on his body, before a huge fire on shore.

"When we got warmed up we went into the shack and had a good dinner," he said later. He had to return to the icy water to replace the mended clevis.

There was plenty of water to fill the boilers by that time, and plenty of dry wood for fire to get up steam. The syphons were started. In a couple of hours the *Marquis* was ready to limp down to Prince Albert boat landing to have her rudder repaired. Three days later Captain Dogle took her downstream to the Forks and up the South Branch to the aid of the SS *Northcote,* which had just lost her funnels in the Battle of Batoche.

The *Marquis* played quite an important role in the Northwest Rebellion. General Middleton decided to use her and the SS *Northwest* to transport himself and detachments of men and equipment to Battleford. The *Marquis* being the larger and more pretentious boat, the general and his staff officers traveled aboard her. When the two stern-wheelers swung out into the river from Prince Albert the North West Mounted Police under Colonel Irvine fired what was probably the greatest salute ever fired in Prince Albert's history. It was a real feu de joie. The rebellion was all but won. The river was high. Crew and passengers were in fine spirits. To complete the general's satisfaction a tiny bark canoe pushed off from shore below Battleford with Robert Jefferson, carrying Poundmaker's letter requesting the terms of surrender. The trip in the *Marquis* took less than two days, upstream, an agreeable comparison with the downstream journey reported by Dr. James Hector. In 1858, according to Hector, the brigade, leaving Fort Pitt on May 22, took seven days to reach Fort Carlton. That year the boats were heavily laden, drawing one and a half to two feet of water. They were constantly aground and the men had to jump into the cold water to haul them off. Hector claimed that the Saskatchewan at that point was not navigable, except for the smallest craft and then only with difficulty.

The *Marquis* made several trips during the summer of 1885. In July she took the troops down to Grand Rapids to meet the Lake Winnipeg boat, which would, in turn, take them to Winnipeg and the railway. It was her last big season. In 1886 she ran ashore at Prince Albert, where for many decades souvenir hunters helped themselves until there was nothing left but the vague outline of her hulk, barely discernible from the bushes beside the river road. An old paddle wheel is a prized museum possession. Gavels have been made from her fine oak. In the hearts of the few men living who knew her and loved her there are many poignant memories.

Archie Ballantine went from the *Marquis* to the newly

painted *Northwest*, that exciting spring of 1885. His official job was night watchman. He had fired the *Manitoba*, worked on the *Marquis*, and he did a variety of chores on his new ship. He was aboard when the arms surrendered by Poundmaker and his warriors were piled up on her decks, most of them rusted flintlocks about six feet long. Those weapons had meant much to the Indians. Each had been purchased with several beaver skins. They had killed buffalo for food and clothing and provided protection, as the natives thought, from white soldiers during the uprising. But when the *Northwest* stopped at historic Pine Island to take on cordwood the guns, now only useless junk, were thrown overboard into the keeping of the Saskatchewan. It is to be hoped Poundmaker never heard of that.

Captain Sheets of the *Northwest* and his crew had a busy season ahead of them. The rebellion had delayed them so much that there was no time for sentiment. While the Big Bear chase was going on north of the river the *Northwest* had a lot of troops to transport and ferry, detachments of the Queen's Own Rifles, Midlanders, and the jolly, French-speaking Sixty-fifth. Such a time as the strong-swimming boys of the Sixty-fifth had! Outstanding among all the troops they took to the river like ducks. Their aquatic tricks amused the crew more than the constant kettledrumming and complaints about food from the others who had nothing to do. The captain and crew cheered when orders at last came to swing about and float downstream. The only cloud to cast a shadow over that day was the death of gallant Colonel Williams of the Midlanders, who died of "brain fever," and of a young man of the Sixty-fifth, who suffered acutely before his death from "appendicitis" or, more likely, too much swimming in cold Saskatchewan water after a meal of hard tack and beans.

The trip downstream was uneventful. Brief pauses to take on wood broke the monotony of the terrific heat under the burning July sun; the *Marquis* had little in the way of protection for so many passengers, most of whom had to spend day and night on the deck boards. There were no towns to watch. Shimmering in heat waves, the banks slipped by until Cumberland Lake was reached. There Chief Factor Belanger fired a grand salute from the old guns in front of the fort. The soldiers were feted to the limit of the resources of the oldest Hudson's Bay Company post on the river. Then the boys from the East watched the low shores until Cedar Lake and Cross Lake brought them to Grand Rapids. Aboard the tramway the company had built to haul its York boats they crossed the old portage to await the arrival of the Lake Winnipeg boat. The interval of waiting was pleasantly spent, except for the mosquitoes. There was fine sturgeon fishing. The boys had a wonderful time broiling their sturgeon over the campfire and washing it down with good Hudson's Bay rum.

While the troops waved their farewells to the Saskatchewan there was plenty of work for the crews of the *Marquis*, the *Northwest*, and the other stern-wheelers. From the landing, fifteen or twenty feet above deck level, bales and other cargo were slid down inclined oak planks. The *Northwest* took on two hundred and seventy-five tons of freight that trip.

Generally a York boat came to the aid of stern-wheelers ascending the rapids. The first mile or so could be negotiated with the boat's own steam. After that there was often a stretch where hauling was necessary. That was where the York boat was handy. A mile of heavy Manila rope, secured to a stout tree above the rapids, was floated downstream and the steersman tossed the weighted end to the big boat. A few turns around the capstan and she was towed against the current under her own power. For Red Rock Rapid most boats left out their own towline on the way down, anchored to a big buoy, picking it up on the return trip.

Captain Dogle of the *Marquis*, Captain Sheets of the *Northwest*, and every other captain of a stern-wheeler to travel the Saskatchewan prayed for calm weather on the 40-mile open water of Cedar Lake. In the protected river valley stern-wheelers were comparatively safe from wind. They had little protection against a gale on that treacherous wind-swept lake except the small group of islands known as Grieg's Harbor, about halfway across. Many a passenger was grateful for the sanctuary of the low group of islands. Many a settler upriver awaiting a longed-for cargo blessed them.

During their brief era of importance the boats carried most of the necessities for the settlements along the river that were pioneering the parkland and prairie two or three hundred miles north of the railway. Plows, harrows, rakes, hoes, scythes, reaping hooks, carts, and threshing machines were stern necessities. So, too, were flour and bacon and tea, without which some of the hardships of pioneering would have been unbearable. The great treat was sugar. Blankets and tobacco were important items. Indian Department goods had to be shipped. The loss of a boat with such precious cargo would have resulted in serious shortages to the little communities eagerly awaiting the shrill sound of the boat whistle coming around a bend.

The Hudson's Bay Company, eventually having mastered the fine art of handling canoes and then taken to the laborious, practical York boat, in time owned a few steamships as well. The SS *Saskatchewan,* the largest company boat, was a fine, pretentious cabin craft which made many trips upriver from The Pas until she was wrecked in 1907. The *Lilly,* a sturdy stern-wheeler one hundred feet long, lined with oak as were others of these boats, was another Hudson's Bay craft. But in time the small, gasoline-engine boat, cheap and easy to handle, suitable for most rivers including the lower Saskatchewan, proved its worth. With the exception of a World War II landing barge which saw service at Dieppe before traveling between The Pas and Cumberland Lake, the gasoline engine predominates.

Most Hudson's Bay Company people who went up the river for the great postrebellion celebration at Edmonton late in August, 1885, traveled aboard the *Marquis* or the *Northwest*. The water was still comparatively high. Only a few shoals delayed progress. At each wooding place and each settlement on the way up one or more people or entire families came aboard in festive mood. From The Pas they came, and Cumberland House. On the long river bends below Nipawin the fiddlers tuned their fiddles and the passengers reveled in dancing. Strauss waltzes on the Danube were never more thrilling than those gay reels aboard the *Northwest*. The pat-pat of her wheels echoed from the high banks. The amethyst sky was brilliant with stars. In the north glowed the reflection of the sun.

At historic Fort La Corne, at Prince Albert and Carlton, Battleford, Fort Pitt, and Frog Lake Landing more passengers came aboard. Some, nearing Edmonton, brought their horses and carts with them to save time. At Victoria Island, famed for its finds of gold, the boat took on wood. During the 3 hour stop the passengers "panned gold" with frying pans and basins and bowls. The captain could hardly get them back on board after someone "struck it rich" with a handful of brass filings surreptitiously deposited by an exuberant wag.

The banquet was the highlight of the celebration. For it the *Northwest*'s cabin was cleared and long tables were set up, covered with white cloth. Extra lamps were hung. Crewmen were outfitted as waiters. There was so much good food that the tables could hardly be seen. Cases of Hudson's Bay brandy, Scotch whisky, rye, rum, and wines, including a few kegs of champagne, were provided for the people on the upper deck; Night Watchman Archie Ballantine acting as wine steward. For the workers on the lower deck, descendants of men who had manned the York boats and pack straps for decades and those who were doing so still, there was plenty of tea and a few bottles of good cheer. They all came aboard, said Archie Ballantine, "with that air of serious bearing peculiar to people of the company." Most of them remained to visit with freinds and relatives whom they had not seen for years. It was a reunion to be talked about in little groups for many a winter, to be remembered by lonely men for a lifetime.

The Saskatchewan was low when the *Northwest* swung into the river for the last trip of the season. On that early September morning a fog lay along the valley. Perhaps it was a lingering wisp of fog that partially hid the rippled sand of the shoal. Perhaps the engineer had enjoyed too much good Hudson's Bay Company celebration. The captain signaled the "slow ahead." The engineer answered with "full speed ahead." The *Northwest*, without cargo, dropped low in the water with the increased speed. Every rod snapped. The boat humped with the weight of the machinery at each end, cutting off the water supply to the boilers. Steam hissed in all directions. The *Northwest* had cleared the bar, but she was helpless, floating downstream. An enterprising deck hand grabbed the end of a coil of line, put it between his teeth, and jumped overboard. Low water and a strong swimmer saved the day. They tied the disabled stern-wheeler to a tree on the bank and made temporary repairs. Traveling under slow bell the *Northwest* finally reached Prince Albert, where seven teams of horses were needed to haul her up on the bank for complete repairs. A few days later she took off on the trip downstream for the last cargo load of the season, so late that she ran on to another bar above Cumberland Lake and had to spend more precious hours easing herself across with her own capstans and steam.

Down at Lethbridge on the tributary Oldman River and at Medicine Hat on the South Branch, Elliott Galt of the English-financed North-Western Coal and Navigation Company built several steamers and barges to haul coal from the mines at Coal Banks to the town of Medicine Hat on the Canadian Pacific Railway. The company's SS *Baroness* was pressed into service during the uprising and made one of the slow, laborious trips to Batoche with supplies. But Mr. Galt, an able businessman who materially helped in developing the West, soon decided against trusting his company's fortunes to variable prairie streams. He found a much more valuable use for the river waters and dropped the word "navigation," to use, instead, "irrigation."

There was, too, the *May Queen*, captained by Mr. Andrews, a trim little pleasure craft of thirty-five feet, built in Selkirk, Manitoba, and shipped west by railway. The sharp-bottomed *May Queen* drew five feet of water when loaded, a fact incompatible with the river's average depth of four feet most of the way. Only when she had the current behind her did she make any time at all. The Temperance Colonization Society, which owned her, decided to find other means of transporting goods for the town of Saskatoon, which they hoped soon would be booming. After two or three seasons the *May Queen* made her last trip, with a little coal and a cargo of groceries to open Saskatoon's first store. Her engine was taken up to Prince Albert and put in a flat-bottomed boat. Her hulk was left on the riverbank, where after three or four years of ice and floods, wind and current it became driftwood.

A small vessel on the South Branch, meeting the train at Medicine Hat, looked like a first-rate alternative to the longer, more tedious boat trip up Lake Winnipeg to Grand Rapids and then up the main river to the settlements. It ought to be less expensive for pioneers who did not have the $230 fare for the longer trip. The charge of $230 a passenger, plus 14½ cents a pound for freight, was far beyond the average settler with a family. Besides there was always the possibility that low water would prevent any trip at all, as happened to James Clinkskill. James Clinkskill, native of Glasgow, rented a building at Prince Albert sight unseen, and shipped up supplies for a grocery store. When Mr. Clinkskill reached Grand Rapids he was told that the boat would not be able to go above Cumberland House, the river being so low. That meant storing his supplies on the lower river while he returned to

Winnipeg for another supply which had to be sent overland. It was an expensive venture.

The long stretch of water below Medicine Hat intrigued any man with a yearning for water traffic. Captain Horatio Hamilton Ross, son of Sir Charles and Lady Ross of Rossie Castle, Scotland, had built a hotel at Medicine Hat in the nineties. The captain found Medicine Hat much too static. He wanted to travel and he liked to have his friends travel with him. The result was the SS *Assiniboia*, built in 1898 and named for a sister river. With a party of friends the captain made a merry trip downstream as far as Cedar Lake. Here the *Assiniboia* ran on a shoal. The season was getting late and the winds blew cold. So the *Assiniboia* was abandoned. Its owner gave the food in the galley to a couple of Cree Indians to stand on guard for the winter and left for Egypt. Spring ice and floodwaters left nothing but the boilers.

Captain Ross still yearned for a boat to travel the Saskatchewan, so he built the SS *City of Medicine Hat* in 1906, a fine boat 130 feet long. For two seasons the *City of Medicine Hat* survived shoals and spring ice and floods. Then, while on a cruise in 1908, she hit a cable strung along the big bridge at Saskatoon and keeled over. The captain decided to move farther downstream where boating looked a little safer. And he took to smaller craft. He formed the Ross Navigation Company of The Pas, and for years owned many boats which served the lower Saskatchewan from pleasure cruising to hauling ore from the copper mines of northern Manitoba to the railway. There was the *Sam Brisbin*, a lovely little pleasure craft, the *Minasin*, the *Notin*, the *Nipawin* with staterooms for twenty passengers, the *O'Hell*, and last of all the *Tobin*, to handle the dwindling traffic of the new era of trains and planes. The hulks of every one lie beside the Saskatchewan that wrecked them. Even Captain Ross, who spent most of his life along the river, lies buried in sight of it, at the Big Eddy.

Time was, as The Pas *Northern Mail* reports, when

"every man who could afford it had a canoe or motor boat. They lined the river bank from the bridge to The Pas River dock. Shrill boat whistles could be heard day and night. Boats were used for picnics and berry-picking. When the ducks began to fly men went by boats to the same places they now go to by car, taking their pals, their best girls and their wives." With a billy for tea or coffee, a frying pan, or even a can of pork and beans, they made their fun at The Pas in summer just as they have long enjoyed fine winter sport with their renowned dog teams.

On May 24, 1907, the mailboat nosed upstream toward Fort La Corne, the rail point then nearest The Pas. It took the place of the dog teams that had carried mail over the ice all winter. Next year the service was discontinued. Trains brought mail to The Pas.

Now the tourist or prospector can fly, drive, or travel by train into The Pas and engage a motorboat, barge, or canoe to take him wherever he wishes to go through the country's maze of waterways. Most likely he will fly, taking off from Grace Lake near the Saskatchewan River, unless he wants to do a little shooting in the autumn. Great catches of fish taken in northern lakes are flown to railhead, quick-frozen, and packaged for use in cities as far off as Chicago and New York.

Crossing the Saskatchewan has been almost as difficult as traveling up or down it. The Indians made bumboats for crossing. Pioneers constructed rude scows or ferries which had to be towed upstream to counterbalance the current. Usually they were harnessed to a horse while a man aboard poled them off the bank. In spring and fall crossings were always dangerous and often impossible. Ferries could not be used. Getting a message across was a problem, as General Middleton discovered during the uprising. When Middleton wanted to communicate with the police at Prince Albert he sent a strong young man named Hourie. The ice was breaking up as Hourie made his way down the sloping bank to the South

Branch near Gabriel's Crossing. Great chunks swirled by, crunching against one another. The river raced angrily. It was an awesome sight. It meant taking his life in his own hands literally. But the message had to go through. Hourie took off his clothes, piled them in an improvised raft, Indian bumboat-wise, and swam through the bitterly cold, treacherous current, or leapt from chunk to chunk. His body was bruised and cut. His feet were raw. Strong man though he was, he never quite recovered.

On April 15, 1904, the citizens of Saskatoon heard a fearful crunching sound. As they rushed to the river they saw first one and then another span of the precious new Canadian National Railway bridge topple into the churning mass of ice and water, the first big bridge across that section of river. With trainloads of settlers on their way west, with boom and expansion on every lip, it was a heartbreaking spectacle. Optimistic as they were, the pioneer citizens could not possibly predict that in forty years Saskatoon would be known as the city of fine bridges. Yet, as recently as 1947 flatcars of gravel had to be rushed to the railway crossing at St. Louis, below Saskatoon, when the strain of ice threatened another catastrophe. On the Saskatchewan bridges are always in danger from the spring ice, just as the boats were.

At Saskatchewan Landing each spring a bus or truck or car plunges through the ice. Too many drivers are hopeful that they can cross before the ice gets too thin. The chance seems worth taking because the nearest ferry is many miles away and to be reached only if the roads are good, which is seldom the case at that time of year. The nearest bridge would take the driver more than a hundred miles out of his way.

Back in the eighties and nineties local ranchers operated a ferry which was used by Indian bands, métis, cowboys, oxen and carts, as well as themselves. In 1891 rancher Jim Smart operated the homemade ferry, which often succumbed to the

Saskatchewan's ardor and, breaking its cables, slipped downstream with her. When the river ripped away the cable resourceful Jim Smart wound a new one from local telegraph wire, spinning it on a wagon wheel. The old homemade ferry is gone, and the new one can handle only three or four cars or trucks at a crossing. Now on a summer day there are often two hundred vehicles to cross.

Waiting in line for the ferry, a lot of people ask themselves if they are not stuck on a political shoal. To them it doesn't look as though much progress has been made since the troops of '85 awaited the arrival of the steamer to ferry them to the north bank and the last lap of their march to the relief of Battleford. Forty-niners at Saskatchewan Landing have heard so many promises about a bridge over the South Branch that the very real piles of the new bridge are often mistaken for a mirage. They won't believe it until they've crossed the new bridge half a dozen times.

CHAPTER NINETEEN

Gold!

"THERE's gold on the Saskatchewan!"

The news traveled faster than the river in 1870. Down at Prince Albert and Fort Carlton they heard it. Farther away on the Red River and in Montana the word "boom" was added. Miners and prospectors, settlers and English remittance men made the long journey upriver or across country. There were never many of them, even during the fabulous days when a man could make as much as $16 a day. In 1870 gold was worth $16 an ounce.

Jim Gibbons was one of the first Saskatchewan River gold miners. Gibbons made himself a dugout dwelling place in the riverbank below the present site of the city of Edmonton. Between gold-mining seasons he traded goods with the Indians, especially liquor, which was officially contraband and hunted down by the North West Mounted Police. He was an educated white man who had degenerated, or liberated himself, according to the set of comparisons used. There were many of his kind in the mushrooming communities along the Saskatchewan. They disliked civilized society's veneer and wanted personal freedom at no great cost.

In the eighteen-seventies a real gold strike was expected any year. The gold found along the sand bars had to come from somewhere, argued amateur and professional prospectors alike. They are still arguing the same way, after seventy years. And getting about the same amount of gold.

Some claim the mother lode must be a few miles above Edmonton because they have not been able to find gold farther up the river. Yet at Rocky Mountain House others have made as much as $5 a day. But the main scene of gold mining is along the stretch of river between Edmonton and Fort Saskatchewan. There the average earning remains about $5 a day—for the experienced, hard-working miner. The amateur seldom makes as much.

The place to look for gold on the Saskatchewan is on a gravel bar in the river or in the sand or gravel on the inner curve of one of the many meanders. The best time is when high water has subsided and left the river grasses dank and strained toward the east. Then the receding water has dropped its particles of heavy gold where the gravel lies packed. The season is a short one, from about the middle of August until freeze-up, perhaps not more than three months. A grizzly is generally used. In the days of Jim Gibbons and his friends a white Hudson's Bay blanket was preferred to catch the precious dust. And in the days of Jim Gibbons and his friends a wise man buying a nugget split it open with a chisel to be sure it had not been weighted with a handy nut or bolt.

There may be pay gold in the banks. The Saskatchewan has been cutting its course lower and lower since the Ice Age. Unless the main ore body, if there is a main ore body, is far below the high plains, there ought to be some gold deposited in the countless layers of river sand that make up the valley.

That is what many a hopeful miner argued during the depression of the thirties when he tried to make a living at washing gold. That is what many a down-and-outer still tells himself as he lies in his dugout while modern traffic whirs over "suicide bridge" high above him.

University students, skiing in winter, often see a spot where the snow has melted, and track past the tiny spiral of smoke that denotes the location of a dugout. Modern dugouts in the Saskatchewan's bank, especially those near Edmonton, are a great improvement over those of the eighteen-seventies. Many have some sort of window. There is at least one ingeniously contrived dugout with a window that lets in a mellow, deep-sea-green light, the sort of light that filters through a "pane" of green-glass beer bottles.

Bigger business has tried washing the valley silt and the gravel above high-water mark with power machinery. It has not paid for the effort and enterprise. Someday it may. Someday the unco-operative Saskatchewan may become co-operative. So far it has paid grudgingly only after grueling labor, and not always then. Miners have lost their lives in its tortuous current just as fur traders did in the earlier attempt to subdue it. But while there is a particle of gold in its gravel and while the Saskatchewan goes on its annual rampages, men will be lured to its banks, especially men who have no taste for the truly hard work of ranching or farming, men without women.

CHAPTER TWENTY

Free Land, White Women, and Wheat

THE woman picked up the stick of firewood from the box under the kitchen window. Mechanically, as she had done for months, she glanced outside at the endless miles of snow, to the far horizon. Easter morning . . . just another day. Would the winter never go? she wondered, the stick still in her hand. And then, slowly, she realized that it had happened. The snow had changed. It was as though the unmarked whiteness had been sprayed with soft, gray rain. Her eyes could bear to look at it now. The dazzling brilliance had disappeared.

Thank God it's going, she thought, and felt guilty. God knew how much they needed the heavy snowfall.

There was no mistaking that faint honeycombing. Spring was coming, and spring reminded her of other Easters long ago—Easters in a city, Easters during their first optimistic prairie years. A half-smile played about her eyes as she remembered. It disappeared as she thought of last spring with the outlines of buildings and implements blurred with driven sand. Drought! She turned from the window. As mechanically as she had picked up the stick of wood she put it in the stove.

I must fill the boiler with snow, she told herself. Instead she stopped by the window again, fascinated.

"Goin' to stay there all day, mother? What's up?"

She had not heard her husband move in his socked feet.

"Oh, I . . . I guess the snow's started to go. Looks nice to see a change." She made way for him beside her.

He looked intently.

"Guess you're right. Does look different." After a moment he went back to the bedroom and pulled on his clothes. The horses had to be fed and watered. "Any snow melted?" he asked.

They were quiet over their breakfast. When they were nearly finished she said:

"It's Easter Sunday."

The man looked at the lithographed calendar on the wall beside the crackled mirror, at the picture of glorious mountain scenery above "Compliments of Massey-Harris Company Limited." It took him a little time to realize that this differed from other days. "So it is . . ."

"They said there'd be a service if the minister could get through."

"Like as not he won't. Still, if he does make it we ought to be there. Want to go?"

Her eyes brightened. A little flush suffused her face weathered to the color of fine old leather.

"Sure! I'll warm the irons and you could put some straw in the sleigh."

It was cold in spite of the hot irons and the straw, a damp cold chilling to people accustomed to dry cold. The woman shivered and looked toward the river valley as her husband eased the horses around a huge snowdrift. She said:

"Next year I'm going to see what it's like on the other side."

"Might as well save yourself the trouble. It's just the same as this, only harder to get at."

"I know, but I just don't like living on this place twenty-four years and not crossing the river once."

It was an old thorn of discussion. To change it he talked about the weather. The wind had softened. He sniffed the air.

"Feels like a chinook."

"It does too! Oh, I hope it won't lick up all the moisture before things start growing . . ."

"Now, now, mother, everything's going to be fine this year!" Clumsily he patted the place where her knee was under the robe. "All this snow's going to fill our new dugout and save hauling water from the river. We'll have a garden when the kids come home for holidays. And," he whipped up the horses as they neared the weathered little town with its grain elevators serrating the blue sky, "this year we'll have a crop. Can't help it with all this snow. Wheat! Three hundred acres of it!"

He unhitched the horses and led them to the shelter, scoured as free of paint as was the church by the wind and sand of many years. Inside they greeted friends. Around the crackling, pleasant-smelling stove they talked about crop prospects for the coming year. The chinook, merely the eastern edge of it, had stirred the perennial optimism that is part of a Westerner's outlook. The cheery group stopped talking only at the sound of loud thumping on the door.

"Here, one of you help me with this," called the minister. "Careful. It's valuable."

They crowded around. They took his old raccoon coat and muskrat cap. They answered his friendly questions as he unwrapped the square bundle. With a deep, concerted breath they realized what it was. A radio!

The minister talked on, ignoring the swift tears that

welled to the women's eyes, not noticing when men cleared their throats. He had seen people like this before, and knew the privations of dry years on the prairie. Tactfully, he invited the men to rig up his aerial. They examined the batteries. One or two talked about the cats-whisker sets they had at home while he put on his robes.

"I'm going to preach the sermon," he announced. "Then when it's time we'll hear some music from a great city cathedral—I hope."

They all hoped so, too. Some bolstered their hopes with prayer. They could not bear disappointment today of all days. Tensely they listened as they watched the minister turn the dials. Their silence heightened the first harsh discords. Pulses stopped when the discords stopped. They started again with a few strains of organ music, raced and wavered with far-off voices. And then it came. To the little group in the little town beside the Saskatchewan it was a modern miracle.

"Christ the Lord is risen today,
Alleluia!"

They sang with the unseen choir, every man and woman and child and the minister. No exquisite carved chancel, no fragrant flowers, no stained-glass windows, not even a new Easter bonnet, only a few people in a small prairie church with chipped walls that badly needed painting. But the hymn soared to the pitched roof, exultant, full of hope. Through the window, open as little as possible to let in the aerial wire, came the touch of the chinook, like a wisp of heaven itself. Another new era had come to the South Branch country. Another radical change had occurred.

There are those who claim that the métis uprising of 1885 did not in itself warrant the status of a revolution. It was merely a part of the real revolution that commenced about the same time. Fundamentally there was the clash between the cultures of the red man and the white. But so long as white men limited their activities to trading consonant with Indian habits, the clash was seldom serious or outstanding. The real revoluton dates from the Dominion of Canada's policy of granting free land to settlers. The cry "Free Land" to a land-hungry world was a magnet drawing men from all parts of the older world to the new Canadian Northwest. And when men came as settlers they brought with them their white women, their wives and mothers and daughters. That underlined many changes. The other major factor was the discovery that quick-maturing wheat, Marquis and Red Fife, could be grown on the vast prairie land through which the Saskatchewan, especially the South Branch, meandered.

Free land, white women, and wheat! They are the elements that changed the great lone land of the Plains Crees and the Blackfeet to shimmering wheatfields which stretched from one far horizon to another. They obliterated deep buffalo trails with the plow. They built new railways, new roads, new towns. They brought or brought about their own problems, soil erosion, depression, mortgages and debt, problems which white men had to solve—or get out. They contrived, in time, $2 wheat, world titles, material and spiritual satisfaction. White women, as well as being partly responsible, continued to be a part of it all. Like a great sounding board they caught every failure and every triumph, every moment of beauty and every long, dreary hour of deadening loneliness. The story of homesteading in the Saskatchewan River country is part of the story of each white woman who looked out across the prairies and called them home.

The métis uprising was not over when settlers started to come, a few more each year, feeling their way. From 1874 until 1900 approximately 88,000 homestead entries were filed. The turn of the century saw a great influx of newcomers as a result of the energetic immigration policy of Clifford Sifton, himself a Westerner. In 1905 over 30,000 entries were made, which represented 77,550 people. By that time the homestead acreage neared the 5,000,000 mark.

As minister of the interior charged with the responsibility of peopling the Northwest Territories of Canada, the Hon. Clifford Sifton scanned the world for likely settlers. He looked for men and white women who would take naturally to the soil. He wanted people accustomed to work, hardy, enterprising, longing for land they could call their own. He found them in greatest numbers in Middle Europe in the group that soon came to be known as "Sifton's Sheepskins": "the man in the sheepskin coat with the big, broad wife." But there were many others besides the sturdy Ukrainians, who included Russians, Galicians, Ruthenians, and Hungarians. Magyars came. There were people from the British Isles, from eastern Canada, from the United States. A few emigrated from China and India. There were Mennonites and Doukhobors. While communities spoke the Scandinavian tongues. In some sections French was heard, with or without a large proportion of Cree. But there was room for many more. There were still great open spaces so that many of the white women who came with their husbands and the wheat to the free homesteads of the West lived isolated, lonely lives. That is why a radio, a telephone, and a car were regarded as modern miracles.

The prairie, except along the river, east and west, and the climb from one steppe to the next, roughly north and south, is monotonously flat. People talk of their 40-mile horizons proudly, or defiantly. The beauty is vast and impelling, comfortable when one is used to it, fearful unless it is understood. In the early days it was difficult for a white woman accustomed to hills and woods and people to find any comfort beyond the rude sod shack, any delight in the endless space except to see her man returning when he was still far, far away. For decades, until windbreaks were planted and replanted after prolonged drought and finally survived, there was no protection from the blistering, dancing heat waves of

July. In winter, during a blizzard, the only safe way to go from house to the barn was to grasp the clotheslines stretched from one building to the other. When Northern Lights crackled to the zenith of the sky or sundogs hung menacingly beside a setting sun the very spaces cried out for the sound of a human voice. With a radio the sense of isolation disappeared. The prairies became friendly.

There was the summer procession of clear, star-studded nights, beautiful sunsets, the fragrant magic of yellow-blossomed, gray-leaved wolf willow borne on an evening breeze. Soon, after the settlers' arrival, a strip of dark-brown or black earth widened day by day and week by week as the plow turned the tough roots of virgin prairie grass, the era of the sodbusters. Wheatfields, a mile square, mile after mile, lay green and then ripening and then ripe in the swift growing season that earned for the Saskatchewan country the title of breadbasket of the world. New lumber houses replaced the old sod shacks, left to the leveling influence of wind and weather. Children went to school, carrying their lunches, killing gophers on the way for which they would collect a bounty of a cent a tail. In some areas the baker, in a tin Lizzie, began to call regularly.

But many a farmer's wife has never given up making bread. That chore is too satisfying to be relinquished entirely. Growing fine wheat and making fragrant loaves of light, crusty bread is too fundamental, whether or not you use the actual wheat that has grown on your own acres. Women troubled by constant prairie wind, by worry about crops and ill-health, by loneliness or even boredom find bread baking the world's best occupational therapy. They know that using head and hands together in the fine art of preparing good food ranks high in human experience.

In the early days of settlement when people in the west began to eat bread as well as meat, and before the era of quick-rising yeast, they used to set the bread overnight. Keeping the dough warm was a problem in winter, in a house without a furnace. And it had to be kept warm if the bread was to be light and tasty instead of heavy and sour. Whether or not to use potatoes as an ingredient and the water in which they were boiled came up wherever women met together. How much milk should be added to the sponge was another topic for discussion. Was softened lard or butter better for preventing a dry crust on top of the dough? But they all agreed on one item, "His" fur coat was best for keeping the dough warm at night.

Such holding of breath as accompanied the careful lifting of the coat and the clean tea towel next morning! Such relief when the dough had risen to the top of the pan! Such delight in kneading it down! That was when you could tell how good the bread would be. If the dough was still as warm as the inside of your elbow, if it squeaked as it was handled, if it had that special smell, that fragrance of sweet bread dough, the outlook was good. But it was not assured. The dough had to rise again. Cunning, competent hands had to knead it and shape it into loaves and brush the top of each with milk. The pans were set to rise in a warm place protected from drafts. And then—the oven. It had to be right. After all, it was the finishing touch. A good bread baker knows when the bread is done almost by the look of it. But just to be sure she will turn out the loaves and tap them on the bottom. The sound and the fragrant smell mean as much to her as to a potter firing an exquisitely shaped vessel, for to the woman who loves to bake bread every loaf needs as much care as though it were to be entered in the baking contest at the local fair or rodeo.

Getting the oven right on a prairie farm calls for a nice combination of skill and good fortune. There is nothing better than a good wood or coal fire for baking bread. But a strong wind in the wrong direction can bedevil oven temperature. Green poplar wood smokes. The best thing, on the prairie, is good coal from some of the world's largest deposits along South Branch tributaries. At Lethbridge, on the Old Man, one great open surface flares up at night in a Dantesque

Saskatchewan Wheat Land,
Winter Night

inferno that has been smoldering since the first white man saw it. At Drumheller on the Red Deer rich coal veins are worked side by side with the delicate mining of fossils ranging in size from tiny seeds and nuts and clusters of figs to enormous trees and dinosaurs. This part of the world has produced well for millions of years. It still generates hearty, healthy appetites together with the means of satisfying them.

Basic foods are abundant on the prairies. Bread and meat. Nowhere is there better lamb or, for fine flavor and good eating, such well-matured mutton. Carefully finished prairie beef is flavorful, well fatted, tender. Perhaps it is the almost constant sunshine that develops such excellent pork and bacon, such delicious, meaty turkeys. Green peas, corn on the cob, roots and greens, strawberry rhubarb and strawberries, roots and salad greens—given enough water, either by natural rainfall or conserved spring runoff, they all do so well that their absence in dry years or on farms where there is no water conservation is tragic.

They were fortunate, the women who lived near the wide valley of the South Saskatchewan. Its coulees broke the monotony of wide horizons. Its bottoms provided hay and grazing for cattle. There was even a little wood, mostly poplar. Best of all there was the river itself, water flowing in a land of very little water. Somewhere for picnics. Somewhere to go. The woman who had lived above the steep banks, not two miles from the stream, and who had no way of crossing it, did not know where it came from nor where it went. Often she wondered. Often, in summer, because the day was too hot and she had not the energy to make her way down to the water's edge and climb up again, she sat on the high rim of the valley and watched the shining, tawny river coming from one bend, disappearing to the northeast around another. Where did it go? Had it indeed cut this deep wide valley? How many millions of years had it taken? Sometimes the thoughts made her feel puny and insignificant. Sometimes they instilled in her a peace which was eternal and satisfying. In the early days she used to bathe in the river, cautiously, because of all she had heard about its dangerous currents and shifting sands. When the children were old enough to go down to the river alone they never went without the old familiar cautioning to stay behind the sand bar.

"Now, mind! That river's dangerous! Lots of good swimmers have been drowned in it!" It became a family joke.

Prairie fires threatened in spring and fall. The acrid, sweet smell of burning grass came quickly on the fast wind. At first they used to blame the Indians, and not without reason. Setting the grass afire was an old Indian custom, resorted to as a means of defense and, sometimes, for little reason at all. "Burned out!" That was a phrase to chill a settler's heart. Very soon he learned to plow wide fireguards around the little homesite. Often a double guard was plowed on the side of the prevailing wind. There was no natural protection. No handy water supply. The river was from two to five hundred feet below the prairie level, a hard, tough haul for horses in a hurry. It is easy to understand why a farmer, burned out, hated the stream flowing arrogantly, carelessly by; hated it and built again, and wished he could depend on it.

Yet after a prairie fire, how quickly and how gloriously the crocus bloomed in spring! Somehow wild roses survived. Tiger lilies grew. It is always that way along the South Branch. Bad luck. Misfortune. Heartbreak. And then wild flowers that make you want to smile with the sheer joy of living. You can woo the prairies, too. Patiently, carefully studying the land contours, you may construct a dugout to hold water or throw up an earth dam across a coulee. Sun and a fairly stable water supply will do the rest. Vegetables and flowers, huge spikes of showy gladioli which make Saskatchewan gladioli shows the envy of the continent, sweet peas to scent the entire house, petunias and incredible snapdragons, colors that have to be seen to be believed—they are the highlight of the short, swift-growing season. For the most part they are the work of white women who came and made the prairie of the South Saskatchewan home. Perhaps it was for such women that Andrew Graham wrote his tribute

To a Prairie Wife

"We broke new trails, wild roses at our feet,
And by the banks of the Saskatchewan
We found the thorny brakes as scented sweet
As any incense Eden gave to Man;
And each new spring, the slowly melting snow
Pours fresh life into this sanctuary—
And through its wilderness the soft winds blow
Till their warm kiss stirs the anemone."

Arthur Stringer wrote about the drab, harsh, lonely life of the prairie woman, cutting notches in the window frame to note the passing of the days, especially the lunar cycle. The picture is true. The Saskatchewan country is no cloying Eden of boundless ease and happiness. Women have gone mad, slowly, hopelessly, incurably mad because it was stronger and bigger than they. There are poets of sorts to record their passing. As well as those who write of beauty there are those who, like Hamlin Garland, see the other side, in

The Farmer's Wife

"Born an' scrubbed, suffered an' died."
That's all you need to say, elder.
Never mind sayin' "made a bride,"
Nor when her hair got gray.
Jes' say "born 'n worked t' death";
That fits it—save y'r breath.

Men succumbed to its harshness, too, as well as to its charms. The weak wilted, their moral or physical fiber not strong enough to struggle against grasshoppers, early frost, hail, sawflies, rust, drought. Slowly their bodies bent with the wind. Their hopes faded. Their eyes lost the sparkle of optimism. Yet not every farmer who, superficially, looked down and out was actually beaten. If you looked carefully, especially at his eyes, you might see a quiet determination, a spark which would rekindle into action at the first promise of a good crop. Artist Frederick Steiger looked carefully at a typical prairie farmer of the thirties and immortalized that spirit. Drab overalls and skin the color of wind-blown soil, at the first glance you wonder why the picture was hung on the walls of the Art Gallery at Toronto. Yet no one, once he really saw that farmer's eyes, wondered again. No one knowing even a little of the way most South Branch farmers meet drought conditions missed the "Drought," a dramatic, heart-stirring story told by that crisp caption.

That is the South Branch country. It is a land of contradictions and extremes. Captain Palliser, making his survey for the British government in the eighteen-fifties, reported most of the prairie through which the South Saskatchewan flows as unfit for agriculture. In the nineteen-forties South Branch people refer to Palliser's Triangle with an amused laugh, during cycles of adequate rainfall. Little Palliser knew of what the prairies could produce! During dry cycles, periods when the press and radio use the term "Dust Bowl," when tumbleweed or Russian thistle scurries down the roads and dams up wind-blown dust along wire fences, they refer more respectfully to Palliser's recommendations. Extremes of temperature. Extremes of fortune. That is the South Saskatchewan country, well inland on the continent, its altitude from fifteen hundred to over two thousand feet above sea level. It is far more given to extremes of fortune than the North Branch or the main river. Even Saskatoon, at the edge of the triangle, is more equable. Prince Albert, the Battlefords, Edmonton—all are famed for their fine mixed farming communities, their generally reliable crops. The South Branch, at least to the dawn of modern irrigation, was an all-wheat, all-or-nothing territory, except for the immediate valley.

Seager Wheeler homesteaded near Clarke's Crossing in

the eighteen-eighties, living in one of the sod-roofed, log shacks familiar to all prairie pioneers. He broke his first furrows with a yoke of oxen and a hand plow. His first grain crop was sewn broadcast by hand. But whether his fields were small or large Seager Wheeler sowed the best seed he could procure. Carefully he picked it all over by hand, discarding foreign grains and weeds. When, after a few years, he moved to a better farm near Rosthern, still close to the South Branch, he followed the same painstaking practice. At Maple Grove Farm he planted poplars and soft maple, willow and caragana, as well as wheat.

To Wheeler seed production became not only a means of livelihood but an impelling quest. Through hailstorms and drought, through years when his experiments failed to keep pace with his hopes, he persevered. Eventually in international competition he was proclaimed wheat king of the world. The honor was repeated. Seager Wheeler was the world's champion wheatgrower not once, but five times. Over the years his scrupulous selection of seeds and patient research brought fame not only to himself but to the entire Canadian wheat-growing industry. Queen's University at Kingston, Ontario, awarded him the honorary degree of Doctor of Laws in recognition of his outstanding efforts to produce a hardy wheat acclimated to Canada. There are others like Seager Wheeler in his country.

Most land filed at the turn of the century was in free, quarter-section farms owned by individual settlers who built their houses and barns and cultivated according to the terms of the Dominion Land Act. A few secured whole sections of 640 acres, a square mile. There were, however, several comparatively large land enterprises. The Hudson's Bay Company and the Canadian Pacific Railway had huge tracts of land grants for sale. Hudson's Bay Company land seldom sold for less than $7 an acre, the old company being well established. The C.P.R. faced a different set of circumstances; people were necessary. To secure farmers who would bring revenue it sometimes vied with the government in making free land available.

One of the largest land companies was incorporated in 1888 by Sir John Lister-Kaye, a British adventurer who had, with British capital, organized large and successful land ventures in the States. Sir John bought several 10,000-acre blocks of prairie land from the C.P.R. at a dollar an acre, the dollar to be rebated for every acre cultivated. Headquarters were situated on the farmsite on Swift Current Creek, some thirty miles south of the South Branch. Sir John Lister-Kaye did not take active charge. He relegated that to Lord Hubert Pelham Clinton, youngest son of the Duke of Newcastle. At the turn of the century the Northwest Territories served the empire well as a place for younger sons of old and proud British families to make their fortunes. Lord Hubert Pelham Clinton in turn engaged South of England Jim Smart to hire farm hands and carpenters for the venture so typical of projects in the expanding British Empire of the late nineteenth century.

Clinton and Jim Smart worked hard to justify the dreams, and capital investment, of Lister-Kaye and his associates. Hundreds of men were brought out from the old country. Carpenters built houses for the men and barns and granaries adequate for a farm of 10,000 acres. Livestock was imported—2,000 sheep, 500 head of cattle, 50 mares, and hogs for each farm. Because the first cattle purchased in the States carried the brand 76, that name was given to the Swift Current farm of the Canadian Agricultural, Coal & Colonization Company, the original home of Sir John's venture.

Those large herds of cattle did well on the nutritious prairie grass. Lord Hubert Pelham Clinton and Jim Smart looked on them with joy as they were brought in to be killed and dressed for shipment east. Special arrangements were made with the C.P.R. for cars. It was the first potentially big-paying crop. Already dividends were in sight. But there was one factor neither Clinton nor Smart had considered—the lack of refrigeration. An unexpected mild spell on the long trip east to Montreal thawed the carloads of fine beef carcasses. Most were completely spoiled. The loss was great enough to cause a reorganization of the company. In 1893 it became the Canadian Land & Ranch Company under the managership of experienced cattleman D. H. Andrews. Once more dividends were talked about.

Huge flocks of sheep had been imported by the company, as many as twenty thousand at a time. Like the beef cattle, they fattened well on prairie grass. A carload was selected to send to the Chicago Fair of 1898. In the spring Andrews engaged extra shearers, among them two lithe, dark-skinned youths from the Argentine, still wearing the overalls they had used in South America. No one on the Canadian ranch knew that the shearers had handled sheep affected by anthrax. None realized, either, that anthrax could be carried on overalls, not until it was too late. Thousands of animals were affected, including the flock chosen to compete for world-wide honors. That catastrophe decided the old-country investors to go out of business before they lost any more money in western Canada.

The prairies were being settled by people who wanted freedom for others as well as for themselves. Most of the men brought out by Jim Smart for the Lister-Kaye farms remained after the company was wound up. They took over the land to which they had come as employees. On a smaller scale they made the Englishman's dream come true. It was a scale better suited to the new land than the Old World custom of a landed aristocracy worked by hands and tenants, a condition from which most emigrants were actually fleeing. Yet today larger farms are returning to favor, largely because they are more economically handled with expensive mechanized equipment. Co-op farms are increasing every year, and though they are popular with women as well as with men they are still an experiment. In a country where large acreages are necessary to provide a living for a family the co-op cuts out isolation. It makes for a happier social life. It promises relief from the unsecluded little outhouse endured so long, because expense prohibits plumbing under small, single farm conditions. The co-op ought to be popular along the Saskatchewan.

The swing from small farms to large is part of the necessary adaptation that has had to be made in the South Saskatchewan country. It is symbolized by the engineer's cap the farmer wears instead of a straw hat, by indoor plumbing in place of the era, not long past, when Indian women squatted on the open prairie because there was no private way to answer nature's call.

There was a lot of disagreement about using land in the vicinity of Swift Current Creek for wheat growing. Man like Jim Smart who favored ranching saw little future in wheat. Others thought, and acted, otherwise. Probably both opinions were right. Some of the land was suitable for wheat growing and produced fabulous crops. Some of it was too light and ought never to have been plowed, as time proved. That was one of the struggles that colored the early settlement days of the country in what is now southwestern Saskatchewan. Farmers insisted on fences. Ranchers stanchly defended the open range. Politicians seeking votes saw more people to the square mile by farming and favored wheat at the expense of cattle, especially in areas along the Alberta-Saskatchewan border, where as much as forty acres a head is needed for open range.

Many a "first" farmer is still on his farm in the South Branch country. After forty or fifty years he is ready to relinquish active work to his son or son-in-law, or even to sell out and move into town or to the Coast. But the farm is still there, the land. And that one man has adapted himself from oxen and the slow, laborious plowing of pioneer days to the rubber-tired power combine. From the primitive seed drill he has progressed to a one-way seeder with which he can work 640 acres. He may be one of the combine owners whose crew regularly travels to the wheatfields far south of the border, where crops mature earlier, working north in time to combine his own crop. For, as a result of wartime co-operation between the United States and Canada, there is a yearly agreement whereby a definite request for the amount of aid needed is placed in advance, practical form of neighborliness.

The beauty and significance of a swather and combine on an enormous, shimmering field of ripe wheat is stirring beyond imagination. With world population increasing in spite of war and disease, bread assumes a more important economic role every year. Wheat is fundamental. But wheat farming on the Canadian prairies is dry farming, a hazardous occupation. No one can know whether the crop that is sown with such high hopes will ever need the combine. There may be no crop at all. That is the chance that must be taken. The odds are long. With grain growing forming so large a proportion of the Saskatchewan country farm income, it is the conditioning agent that buys a tractor this year and hopes for a big crop next year—to install a wind charger for local electricity, or indoor plumbing.

Wheat interests Saskatchewan farmers and everyone else in the Hudson Bay Route Association. Only a few prairie people dream of using the Saskatchewan as a commercial waterway. All realize the economic value of a seaport a thousand miles nearer than Montreal, seventeen hundred miles nearer than Halifax, because freight rates are another of the nightmares against which prairie farmers must contend. Though Port, no longer Fort, Churchill is open but a few months of each year, it can handle a lot of freight during those months. As in fur trade days, it is much the nearer route to Europe, where millions need the wheat stored in Canadian granaries and elevators, the rye that grows so well on submarginal land, oats and barley and those glorious fields of flax, as blue as the skies they reflect.

For long it was all wheat, until the terrible drought of the thirties. Wheat was an easy crop to produce. A few weeks' work in the spring, a few weeks' work in the fall. Grain in the granary and elevator, money in the bank, winters in California—that was how it went for a time and for a fair number of farmers. No trouble with rusted implements; in that dry climate farm machinery could be left outside all year round. Even grain could be left on the ground if the granaries and elevator were full.

But the soil became a little drier. Eddies of dust whirled up from fields and danced across the prairie. Without an anchor of roots, wind played flagrantly with rich topsoils, increasing in size and frequency. Next year there were clouds of dust, greater than anyone remembered having experienced before. They blotted out the blue sky. They rolled across the land in thick yellow fog. Farmers who did not take special precautions, such as strip farming, rough cultivating, or planting holding crops such as spring rye, lost their topsoil. It was blown onto the next farm, dammed up against fences and buildings and implements and windbreaks, blown high in the sky for hundreds of miles. Once-wealthy wheat farmers hung on grimly or talked of moving farther north. The Bennett buggy, named for Prime Minister R. B. Bennett, appeared on the roads, often a fine Cadillac drawn by horses because the owner had no money with which to buy gasoline. The dominion government again had to remember that it had territory in the West. The now-famous Prairie Farm Rehabilitation Act resulted.

It was no longer considered funny to sing "Dust Gets in Your Eyes," not with fields which were blown sky high or grew nothing but a crop of Russian thistle. The exquisite silky flowers of the great yellow cactus and the smaller red variety became, for the time, symbols of the desert rather than objects of visual delight. Some farmers lost carefully grown windbreaks and hedges and gardens. There were others, across the road perhaps, who managed to save the results of years of hope and effort. They may have cultivated their fields more scientifically. Possibly they had constructed larger and more efficient dugouts and dams to hold water or employed contour plowing to lessen moisture runoff. Yet saving even gardens did not depend entirely on the farmer's initiative or that of his wife. The type of soil had much to do with it. Too-light soils blow easily. Heavier soils can be made to stay. Solving these and similar problems has made the Dominion of Canada Experimental Station at Swift Current world famous for scientific investigation of areas of low moisture. There drought has been studied. Drought-resistant methods of farming have been developed which include new plants, soil cultivation, and moisture retention. With perennial faith in the country, people living along the South Branch now look forward to the next dry cycle with reasonable hope; they long ago accepted the fact that cycles of drought alternate with those of just enough moisture to produce a bumper crop. Many realize that this is merely another of the struggles common to the Saskatchewan's story.

Struggle is not new. In the early days it was between men of rival fur interests. Later it was between the native and the invading white man. Always there has been struggle between the river, its currents, shoals and ice, its extremes of climate, and man. The struggle has left its mark on the people. They are tough, independent, resourceful, friendly. They are resilient. The number of young men from the Saskatchewan country who manned the Air Force and Navy during World War I, as well as World War II, is almost incredible considering the population. These people tackle huge problems. They believe that the steepest hill levels off as you drive toward it. Because they are accustomed to sunsets and dawns and blizzards, as well as fields a mile square, they are part of an enormous, spacious beauty which is sometimes too large for the appreciation, even the perception, of those accustomed to tiny, tidy fields and the streets of huge cities. This is the great blessing that offsets some of the hardships.

CHAPTER TWENTY-ONE

Branding Irons

NO WISE chronicler of the Saskatchewan River would dare say which was its first ranch or give the date thereof. Up on the North Branch Battlefordians are confident that the first prairie ranch was owned by North West Mounted Police at the site of the present city of North Battleford. On the South Branch half a dozen communities not only claim the distinction of having had the first ranch, but can recite the names of their pioneers and recount a few exciting episodes as proof. Saskatchewan Landing, Medicine Hat, Bow Island, and McLeod were all "firsts," though McLeod has a little edge in that it was officially "Stock District No. 1," under the ordinance of 1878 "respecting the Marking of Stock." Probably they are all right, for a few cattle and horses were run at all these places in the early eighties. Yet two years before the North West Mounted Police arrived John and David McDougall of the famous missionary family had a herd at Morley up in the foothills west of today's city of Calgary. The McDougalls were busy protecting their cattle from timber wolves or they might have thought about using the year of their arrival, '71, as a brand instead of their initials, thus saving several groups of future citizens a lot of trouble.

No one argues about it. Arguing would be superfluous. Instead, each community takes pride in its own "first families," quite forgetting the greatest ranching enterprise the country has ever known, that of the Indians and their enormous herds of wild buffalo. No white man's roundup ever equaled that combination of millions of acres of range, superb riders, wild horses, and wilder animals. But that was all long, long ago in the swift-paced story of the Saskatchewan. Actually the less extreme climate of the chinook belt attracted ranchers before anyone thought of using the range along the South Branch.

There is, too, the problem of determining when a ranch becomes a ranch. Very few started up business with a flourish. They just happened. The Mounted Police needed beef for their men, or remounts, and in a few years there was a ranch. Perhaps some man and his partner—there was usually a partner—secured a contract to supply them. Another ranch got under way. Or else a couple of cattlemen from Montana trailed in a band of horses or cattle or both, and for various reasons stayed. Early storekeepers often found they had not enough to do, so they herded a few cattle. Generally it was the natural progression of cattle and cattlemen following the range north from Texas. Just what constituted the founding of a ranch has never been settled, whether it was five hundred head of stock or a thousand, whether it meant the first night spent in a dugout or shack or the registration of a brand. Prior to 1875 there were no ranches on the Saskatchewan or its tributaries. By 1890 hundreds of thousands of acres were under lease, great herds of cattle and horses and sheep were being run, millions of dollars and pounds sterling were invested. The cattle business had spread to the Canadian prairies.

Brands were first legally registered along the Saskatchewan in 1878 at the second session of the Council of the Northwest Territories at Battleford. In those golden days of ranching there were no fences between the Missouri and the Arctic Circle. The short-grass country belonged to the rancher, and the rancher's brand was his coat of arms. Spring and autumn roundups were the highlights of his social and economic calendar. The first big roundup took place at Fort McLeod when sixteen men rounded up several hundred head of stock. There ought to have been more stock, but the natives were short of food and a good steer was almost as tasty as a young buffalo cow. Brands were new to them then.

That important coat of arms, forged by the blacksmith, came up from Texas along with the stockmen, the horses and cattle. The 3- or 4-foot handles of the various brands thrust into a fire have been staple equipment at every branding from the days of the big open roundups to today's fenced private and community pastures. Like the smell of burning hair and hide, they stand for corrals and bawling cattle, dust and white clouds scudding across a clear blue sky, expert riding and sweating men working beside a big board, on which, like a calendar, the community's brands are burned. Even on the most modern ranches where branding tables are used the brand is still employed.

Early ranchers often chose their initials as their brand. Missionary the Rev. John McDougall used JM, the Hudson's Bay Company HB. Sometimes a brand was merely one initial distinguishable by the manner in which it was used. Famous among South Saskatchewan ranches for a number of years was the "Flying U" of the Matador, which had huge leases north of Saskatchewan Landing. But several other ranchers might use the same letter without confusion. If it was employed on its side it was known as the "Lazy U" ⊂; inverted it could be the "Crazy U" ∩; leaning at an angle of 45 degrees it became the “Tumbling U”; riding on a quarter circle, its owner’s ranch was doubtless known for hundreds of miles as the “Rocking U”; and in the case of the Matador, the flare at the top made it the “‘Flying U” Circles, diamonds, dots, and bars contributed to the calligraphy of the industry, the bars being especially popular as in the case of the “Bar Nothing” brand. The popular modern word “barbeque” had its origin in a Texas brand, which gave rise to a custom—perhaps with adaptations—in use on ranches along the northern river almost as much as along the Rio Grande. Like the brand, many of the old happy uses remain even though times have changed and fences, anathema to old-timers, are now accepted without comment.

In the eighteen eighties an enterprising man, and his partner, could trail in a few hundred head of horses or cattle or sheep from the States or overland from Winnipeg without knowing that there was another white man for hundreds of miles. That is how it was with some of the earliest ranchers. One drove the cart or wagon with food and a few meager supplies; the other trailed the stock. When they eventually came to a location that suited them they squatted. The grass was long and lush and stretched far beyond the horizon. The Saskatchewan or its tributaries provided water. It was as simple, and as difficult, as that. Generally those who pioneered as ranchers were men who previously had known the country in other capacities, as mounted policemen, surveyors in the employ of the Indian Affairs Department or the Hudson’s Bay Company.

James Hargraves entered the service of the Hudson’s Bay Company on the advice of his uncle, James Hargraves, factor at York Factory on Hudson Bay. Eventually the nephew came to know the Saskatchewan well and served as factor at several important factories including Cumberland House. At the time of the Northwest Rebellion he and several other company men had realized the ranching potentialities of the rolling country above the forks of the Red Deer, once site of old Chesterfield House, and near the Cypress Hills. James Hargraves and his family were already living in the upper South Branch country when one of the first overland pioneers, a Scot named Robert Mitchell, reached the lush flats below today's Medicine Hat; Robert Mitchell had driven his wagon from Regina while his son, Jimmie, then thirteen, trailed their cattle. The Mitchells built themselves a dugout in the riverbank and prepared to make a home for the rest of the family. They soon came to know their neighbors, the Hargraves. Often, during the winter, they visited together. That was how Jimmie Mitchell came to know James Hargraves's daughter, Helenora.

In spite of what later generations call hardships it was a wonderful life for young people, especially young men. Medicine Hat lays fair claim to more hours of sun throughout the year than most places on the North American continent. It is blessed by the chinook, no mean blessing. In those early ranching days the grass grew longer and the cattle bigger. The hills have always been a colorful rhythm of incomparable grandeur. And there was the river. When Jimmie Mitchell was nineteen he squatted beside it, ten miles north of the 10-year-old town of Medicine Hat, later taking up land in the regular way. In time he acquired some 45,000 acres on lease and 5,000 acres of deeded land which included two tracts farther downstream, the Cold Storage and White Rock summer ranges. But that original site was the Home Ranch, and no one contributed more toward giving meaning to the word "home" than Helenora Hargraves, Jimmie Mitchell's wife.

True to their Scottish background, Jimmie Mitchell and his father never entirely relied on the grass that nature cured right on the ground. From the first they put up hay so that their stock would have feed when the snow was too deep, or during dry years. Cutting and stacking hay was hard work, but it was insurance against the lack of feed which, in drought years, sent many another rancher back east or over the border into Montana. The Mitchells stayed, and the Mitchell brands, 7-T (seven bar tee) on the left ribs of the cattle and on the horses' flanks became well known through the upper South Branch country.

The Mitchells, like their contemporaries, had more to do than spending their days in leisurely riding and their evenings listening to cowboys strumming guitars beside flickering campfires. Drought and heavy snows were natural problems. More complicated were some of the human relationships, range rights, and the incompatibility of grazing sheep and cattle together, eradication of mange, which soon reached serious proportions, the steady influx of settler-farmers with their demands for fences. Big issues were linked with all the romance of the golden days of ranching, of cowboys and hard riding, roundups, and the sharp smell of branding time. These big issues became a part of the government of the cattle country. Gradually they were woven and interwoven with the needs of farmers and townspeople, of marketing and irrigation, of rodeos and the greatest cattle show of them all, the Calgary Stampede. They led to the Alberta Stock Growers' Association, which in time became the Western Stock Growers' Association numbering among its membership vast ranches developed by foreign, usually British capital, and the slightly smaller private outfits owned by men like Jimmie Mitchell.

"Forty acres to a critter" was the rule for the dry short-grass country of southern Alberta. That acreage was necessary, year in and year out, if the range was to be adequately maintained, and in time was recognized by an order in council regulating leases for grazing. Farther west in the foothills the limit was ten acres. Over two million acres were under lease during the early eighteen-eighties, making comparatively large roundups necessary.

Medicine Hat ranchers formed their first stock association in 1896 to handle their first roundup, one of the best they ever held. In those days, say the old-timers, the country was so wide and open and the grass so rich that cattle grew bigger. Steers had to weigh 1,400 pounds before being sold; if a steer was not heavy enough at four years he was kept on the range until he was. Grass was all but free. A 4-year-old, 1,400-pound steer brought $40 at Winnipeg, where most of the cattle were shipped. No one thought much about breeds. A few years passed before ranchers went in for purebred shorthorns, Aberdeen Angus, Hereford, and the famous Galloway cattle, bred for stampedes and rodeos because they were wilder than any other breed. That first roundup was a natural.

Its area stretched down the Saskatchewan from Medicine Hat to the Red Deer Forks, angling southeast to near Maple Creek and then back along the railway. Neighboring roundups from Maple Creek, Cypress Hills, Red Deer, and Lethbridge sent their "reps," riders who would look after exchanges for their districts. Each rep brought his own horses, usually the best cow ponies he could get and several of them, and his own bedroll. His saddle was his pillow. There were twenty-five men in the party with a cook and a cook's flunky, a day wrangler to herd the cavvy of horses and a "night hawk" for night duty. Camp equipment consisted of two wagons, a bed wagon and a chuck wagon, each drawn by four horses. The cook drove one and his flunky the other. A tarpaulin covered the chuck wagon's table and box of food and dishes. Traveling, the stove was lashed on behind with the stovepipes and tent poles along the sides. Any cook who lasted to cook for a second roundup had his stove lowered to the ground, the awning up, and a meal ready in shorter order than most cooks would care to match. There was a reason for the hurry.

Spring roundups lasted four or five weeks. During that time the entire work of the roundup had to be completed, cutting or sorting according to brands, roping, branding, castrating, dropping cattle that belonged to neighboring ranches and moving the others to grass and water. It meant getting up before three in the morning, at which time the cook had breakfast ready. Immediately afterwards the captain called together his riders to divide them into groups to go out on "circle." They were a businesslike lot, too, in their blue jeans, cowhide chaps, and high-heeled cowhide boots, buskskin jackets, regular cowboy hats with a thong trailing under the chin and over a knotted neckerchief. Many wore the wide mustaches affected in the late nineties. All rode stock saddles. In the first light of the morning ropers gripped their lariats as they quieted their horses and listened to the captain's plan.

Jimmie Mitchell was captain in his day. But before that he had often ridden with the boys, circling as much as sixty miles before coming in with his bawling charges for a 10:00 A.M. lunch. The riders ate their lunch, meat, tea, sourdough bread, and pie and then went right back to work. As soon as the last man had eaten, the cook and his helper had the stove up on the back of the wagon, the pipes lashed alongside, the bed wagon loaded, and were driving their two 4-horse teams across country to the next meeting place, raising almost as much dust as the bawling, restless cattle. That was the origin of the chuck races that are now a feature of every stampede and rodeo. It was continual packing and unpacking to get a lunch for the night wrangler at midnight, breakfast for the riders at three, lunch at 10, dinner and supper, with those dust-raising, wild 4-horse teams racing across the trailless prairie to meet up with the constantly moving roundup. Cooks had other troubles than setting up the cookstove, racing across the dry, short grass, and serving meals. When riders and horse wranglers dipped into the pies set out for the night hawk the cook had to find his own solution. During the first roundup he resorted to a sound, if old-fashioned procedure. Holding his pistol over the recalcitrant he made him eat so much pie that he never wanted to see another. There was pie enough for night hawks after that.

Spring roundups are necessary for sorting and branding stock, and dropping them on the owner's place. The fall roundup is similar except that its purpose is to collect beef for market. Actually there is little change over the years. The roundup that used to take place over open range is now limited to the owner's fenced lease and deed land. In the Saskatchewan country there never was much need for a cowboy to carry a gun. If he did carry one a Mountie usually met him on Central Avenue.

"Let me take that till you leave town," the Mounties used to say. "It might get you into trouble."

The cowboys drank and chewed, smoked and gambled. Sometimes they yipped down Central Avenue or crooned a sentimental love song. But most of the time they worked hard, as they do today. They spent long hours in the saddle in biting, cold winds and in the heat of summer, in snowstorms and rain. Fancy saddles and custom-made shirts have always been a craze with some of them. They are sentimental and cling to old habits and phraseology. That is why many an old cattleman survivor of Jimmie Mitchell's day delights to brand Saskatchewan's Canadian Commonwealth Federation government, commonly known as the CCF as the "double cee eff."

Jimmie Mitchell specializes in white-faced Herefords. On the Home Ranch a gas well supplies power to pump water from the river to irrigate alfalfa growing on the flats. When there is a good "rainy" year, wild hay, or deep grass, is cut and stacked as well. The combination of putting up native hay in good years and irrigation has cut down considerably the acreage required as range for each animal. Feed lots are important.

No cattle ranch exists without horses and Jimmie Mitchell early showed his fondness for a good horse. Among pioneers a boy becomes a man early, and young Mitchell was only in his middle teens when he started buying outlaw horses, breaking them thoroughly, and then selling them. It was a good beginning for the man who was later to win the world's relay race championship at the Calgary Stampede, to judge bucking horses at the same show for nearly thirty years, and to become president of the powerful Western Stock Association for five years.

In many ways James Mitchell was typical of ranchers along the South Branch. He arrived in the all but untouched short-grass country with nothing but what he brought in his own hands, his own mind, and his own heart. When he died in 1942 they said he was probably the best known rancher in the Canadian West and far south of the border. Like all real ranchers, he was an individualist. He became a big businessman. Rolling hills and wide horizons, many acres and few people brought out the best in him, making a warm friend, a generous neighbor, and an extremely public-spirited citizen. When he arrived on the South Branch there were few old people there. Not a grain elevator broke the sky line. No fences divided the territory between the border and the arctic. The rancher was king.

When James Mitchell went on his last roundup nearly everything had changed. Ranches were mechanized. Ranchers had big cars, an old Ford, and possibly a light plane as well as the saddle horses. Their sons and daughters received their education at a different university from that of hard experience which had taught the old man. Yet it was a sound, practical education many of the first ranchers received. Scientific soil surveys and economic studies have shown that they, as well as Captain Palliser, were at least partly right. Much of the prairie land should never have been plowed, even with irrigation as a potential aid. Fenced areas of a quarter or half section are too small for profitable farming, and certainly much too small for profitable ranching and a rancher's horizon. Jimmy Mitchell's 50,000-acre ranch, now owned by his son, is an indication that everything has not changed.

Like James Mitchell of Medicine Hat, James Smart of Saskatchewan Landing, farther downstream, had strong opinions about the relative importance of ranching and farming along the South Branch. Jim Smart was on his place in the nineties. He was riding cattle one day when he met a prospecting farmer from the States, busy digging holes to see what the soil was like. Jim Smart reined in beside him. He greeted the stranger pleasantly and asked him to have a drink. They had supper together, grilled antelope steak, sourdough bread and tea, and talked about things in general. When they had both lit their pipes a breeze sent a drift of wolf willow fragrance to mix with the smoke from their fire. Jim looked the other man in the eye. There wasn't a chance, he opined, that wheat would grow in South Branch country, not a chance. Mixed farming was out of the question.

"This country is so dry even the gophers are getting scarce," he went on. "It's so dry public citizens are out to preserve the remaining gophers as specimens for a museum. I'd suggest," Jim tamped the tobacco down in his pipe, "I'd suggest as a neighborly gesture that you save any you come across before you leave for other parts . . ."

Tradition has it that the prospective farmer took another drink, thanked rancher Smart for his good advice, and decided to settle right there!

With Jim Smart, the South Branch country was a case of love at first sight, a love that lasted through struggles against fences as well as settlers, drought and depression, good years and bad. An advertisement in a South of England newspaper by British promotor, Sir John Lister-Kaye attracted his attention in 1885. The advertisement read: "Wanted a young man to assist in bringing men to Canada." Jim Smart applied, got the job, and came to Canada with the men who started the old Lister-Kaye outfit, the "76." The men were offered $10 a month and board, starting when the boat sailed. Many of them, accustomed to England's neatly tilled fields and friendly villages, faltered when they saw the untouched, treeless prairies. Remembering tall Russian tales of attacks by wolves, they quailed at the sound of coyotes at night. But those who stayed learned that the prairies can be friendly and that the worst thing about a coyote is his blood-curdling howl. Many, like Jim Smart, became the first ranchers in the country along the South Branch, north of the embryo town of Swift Current.

Jim Smart soon left the Lister-Kaye employ. He had seen a stretch on the South Branch near Saskatchewan Landing, a wide valley with a lot of deep natural grass. He had thrilled to the bluffs along the coulees, to the mad whirl of crunching ice at breakup. Down a trail laid out by an old Indian woman before the day of surveyors he went to the spot that was his home for the Canadian part of his 90-odd years.

Jim Smart built a snug ranch house on a knoll in the valley, married pretty Elizabeth Richardson, and in no time their home was a social center for the community. Like the Brunyee Ranch and Colonel Yates's place at the forks of the Swift Current Creek, it became famous as a picnic center among young townspeople and settlers living away from the river. When the prairies were hot and dry, when winds tumbled the tumbleweed and filled the air with gritty dust, those ranch homesites in the valley of the South Branch were a series of oases. They were more than places where fried chicken, incomparable potato salad, and strawberry shortcake might be enjoyed around long trestle tables set up under the cottonwoods. They were symbols of hope. The strawberries grew in irrigated plots. So did the greens in the tossed salad. It was interesting to watch the sheep grazing along the north bank. After lunch, guests liked to stroll out to see the cattle or mount one of the saddle horses to explore the coulees.

"We never used to bother milking," said Jim Smart, his deep-set blue eyes twinkling. "The calves did that till the ladies arrived to civilize ranching."

Perhaps they are among the most civilized people in the

world, those ranchers who built their comfortable homes along the river. Many are exceptions to the too-often-true gag that the West is a place "where men are men and all the plumbing is outside." Opportunity to think and enough space accent the blessings of radios and record players and books as well as the satisfaction derived from breeding and owning Palominos, Herefords, and sheep that produce good mutton and fine wool. Perhaps they realized, Jimmie Mitchell, Jim Smart, Bill Brunyee, Jim Yates, and others who chose to live along the South Branch, how hopeless the Canadian prairies would be without the great angle of the Saskatchewan watershed.

The huge, impersonal company ranches never took to the South Branch as they did to its tributaries in the foothills. The old feudal attitude of absentee owners collecting dividends was out of step with 40-mile horizons and all that land which might be owned by a man who liked independence and was willing to invest some risk and work to secure it. Even the Scottish-owned Matador took on much of the personality of its long-time resident manager, "Legs" John Roscoe Lair, who followed the famous Scottish manager Murdo MacKenzie. Lair was a Texan who had worked on the Matador's large American holdings, a man with a voice to match his 6-foot-6 height, and a heart to match both. His beautiful Texan drawl was the envy of many a local cowboy. So were his hounds, for to Lair good dogs belonged with good horses, and a hound is fine for running coyotes. They used to say of him that he would as soon run a coyote as eat any day. And many were the fine runs enjoyed by Lair and his friends.

When the Matador first leased six townships of grazing land north of the South Branch, Legs Lair cursed the cold Canadian winters. The country, he opined, was fit only for Indians and Eskimos. Certainly it was no place for a Texan. Yet it wooed and won him. He had spent most of his life with the Matador. When, in 1922, the company decided to pull out of Canada, Lair remained. He bought a small place of his own and Canadians interested in the cattle industry discovered that a lot of the sound business and excitement that had been associated with the Matador really stemmed from Lair. At his own place, as at the large ranch on the north bank of the South Branch, the latch was always outside and the coffee-pot on the stove. That coffee, his friends used to say, "would float a spur rowel!"

With the Matador went the most representative capitalist-owned ranch along the South Branch. Currently the tendency is a return to larger leases, up to fifty and a hundred thousand acres. The sight of a large herd fording the river still reminds all who saw the last of the Matador herds returning to Montana of the late Legs Lair. There was something about that big herd which was like Lair. It moved massively down the coulees to the river in the valley, just as the buffalo herds had moved. At first, in the distance, you thought it was the shadow of a great cloud. And then you felt it. As though a great choreographer had planned it, the herd came down from the prairie and riders circled it, keeping it in formation. Across the river they swam, still in that loose, yet massive formation, always moving forward and, it seemed, in all directions at the same time. Then the herd left the stage, the valley, and disappeared up the coulees to the prairie again. The dust of thousands of hoofs lingered. A great trampled path marked the short grass.

Sheep coming to the river do not take up so much space as a comparable herd of cattle. Yet, like the cattle, they look like the shadow of a cloud as you see them in the distance, often herded by dogs. Down near Maple Creek sheep rancher W. H. ("Bill") Martin uses border collies on his 55-section ranch, dogs which he has trained to answer to whistle signals, and which will guide sheep from a distance of a few feet without frightening them. They are the collie dogs that thrilled audiences in New York's Madison Square Garden, Toronto's Canadian Royal Winter Fair and in small Saskatchewan rodeos. Often Bill Martin has had to wait until the applause died down before his dogs could hear his signals to continue the sheep-herding exhibition.

Large sheep ranches and lambing and shearing are a part of South Branch life, especially in the rolling steppe land from the Red Deer forks south to Maple Creek. There the ancient picture of a shepherd with a flock is highlighted by the wind charger, which provides electricity for the ranch home and barns, and by modern, scientific methods of shearing and disease control. Only the market remains geared to the equally ancient law of supply and demand.

There is going to be grazing for more sheep as well as cattle when the surplus wild horses of the Saskatchewan country are under control. Wild horse herds annually crop range land which would maintain upward of forty thousand cattle. The solution was summed up in a recent rodeo at Swift Current when a horse appeared in the opening-day parade with the caption "Only one life to give for a hungry world." At Edmonton and at Swift Current large herds of wild horses graze in fenced pastures awaiting their last roundup. Packing plants at the two cities have prepared millions of pounds of horse meat for Europe. Under UNRRA more than five million cans have gone to Poland alone. Mane and tail hair goes to Belgium. Meat unsuitable for human consumption feeds fur-bearing animals. Hides and bones have good commercial value.

There are a lot of factors behind those wild horse herds. Mechanization is chief among them. Time was when ranchers played a fair bit of polo. No one plays much polo now. It may even be that there are more men than gentlemen, in the polo-playing sense of the word, along the Saskatchewan. Specialized breeds are needed, heavy draft horses for farms, reliable cow ponies for herding, saddle types such as Palominos and Appaloosas, horses that will do for the local light-horse cavalry units, for pleasure riding, for show, and of course, for rodeos, and stampedes.

Ranchers will tell you that there is a vast difference between a stampede cowboy and a cowboy doing the routine work of the cattle industry. Yet there is a symbolism that is sound. Long days of hard riding in all kinds of weather and equally hard economics highlight the comradeship and holiday atmosphere of every local rodeo. You can detect it in the eyes of old cattlemen and their kindly, poised wives as well as in the eyes of their lean, lithe, narrow-hipped sons who ride in every show and wear chaps and sombreros and sport fine saddles and custom-made shirts. For the fundamentals of ranching have not changed much since the days of the open range. The old fascination that accepts a lot of hard work and roughing it is part of the lure that annually draws increasing thousands to each rodeo and agricultural fair in the country.

The modern rodeo is an exciting, noisy, friendly, competitive, dangerous get-together. At each grandstand, crowds provide all the thrill of a first-night audience. At the chutes, riders and horses and bawling cattle put on the show. Because most rodeos take place in June, July, and August, nature provides a dramatic scene. Invariably the weather is dry, sometimes too dry. White clouds sail a blue sky, unless the day is so hot that the sky is copper colored, and dapple the sunny prairie with shadow. The hotter the day the better is the rule for stampede weather. Local bands play. Over the loudspeaker someone makes the official announcements, repeats the imposing prize list, says a few friendly, banal words of welcome. And then—out they come!

At the far end of the stand, amid dust and the bawling of cattle, the first rider cavorts out to contest the saddle-bronc riding title. With a whoop the boys urge him on. An experienced cattleman, the announcer follows him while the crowd applauds. This is no pastime for an amateur. That bronc twists and rears and leaps to shake the rider. The boy's hat is still rolling down the field. His red shirt balloons out behind him. Will he hit the dust? asks every spectator. Can he hang on, just once down the field? He does! Cheers! Yipping! Applause! It was almost as quick as the eye could follow. And before he has left the field the next rider is hurtling out the chutes. The crowd gasps its unspoken appreciation of the wild rhythm of a wild horse and a young, competent rider.

On the program the list includes typical rodeo events—steer decorating, bareback riding, calf roping, milking a wild cow, riding a wild steer. Occasionally a rider is thrown or a horse is hurt and the crowd waits tensely for an announcement. Then the show goes on, faster, dustier, hotter, noisier, in a crescendo of excitement; friendly because the riders know one another and the entire community knows them by reputation if not in person; keen because competition is the keynote. There are cowboy heroes, riders who are top all-round men, whose colored shirts, intricately tailored, hand-made boots, and hand-tooled saddles are copied and envied by every youngster who sees them. There is romance. There are purses and reputations at stake. It's an occasion worthy of the "Hi, Neighbor!" slogan so popular on rodeo programs.

Rodeo and roundups are important dates on a rancher's calendar. So are the various sales, cattle, sheep, bulls and horses, which decide whether he is going to stay in business or not. Mighty exciting events they are, too, to visitors as well as to the man whose stock causes the rapid patter of the auctioneer and those silent, barely perceptible bids which indicate so much. Neatly dressed men from the big packing outfits, racy-looking individuals who want prize stock for their own gentlemen's farms, small buyers for local firms, men who will bid thousands of dollars for a good bull—they are the "other half" of the sales to which ranchers go with their year's harvest. Such buyers are vastly different from the itinerant buyers who roamed the prairies at the bottom of the depression of the thirties offering such shockingly low prices that more than one rancher ordered them to "Get the hell outa here before I kick you off . . ."

Dry years are hard on ranchers. Some have lost everything during prolonged drought. Some cut down their herds, retaining their best breeding animals to build up again when the next good cycle returns. Irrigation helps many to provide sufficient feed to tide them over. In fact, small irrigation projects and improved ranching methods have lowered drought hazards to a comparatively safe level so long as prices remain stabilized. In the days of the open range, cattle fended for themselves during the winter. Now feeding is taken for granted.

Short, crisp names recall men who have adjusted themselves and the ranching industry to Canadian prairie conditions. They are simple names, easily remembered, typical of the quick, friendly attitude of the South Branch country. Picked at random you will find Jimmie Mitchell, "Rube" Gilchrist, "Legs" Lair, Jim Smart, Bill Brunyee, Neil Janke, Harry Minor. Farther west, along the tributaries and in the foothills, there are more as easily recalled—Pete Knight, Pat Burns, George Lane, Archie McLean, A. E. Cross, Guy Weadick, who was in at the beginning of the Calgary Stampede. They are typical of the cattlemen, some of them cattle barons, who solved the difficulties of pioneering and made the industry great. Their sons are as enthusiastic and as competent. Most have been to university. Few know anything about hardship as their fathers and grandfathers knew hardship. But that does not mean that their lives lack challenge.

The new challenge is merely of a different order. It has to do with producing better breeds, meeting the competition of international markets, and the steadily increasing demands of a steadily increasing population for more meat as well as for more bread. It is a challenge for which cycles of adversity and quick, easy harvests have equipped men and women living in the Saskatchewan country.

CHAPTER TWENTY-TWO

Rod, Gun, Camera, and Shovel

WHEN you first enter Num-Ti-Gah Lodge at Bow Lake smoke gets in your eyes, faint, pleasant wood smoke. In no time you are accustomed to it. In no time, too, you feel at home in the warmth of the greeting of Mr. and Mrs. Jim Simpson and their family. Four-foot logs crackle in the stone fireplace. Superb heads of mountain goats and sheep, bear, deer, moose, and other animals adorn the peeled log walls, animals shot by Jim Simpson during his fifty years' hunting in the valleys and slopes about the sources of the Saskatchewan.

"Num-Ti-Gah" means brown marten, dark, beautiful

"Mrs. Jimmie" will tell you, her rich voice proudly proclaiming her Scottish birth. When she arrived as a bride in 1917 the only link between Bow Lake and the outer world was the pack trail up from Lake Louise, or, as it used to be known, Laggan Station. Now there are the Columbia Icefields Highway and the fire rangers' telephone line, great improvements which have meant little change to the valley itself.

Wild life still abounds in the sanctuaries of Banff and Jasper National Parks. Deer come down to the corrals at Num-Ti-Gah as tame as the riding ponies. Bow Lake provides some of the best fishing in the world. In summer Rocky Mountain bluebirds are there to turn Maeterlinck's fantasy into fact for truly, if there is a spot on earth where happiness might be expected to be found, it is in the high, exhilarating valley near Bow Pass, where the blue-green waters of Bow River tumble down to meet the South Branch and the milky streams of the North Branch drop swiftly to the foothills and the prairies below.

For the hunter who seeks to capture and record beauty with a camera there is scenery unsurpassed. Moose feeding in the Waterhen Lakes pause to lift their great heads as the car or bus pauses within easy photographing distance. Mountain sheep and goats beckon from the highest crags. Wild flowers from fringed gentian to exquisite, minute alpinae star the slopes. And, as Jim Simpson will tell you, discriminating hunters come from all over the world to shoot big game in the passes just beyond the park.

Years ago, before anyone dreamed of making the headwaters of the Saskatchewan into a national park, Jim Simpson trapped marten, wolverine, mink, bear, ermine, and other animals where but a few years earlier Sir James Hector had come as one of the earliest explorers. There is little that Jim Simpson has not hunted or acted as guide for others to hunt in the great valley. It was he who guided Sir James Outram, first man to make the ascent, to the Columbia Icefields. Geologist A. P. Coleman rode in with him. Year after year scientists come to see with him the mountains and valleys and glaciers that he knows as most people know their own road. Jim Simpson enjoys the hunt as well as the quarry.

The mountains about the river's source are a hunter's paradise no matter what he pursues. Winds that moan and whisper about high peaks are music worth a long, long journey! Once you have heard that unforgettable symphony you know that if ever geography enters into your relationship with God, it is here. Down in the foothills, out on the prairie and parkland and forests to where the mile-wide river narrows to pour into Lake Winnipeg, there are successive paradises of but a lesser degree. Sport, beauty, variety. It could not be otherwise with a river that cuts across the waist of a continent.

Hunters eager to shoot big game in the mountains may start from Num-Ti-Gah Lodge on the Columbia Icefields Highway or they may go by train or car to Rocky Mountain House and up the old route traveled by Duncan McGillivray, David Thompson, and the fur traders and explorers of the nineteenth century, crossing the river on the Thompson bridge. The Alberta government has plans to develop the rough trail that connects with the Icefields Highway into a modern road commemorating David Thompson. Now the trail beyond Nordegg can be traveled only by pack horse or a sturdy jeep. But it is a trail beloved by hunters. When autumn days are shorter and early snows blanket lower peaks, Rocky Mountain House—"Rocky," to people living in the community—resumes much of the excitement of the days when great brigades left there for the Pacific. Modern hunters travel with guides and well-equipped pack horses. Up on the Kootenay Plain, where the Indians long ago gathered to hunt and dry meat, where Duncan McGillivray enjoyed his first meal of mountain sheep, "the sweetest and tenderest meat I ever ate," today sportsmen come thousands of miles to enjoy that same "sweetest and tenderest meat" and to secure a precious trophy to take home. Local farmers and ranchers and businessmen call it a bad year when they miss their few days' hunt for mountain sheep, goats, bear, moose, or deer.

Down on the prairies nearer Edmonton and in the irrigation country farther south, in the Central Flyway, ducks and geese attract sportsmen from the States and the Pacific coast and down East. With grain in the stook, farmers welcome hunters. Ducks and geese have voracious appetites after their flight from the cold, invigorating arctic. They do enormous damage to grainfields. Farther downstream the Mississippi Flyway crosses the Saskatchewan. There are few stretches where, come September, men and some women do not plan "a few days' shooting." Some drive out the evening before. Most, living nearby, leave their warm beds in the cold predawn and reach their shooting areas with the first signs of day. Before World War II, everyone took his bag to the ubiquitous Chinese restaurant to be plucked. "John" used to pluck birds for as little as five cents each, though a dime was more general. Those duck or goose or prairie-chicken dinners, served with wild bullberry or chokecherry jelly, are something to remember. Up on the North Branch, where winter stays winter, game has long been a staple food as well as a luxury.

Freezing game for winter is a fine old North Saskatchewan custom. They have been doing it since Samuel Hearne was too often short of the only food on the fur traders' diet. With the advent of flour and vegetables and other food, game took its proper place. Senator W. A. Griesbach paid tribute to the custom of freezing birds in his highly personal book *I Remember*. Recalling the good food at the North West Mounted Police Division at Fort Saskatchewan during the eighteen-eighties and nineties, the general does not forget the prairie chickens, partridge, ducks, and geese hung up to freeze on the shady wall outside the kitchen. That is the sort of thing you don't forget.

There is fishing in practically every mountain and foothill stream that eventually becomes Saskatchewan water. Cutthroat trout abound in the Highwood, Sheep, and Pekisko

Creek country where the Duke of Windsor has his celebrated EP ranch. To keep the main streams stocked, fishing in side streams has been prohibited for many years. But special permission was obtained for his Royal Highness during his stay in 1923. As soon as the telegram came through from Ottawa to High River, game warden Sam Smith rode out to the EP with it. Typically the then Prince of Wales asked if such privileges were granted to other fishermen. His comment was typical also.

"Then there won't be any fishing in the side streams while I am here either," he said. "There must be the same regulations for all."

It is a royal sport shared by the old ranching aristocracy who came in prior to 1905 and provincial autonomy, and by newer ranchers, farmers, and townspeople. They all like to take off a few days, between work, for a little fly fishing. And nowhere will you find more ardent devotees of the fine art of tying flies. Bits of colored yarn, feathers, hair, and fine wire occupy a fair number of people for a fair bit of time in the foothills country. Carefully and ingeniously composed and imaginatively named, hand-tied flies are proudly exhibited wherever good fishermen get together.

Along the main river and up the North Branch a few hunters have developed a sport which demands the utmost in skill, knowledge, and tact—the search for old fur traders' sites. They couldn't make much progress while they had to depend on the scant records left by the Nor'westers. They got almost nowhere so long as the Hudson's Bay Company retained its traditional attitude that letters and journals written by its servants were private business and not the concern of either amateur or professional historians. But they have been having a wonderful time ever since the company changed its 250-year-old policy and opened its priceless archives.

For decades trappers, surveyors, and sportsmen-travelers have been on the lookout for likely depressions, all that is left of early sites. Fur traders' houses or shacks and stockades were built of logs and soon fell to wind and weather if they survived burning by Indians. Certain locations are obvious—the confluence of a smaller stream with the Saskatchewan; a promontory, such as at Nipawin where Indian women came to watch for the returning canoes; at bends, where there were good supplies of food and fuel. History confirms these sites. Time and again they appear in the journals of the fur trade and the explorations that went with it. Over the years every protected bottom and every lookout on the highway river had a succession of houses.

The most difficult houses to find were those built below the Forks during the brief French regime. Trees, growing out of silt-covered ruins, indicate age. Hearthstones and chimneys, cellars and old glacières are important finds. The French built their stockades in oblong shape, the narrow part fronting on the river. When the English came they built square stockades. Pedlars' and Nor'westers' houses were made of squared logs set in an upright frame after the custom along the St. Lawrence. Hudson's Bay Company men erected shacks of logs notched at the corners. But the big thing, after years of growth and fire, flood and weather, is to locate a likely depression. Even then the depression may turn out to be merely an early settler's shack.

Several sites already had been found at Nipawin and other points on the main river when the search for fur-trading sites along the North Branch got under way. The earliest was known to be located near the Sturgeon River, some six miles above Prince Albert, locally known as the Shell and by David Thompson referred to as the Net-Setting or Pukkatowoggan River. It was thereabouts that Peter Pond placed his post. The Cumberland House journal of 1777 mentioned this site as the Upper Settlement to which the pedlars had gone to ease the strain of competition. It was on the edge of the buffalo country and, in the fur trade days, a good area for beaver. Alexander Henry the younger said he "camped on a beautiful small meadow where there was every appearance that a range of forts stood many years ago," probably successive Hudson's Bay and North West Company posts. Careful surveyors like Fidler and Turnor and David Thompson measured the distance from the mouth of the Sturgeon to the ruins. Peter Fidler wrote:

"An old Canadian house or Houses burnt down . . . Mr. Blondeau wintered here in 1779 . . . Lat 52.10 as per Philip Turnor . . . about ⅛ mile higher up Sturgeon or Setting River flows in here . . ."

With this information and the fact that Sir John Franklin had described a carefully lobbed willow, the site ought to be an easy one to find, argued eager twentieth-century hunters—amateur and professional archaeologists, geologists, engineers, students of history, settlers, and farmers. But, though they all knew where to look, no one had found the slightest evidence of an old post. For years they hunted until the challenge developed tantalizing proportions. The search went on in spring and autumn, when the leaves were off the trees and before the ground was blanketed by snow. Carefully the banks were examined, the underbrush combed. Then someone looked down from a high bank and noticed that the Sturgeon River had had more than one mouth, that it had had, in fact, two mouths which were silted in and almost completely obliterated by shrubs. Which of the two mouths was the older?

". . . about ⅛ mile higher up Sturgeon or Setting River flows in here . . ."

Which mouth? The hunt was intensified. Once again every foot of the area was examined. For almost two hundred years the Saskatchewan River had been flooding the little outpost site. But the hunters were persistent. Eventually two shallow depressions were found. There was the usual excavating, the careful noting of folds of silting. Finally the hunters came upon flat hearthstones and some ashes, laid on silt. They dug down deeper. Some four feet below the level of the present bank they found what they sought—a semicircular arrangement of flat stones laid on the surface of the ground and not on silt. This, they decided, was the site of the fort built by Peter Pond and his associates. The shovel had been as rewarding to them as the gun or rod or camera had been to other sportsmen.

CHAPTER TWENTY-THREE

Clusters of Light

At night, as you drive toward them, most prairie towns are a cluster of lights. Flying, the effect is even more marked. In the dry, clear air each light is distinct for miles. Sometimes, especially along the South Branch, you may see eight or ten bright clusters in a radius of twenty miles. Often they are small, the lights of a few homes, a few stores, the gas station, hotel, and railway depot. Most urban centers along the river are cities, with a minimum population of five thousand.

There are conditions apart from the dry, clear air to account for the brightness of those light clusters. One is the comparative lack of trees. Trees do not grow naturally along the South Branch, except in protected coulees, though many fine parks and windbreaks have been coaxed into being during the fifty years since lots were sold at auction and the fame of western Canada as a ranching and wheat country was broadcast by promoters who sought, so they said, to create towns to serve the settlers. Along the parkland of the North Branch bluffs dot the rolling country. No forests limit visibility except, perhaps, at Rocky Mountain House and The Pas. Even at these centers, almost as far apart as the source and the mouth, there are no great trees. Poplar, jack pine, lodgepole pine, and willow predominate.

The other factor conditioning the brightness of the clusters is their comparative rarity. There are no large cities on the prairies. In fact, the population of most of the Saskatchewan River country averages about six persons to the square mile, with large areas dropping to less than one. Where people are so few and, because of the nature and vastness of the territory, far apart, every light seems brighter.

Each town and city is new, almost as new as electricity and the automatic telephones that were installed along with the first plank sidewalks. There are still people living who can recall days when the brightest lights along the Saskatchewan were the campfires of the fur traders, Indians, and very early settlers. Now the clusters shine wherever the railway crosses the river, with the railway their natural link instead of the river as in the days of travel by canoe or horse. They shine to direct great international transport and passenger planes as well as tiny fire-ranger and ambulance craft to well-constructed landing fields; if there is no landing strip, one is often improvised on the river or a field, with the lights from a car, tractor, or jeep. Saskatchewan River people are still pioneers when the occasion demands resourcefulness. Their new towns and cities on the North Branch and the main river are bases for today's true pioneering of the northland that stretches to the Arctic Circle and beyond.

The lights of The Pas are familiar to all the great mining interests of Manitoba's hinterland as well as to trappers and lumbering men and their families. Prince Albert boasts that it is the center of the northern two-thirds of Saskatchewan Province. The Battlefords are a regular air stop. Edmonton sends its beams not only into the vast territory of Great Slave Lake, the arctic, and the Mackenzie basin but also, as a base on the northern circle, to the Yukon, Alaska, and Asia. And these are only the literal lights. Metaphorically the two universities of Saskatchewan and Alberta shed a bright and penetrating light on the local problems of a territory to which men, women, and children are still learning to adapt themselves—or the territory. It was not by a whim that the university at Saskatoon inaugurated a Faculty of Agriculture along with its Arts. Nor is it a coincidence that legislators at Alberta's provincial capital, Edmonton, have been faced with and are meeting the many problems of government that occur in a territory, some of whose conditions are still unknown, and whose citizens are absorbed in trying to make the best of them.

They are not haphazard, those clusters of light typical of the Saskatchewan country. They did not develop slowly, this way and that, as people added a street here and there over the centuries. They were installed when the towns were laid out, generally in straight rows, at right angles to one another. The only curving roads were dictated by the curves of the river and these are all met by the neat lines of south-north, east-west streets. A common joke is the retort of the visitor from any large eastern city to the proud Westerner boasting of how easy it is to find your way when all the streets are numbered one way and the avenues the other.

"In a town this size," proclaims the visitor, "you couldn't get lost if you tried!"

Westerners realize that this is merely the narrow-minded attitude common to people who live without enough room to breathe properly, and dismiss it. Or else, like the friendly taxi driver in Edmonton, an astute psychologist, they know you will need the information sooner or later. It saves everyone trouble to hear it repeated.

"It's easy to find your way in Edmonton," says the taxi driver imperturbably. "Remember that Edmonton is in the northwest. The farther north and west you go the higher the numbers!"

Actually, of course, Edmonton with its astronomical street numbers is not in the "northwest," though it used to be. The phrase has been used conveniently, and loosely, ever since the continent was discovered. Each century it has been pushed on a few hundred or a thousand miles, always a little ahead of the awareness of people living down East, or coming from the older settled communities. Mid-twentieth-century Edmonton is in the province of Alberta, or in western Canada, some 350 miles north of the International Boundary. The last northwest is down the Mackenzie River basin or in Yukon Territory. It is a good thousand miles beyond the Saskatchewan.

Modern lights along the river first shone at Medicine Hat. That was about 1883 when the Canadian Pacific Railway Company's first train crossed the pile bridge that was the first bridge to span the river. They were not very bright lights but a promising beginning. To the same railway goes credit for making the initial discovery that Medicine Hat was being built above a vast lake of natural gas, a supply which has made the town rich and famous as a manufacturing center and site of many acres of greenhouses. The railway people were drilling for a water well when they accidentally struck a small flow of gas. The crew heated their section house with it. A few years later the town of Medicine Hat and the railway got together to investigate further. A 65-foot bore gave them a flow of gas with 250 pounds pressure but containing a lot of moisture. The next hole went down deeper. Soon after the turn of the century Medicine Hat proudly announced that it had struck natural gas with a pressure of 550 pounds, dry and presumably limitless. There was so much gas that the street lights were left on day and night. Inevitably the legend spread abroad that Medicine Hat left its lights on because that was cheaper than bothering to turn them off. The legend still has good publicity value, though both streets and homes are now lit with electricity, economically generated by gas. Homes are heated by gas. In Medicine Hat, so they say, husbands are more kindly and chivalrous than elsewhere; they don't have to wear themselves ragged shoveling coal and ashes.

Like most places of even modest fame, Medicine Hat cherishes its legends. There is the one about the famous Cree warrior. There is another about a great serpent who comes up to breathe in the water hole, which is often open through the Saskatchewan's ice even in the coldest winter, due no doubt to currents. The legends provide a poetic background for the city's many industries, built up by that combination of seemingly illimitable gas a thousand feet below the river's banks, more sun in a year than most places on the North American continent, and weather conditioned by the chinook.

Though the area of Alberta served by Medicine Hat is primarily devoted to the largest cattle ranches in the British Empire, and to sheep raising and wheat growing, the city is properly proud of its industrial enterprises. Among them are the potteries, using clays imported from large deposits at Eastend and the cheap natural gas, to make ceramic products known all over the world; a linseed-oil plant; a glassworks, and the extensive sewer pipe and brick works for which the city is famous. The latter are especially fortunate, with enormous deposits of clay right at the factory doors—"enough to last a million years," some people claim.

Redcliff, a few miles downstream from Medicine Hat and distinctly not a suburb of the larger city, is aptly named. Its citizens are intimately associated with the manufacture of extensive clay products ranging from tiles and sewer pipes to building brick. Many work in the glass factories, where they employ ancient processes, with modern adaptations, to blow bottles for numerous utilitarian purposes from milk, preserved goods, and pop to medicines and machine oil. Visitors never know whether they are more fascinated by the dramatic craft of glassblowing or the Dantesque inferno of gas chambers which reach a temperature of 2,800 degrees Fahrenheit. But it is the natural gas, still glowing brightly in a few incandescent mantles at the railway station, that keeps Redcliff's factories humming. It is natural gas that provides employment for many southern Alberta townspeople, as well as a balance between industries which are agricultural and those which are urban.

Saskatoon was the second community along the Saskatchewan to welcome train lights. That sturdy settlement was founded by a group of Toronto promoters who had received a grant of a quarter million acres astride the river, and who called themselves the Temperance Colonists. Down East great meetings had been held. Would-be settlers had heard fine, promising speeches about the territory "where temperance ideals would prevail exclusively." Since the Northwest Territories were officially dry, the temperance angle was superfluous. Even more superfluous was the price—$2 an acre. That brought the cost of a quarter section, or 160 acres, to $320.

There were advantages in living in a community where one's principles would be respected, argued the promoters. The number of zealous temperance colonists eager to come out by the first train, or even by boat downstream from Medicine Hat, encouraged them to talk about a land rush. The first snag was the discovery that there would be no exception to government rules respecting land surveyed for settlement. Even-numbered sections were available for settlers; the colony's strict regulation could not be enforced on them. In every township two sections were set apart for school districts and two for the Hudson's Bay Company. That meant that the Temperance Colony could not hold its land in a huge tract but rather like alternate squares on a gigantic checkerboard. And settlers, if they chose, could take up a quarter section of free land for a fee of $10! The difference between the $10 fee and the $320 asked by the promoters appealed to colonists, who had food to buy as well as farm equipment. Most decided on the $10 fee without the full benefits of a strict temperance community.

At the time there was a lot of disappointment and disillusionment. But the settlers and some of the promoters who had made a little money got together and built a ferry and installed a sawmill. In 1889 they all turned out to welcome Saskatoon's first train. It is safe to say that the railway would not have arrived anything like as soon but for their own efforts.

The little cluster of lights on the east side of the river increased in numbers and brilliance. The community boomed. It was Saskatoon, and in its midst stood the railway station. There was no bridge for trains to cross over to the little group of citizens living on the west bank, not for months, and that irked. Resentfully they looked across the river to the train, the railway station, and the growing community. When the bridge finally spanned the river they celebrated fittingly. The celebration became truly jubilant when the railway company, with incredible lack of tact, moved the station across the river and painted up the name of Saskatoon. Citizens of the erstwhile Saskatoon on the east bank protested the injustice in a manner worthy of a pioneering people. In the same spirit their neighbors understood. Warmhearted, they too felt the slur implied in the railway company's callous unconcern for the nicer sensibilities of territoral citizens. It drew both sides of the river together again. Thomas Copland, agent for the Temperance Colony, enterprisingly thought up a scheme to save face for citizens of the east bank. He suggested a new name.

Nutana, he said, was an Indian word meaning "first born." The gesture was tactful and the name is still used by the large section of Saskatoon on the east and south bank of the river. But the original citizens were not entirely appeased. None of the Crees or Sioux they knew ever used the word "nutana." Naturally they deduced that Thomas Copland had pulled it out of his imagination. But it was a constructive gesture.

Fortunately everyone was too busy with the immediate task of making a living to devote much time to nursing bitterness. Most settlers had come from Ontario and were completely unprepared for the dry farming conditions of the South Saskatchewan country. They had a lot to learn. The handful of townspeople quickly discovered how closely and to what extent prairie economy linked their welfare to that of the surrounding farming community. Together they worked so hard and well that before they realized it the lights of the first train had developed into the lights of a little metropolis. The towns on either side of the river had become one, linked by a vehicle bridge as well as the train and the old ferry. Fashionable ladies in Saskatoon, in common with fashionable ladies in other towns along the river, were donnng wide hats and long trailing skirts to trip along rough plank sidewalks to "At Homes," happily nonchalant when the July sun in a copper sky melted pink ice cream and faltering candles alike. Then the West was booming. Money was so plentiful that nothing less than a nickel was ever used, with quarters preferred as a convenient minimum.

Saskatoon began to think of itself as site of the future provincial university about the time the Northwest Territories were promoted to the status of the provinces of Alberta and Saskatchewan, in 1905. The old rivalry between the citizens of each side of the river was nothing compared with the rivalry between Saskatoon and Regina for the privilege of becoming a capital. But Regina had won that round, with all the business and offices that belong to a capital. Now its people were saying boldly that the university ought to be situated close to the capital. Naturally Saskatoonians disagreed forcefully. It was incredible they argued, that anyone would think of locating a great university along the banks of that trickle of water called Wascana Creek when there was a choice of superb sites along the beautiful South Saskatchewan River.

Back of the Arena
at Medicine Hat Rodeo

They mentioned other factors, including justice and fair play.

The Saskatchewan government in due course appointed a board of governors for the proposed university. The board of governors in turn searched far and wide and appointed the first president, Dr. Walter C. Murray of Dalhousie, a choice with which everyone approved warmly then and in the years to come. The next step was the site. Towns and potential cities were visited. Offers were considered carefully. Eventually all were eliminated except three—Battleford, Regina, and Saskatoon. All three were strong contenders.

The board discovered that some of Regina's land, supposedly a gift from interested citizens, actually belonged to the government. Battleford at once offered an outright gift of a thousand acres. Saskatoon went one better and proposed to donate a choice of a thousand acres in a large, valuable tract. No interprovincial football game ever rivaled the excitement and effort put forth in that three-way struggle. When voting finally occurred in Regina it was behind closed doors. They said afterwards that the drop of a pin would have sounded like a gun being fired during the tense silence of counting ballots. Battleford was eliminated first. A wave of comment broke over the room. And then Regina and Saskatoon were fighting the finals in the second round of silent, secret balloting. No one knew what might happen if Saskatoon lost. No one dared to think about it. Fortunately she won.

At once telegrams were sent to the city along the South Branch, her delegates following by the first train. When they reached home all Saskatoon was out to meet them. Whistles blew. Bells rang. An unacademic procession was formed and everyone made speeches or listened to them until exhausted. A few citizens went so far as to belie the community's early temperance leanings. Next day Saskatoon, and the board of governors, settled down to the important and sober task of selecting the site and inaugurating the University of Saskatchewan. They chose well. The site is a glorous one, high above the east bank of the river, covering more than fifteen hundred acres, its buildings constructed of the native stone that later gave its name to the undergraduates' fine publication, the *Greystone*. Sir Wilfrid Laurier laid the cornerstone in 1910, and by that time the Faculties of Arts and Science and Agriculture had enrolled their first students, the latter soon taking over the educational work of the Provincial Department of Agriculture.

Now it is difficult to say which sheds the greater light on the lives of people living along the angle of the river, faculties of arts and science or agriculture. Agriculture has made so many practical contributions to a better way of living by its investigations into soil conditons, moisture conservaton, crops, economics, grasshopper and other plagues that it is possible for more students to acquire an education in the humanities.

Prince Albert, though founded before Saskatoon by missionary Rev. James Nisbet, did not see the lights of its first train until a year later. Even that was almost a year before the railway reached Edmonton. With his wife and child and a few settlers James Nisbet had spent sixty-five days on the old Hudson's Bay Company route traveling from Winnipeg. Development was slow until the railway reached the river. Then Prince Albert started on its important career as "hub of Saskatchewan's top two-thirds," blessed with good mixed farming land, lumbering industries, furs, fish, tourist business, and the mid-twentieth-century interest in the vast wealth of the Pre-Cambrian Shield. Its brightest lights are those of its airport, base for passenger and transport services that reach far into the northland.

Because the riverbanks are comparatively low at Prince Albert the airport is conveniently located beside the seaplane base. A weir downstream a couple of miles keeps the water level fairly constant, and all air services are close to one another and to the city. Thousands of miles of lakes and rivers and forests north of the river are being aerially photographed. From the river "smoke eaters" take off on their long, careful fire surveys. For the northland is a part of the city of Prince Albert. Because the cluster of lights is nearest and so precious to people living in remote parts of the province, they shine more brightly than any others along that stretch of river. They are a symbol of the transportation and communication by air that has brought the "top two-thirds" to civilization, or civilization to the "top two-thirds."

The Saskatchewan Government Airways provides transportation services for people living in isolated places. It assists in the development of vast natural resources, mining, fishing, trapping and lumbering, and even flies hunters and fishermen to areas previously untouched by white men.

Today, not far from the site of the first fur traders' post on the North Branch, passenger planes arrive from the north to land on the river, from the south and west to land on tarmac. That is in summer. Winter flying conditions are more difficult. In that land of forests and lakes and rivers there are few landing fields. Water is used almost entirely, planes being equipped with floats in summer and skis in winter. Pioneer fliers using the river soon discovered that it never froze in a smooth sheet of ice. At the beginning of winter ice on the North Saskatchewan forms gradually, breaking and piling until finally the surface is so rough that planes can barely take off or land. Back in the mid-thirties conditions were so bad that flier Angus Campbell determined to do something about it.

He applied the principle of a tire and tube as used on car wheels and adapted it for skis. He designed a pedestal which, when the plane hit a rough area of ice, took up the shock through a shoe. Gradually the invention was developed. Civil aviation across Canada adopted it, and the Royal Canadian Air Force uses it in investigating winter flying conditions in the north. Angus Campbell called his invention the Pneumatic Ski Pedestal.

When a city takes an active interest in its historical background it has reached some degree of maturity. For years the citizens of the Battlefords were occupied with the serious problems of handling local Indian affairs for the numerous nearby reserves, making a living, and building their towns. Outsiders generally refer to the two places as the Battlefords. But loyal inhabitants take care to clarify their position. Battleford, according to residents of the town on the high plateau between the two rivers, is the original town, historic site of the first police station and one-time capital from which all the Northwest Territories were governed. The North West Mounted Police Memorial and Indian Museum are situated there, in restored original buildings and stockades. Lord Alexander of Tunis opened the museum officially on Victoria Day, May 24, 1948. The ceremony recalled that other Victoria Day in 1885 when General Middleton arrived to accept the surrender of Chief Poundmaker at Battleford, not *old* Battleford, as its citizens remind visitors. Battleford is conscious of its important place in Canadian history. North Battleford, across the Saskatchewan, is a city of another sort.

North Battleford is the modern town, the bus depot, the railway center, the city of business and the homes of businessmen, at least as interested in the present and future as in the past. Beyond it, to the west, the bright lights of the airport shine at night. To the east lies the provincial mental hospital with its beautiful flower gardens. The mental hospital was the prize North Battleford won in a later intercity struggle for patronage, and quite right, too, as its citizens point out, considering that Regina became the capital and Saskatoon seat of the university.

Spirited contests between settlements on opposite sides of the river are a part of the story of each town and city. No less spirited is the keen competition between the three cities in the angle—Saskatoon, Prince Albert, and the Battlefords—with Regina. Each has seen to it that the honors have been fairly evenly divided. To offset the capital at Regina, the

University at Saskatoon, and the mental hospital at the Battlefords, Prince Albert takes a great pride in the large sanatorium that lies among the pines north of the river. The pride is legitimate, for it is a place of beauty in summer and winter, with a climate that contributes much toward good health. With patronage fairly distributed and local pride upheld, there is a lot of friendly visiting between the three cities, especially by air. Air connections are excellent and not expensive. The mildly bumpy flying typical of the white-clouded blue sky of summer seldom discourages passengers. Winter flying is excellent.

In common with the other river cities, Edmonton's lights began to glow brightly when the railway finally crossed from the south bank. But it was touch and go for a few months whether they would ever flicker. A branch line of the Canadian Pacific Railway angled north from Calgary and, as at Saskatoon, paused before spanning the river. The North Branch at old Fort Edmonton called for a much longer, higher, and bigger bridge than was needed at Saskatoon or Prince Albert. It would be a costly bridge and difficult to build. Quite naturally the railway company wanted to know whether the cost was warranted. It was a momentous period for the little town of Strathcona on the south bank. The lights of Strathcona increased and brightened, much to the chagrin of Edmonton on the north bank. Edmonton was very, very far away from the railway's services. In fact, it was distant by a hazardous, precipitous lurch-and-tumble down to the water's level, an uncertain current-propelled ferry trip across the river, and then a fearful climb up from the valley. Citizens of the proud, ancient site of the old fort snorted and fumed.

They sent delegations to Ottawa. They indulged in a welter of rivalry and conniving before the bridge across the North Saskatchewan was finally commenced. To add to the rivalry, spans were started at each end and the gang of workmen at Strathcona's side went on strike, leaving the citizens of Edmonton in a frenzy and her crew of workmen out in the air. It was a situation demanding the strong, practical methods to which Fort Edmonton's people had long since been forced by necessity. The workmen at the Edmonton side decided to see what they could do about the strike and the citizens took care not to interfere. They were a he-manly crowd. None of them wore gloves, which may have accounted for the success of the strike-settling venture. The two factions met on the riverbank. There was a little plain talk and some much plainer action. Fists found their mark. Legs tangled. Few punches were pulled. Up and down the banks the men surged and struggled till eyes were blackened, bodies and noses bleeding. It was a wonderful fight, an unforgettable occasion. And it lasted all afternoon. Next morning the crew from the Strathcona side went to work, and in due course the bridge was completed. Edmonton sent up a lusty cheer, and its lights began to flicker. Whether the citizens of Strathcona had anything to do with the strike has not been completely established, though a lot of Edmonton's old-timers "could say plenty if they wanted to!" Time has healed the breach and Strathcona is an important part of Edmonton. Sometimes it is even called South Edmonton.

Now Greater Edmonton has a population of nearly 130,000, noble legislative buildings where once stood John Rowand's great house, a university which has sent brilliant graduates all over the world, and a road, rail, and air connection which is steadily increasing in importance. It has a well-planned civic and community center. The Old World beauty of its many-domed Ukranian church is unique in Canada. It is the heart of a vast field of oil and natural gas. Its lights make up an enormous cluster of neat cross lines with the great strings of bridge lights reflected in the river so far below that citizens laughingly refer to their suicide bridges. Though they have shone brightly for over fifty years, none of the lights shines more brightly than those which were lit at Canada's first municipal airport in the late nineteen-twenties.

In 1925 Edmonton decided to have an airport within its limits. A hundred and sixty acres were set aside and a sum said to be about $500 spent in leveling and clearing away willows and other brush. That was all. The city applied for a commercial license. A few Royal Canadian Air Force men who had been experimenting wth fire patrols by air flew up from southern Alberta. They met a few more who had been barnstorming locally and the airport was officially declared open for business. During the first summer some landings were made on the North Saskatchewan, pilots tying their craft up to barges which were pushed out farther and farther as the water level dropped. But generally the new flying field was used. In no time the success of the venture was assured.

The presence of several of Canada's outstanding airmen of World War I in the vicinity of Edmonton may have a lot to do with developing the new airport, men like "Punch" Clennell H. Dickins, "Wop" Wilfred Reid May, and the late Roy Brown. They had to have somewhere to take off and land because they had to fly. To the north of Edmonton beckoned a land of almost unknown lakes and rivers, of woods and mineral wealth, of trappers and mounted police, Eskimos and Indians. There might be some use for commercial flying. By air there ought to be as much scope for exploration as ever delighted restless, questing young men traveling by canoe and dog team a hundred years before. So the youthful airmen thought it out. Events soon proved how right they were. Very shortly the venture developed into a transportation executive's dream come true—pay loads both ways plus an incredible amount of public service.

The Edmonton airport crowd of the late twenties and early thirties believed in safe flying. They did not take unnecessary chances. To them it seemed more logical than courageous to fly to the rim of the arctic without radio communication or the advantages of meteorological stations. In

1927 Punch Dickins inaugurated the fur service, and ever since Edmontonians have been gathering in their broad, bright streets to cheer hero after hero. They cheered when Dickins and Wop May won Canada's coveted, highest flying award, the McKee Trophy. They gathered in great numbers to welcome May when he returned from the trail-breaking trip of flying diphtheria antitoxin to Fort Vermilion to stamp out an incipient epidemic, and when he took part in the Royal Canadian Mounted Police hunt for Mad Trapper Johnson, who had killed one Mountie and wounded three others. May flew the trapper's body out to Aklavik after he had been shot by pursuing policemen. The streets of the city rang with cheers when Dickins and other fliers returned after the long search for the MacAlpine party lost far beyond the rim of civilization, and again when goods were flown to Sir Hubert Wilkins's base during the search for Russian fliers lost over the Polar Ice cap in 1937. The fliers insist that there is altogether too much fuss. But Edmontonians have a feeling for that vast northland of strange lights, a brief summertime of twenty-four hours' daylight, and a long winter of incredible darkness and cold.

They recall those tiny, open cockpit planes in which their intrepid young fliers took off for the unknown north, the open cockpits in which they froze hands and faces all too often. They have enough imagination to compare today's flying with the days when families waited without possible word for men who were days overdue. In a sense they are happy to be able to cheer. And, of course, they are a warm and hospitable people. They like to show their pride and appreciation, as well as their relief.

Yet, though they cheer a lot in Edmonton, they also take much for granted. Men like Wiley Post, Jimmy Mattern, and Howard Hughes brought them out to the streets in crowds eager to offer a hearty welcome and as eager to wish the pioneer fliers Godspeed. Today a North West Airlines Skymaster flying to Tokyo by way of Anchorage, Alaska, comes down to fuel with scarcely a comment. It is largely a matter of familiarity.

At first the boys "flew by the seat of their pants." They knew the Mackenzie and a few other major rivers and lakes. Maps and instruments and radio came later. In 1935 C. H. Dickins flew the director of civil aviation, Dan McLean, on a search for possible air routes and locations for landing strips and, incidentally, to try to discover where the Rockies ended. The important result of that extensive trip was to open the way to the string of airfields that, during World War II, made possible a way to Russia for all the advantages of Lend-Lease.

That original little airstrip cleared of willows and brush in 1925 became, by 1943, a well built 750-acre field which in one 24-hour period accommodated 865 craft. During 1943, 82,000 planes used the airport only three miles from the center of Edmonton.

From that small beginning of flying trappers down north and their furs back to Edmonton, flying mail so that old-timers marveled at seeing newspapers a day instead of many weeks old, air traffic out of Edmonton has increased until there were, in 1948, eight companies running on a daily schedule. Charter trips are commonplace. Back in 1929 Edmontonians were able to boast that more air passengers and more express used their airport than most of the larger American airports. That local pride is a characteristic which warmed many an American citizen during war years when Edmonton was often referred to as the "forty-ninth state." To justify it, and to curtail seasonal delays when freeze-up and breakup prevent float landing, twenty-five airports are already established in the north country beyond Edmonton and new landing strips are under way.

The Saskatchewan is mostly a useless stream now that it is no longer used for navigation. Yet its shores or its high banks have been the starting point for most excursions into the northland. Military exercises such as Muskox were supplied largely from Edmonton. Gilbert Labine in search of precious ore beds flew north from there; now those little bags of ore from Great Slave Lake are a common sight at the hangars as they await shipment to the pitchblende plant at Port Hope on faraway Lake Ontario, which on one occasion was a roundabout way to Hiroshima. A trapper wanting to survey his territory, 1949 fashion, engages a competent pilot and a plane and takes off to note the higher levels where he will set his traps for lynx, and the stream bed likely to be followed by fox. He saves time and money and can be back in Edmonton in days instead of months. Flying in supplies and flying out pelts, he saves not only time but money because he can catch the current season's market with pelts in prime condition. The Saskatchewan does not seem to mean much to him, perhaps no more than to the bishop, the doctor, the mining man, or the pretty little strip-tease dancer who entertains the boys in the lumber camps. Yet every town of any account in a vast section of the Canadian West depends on it for water, for beauty, and for many other essentials. For people gather together where there is water.

Geographer Griffiths Taylor sees Alberta becoming one of the world's most thickly populated centers in the next hundred years. If his predictions are correct, the light clusters along the Saskatchewan will shine brighter and much farther than now. Especially at Edmonton. With enormous resources of coal in the province, with huge oil wells and supplies of natural gas, and because of its strategic position on the route to Asia, Edmonton may become one of tomorrow's bigger metropolitan centers. In the meantime the lights shine brightly enough to suit old-timers. When a town gets too big, they opine, you just can't get to know all your neighbors. And knowing your neighbors is one of the prime joys of Saskatchewan River folk.

They are generally electric, those clusters of light which shine out across prairie and parkland. Sometimes the electricity is produced by natural gas. Often coal is the source. Occasionally, especially on comparatively isolated farms or ranches, there is a wind charger to harness the strong prevailing winds. The other great source of light in the Saskatchewan River country, steadily increasing in brilliance, is that of its oil wells. But they can scarcely be referred to as clusters. There's too much danger that some of them might become conflagrations.

CHAPTER TWENTY-FOUR

Oil!

ALBERTA takes its oil the way it takes everything else, high, wide, and handsome and by divine right. In the foothills country white people quickly took to half-million-acre ranches and many-million-dollar irrigation projects. Land booms were as perennial and as popular as a chinook arch. When, in 1914, oil was discovered in Turner Valley it was just another proof that Alberta was "God's country." Everyone was going to get rich quick, though not many people took it too seriously. The Calgary *Herald* echoed local mood in a list of "regulations" published as part of its tribute to the handsome Palliser Hotel that the C.P.R. had just completed to reign over the smokeless, gas-heated foothills city. The list read:

1. No well shall be drilled before 6 A.M. or after 3 P.M. Operations at that time are apt to disturb paying guests while in the midst of beautiful dreams of vast wealth and permanent gushers.

2. No more than one well shall be drilled in each leather chair, or sofa, during one time interval . . .

3. No well shall be drilled in a tone of voice which is audible within the three-mile zone and causes the skylight to flutter.

4. No well shall be drilled nearer than one foot from any door, window or passageway, and no disputes shall be indulged in or any lease located in such areas.

5. No dry holes will be tolerated in the lobby. All wells brought in must be in the thousand-barrel class, or larger.

6. All shares offered are to be of the gilt-edged variety.

7. No well drilled in the lobby shall stop at shallow sand. Every well must run down to deep pay and represent an outlay of not less than $100,000.

For nearly three decades Calgary's major tourist attraction was a visit to the top of the Palliser Hotel at night to watch the glow from millions of cubic feet of gas burning in the Turner Valley field some forty miles southwest. Now geologists regard Turner Valley as a fluke, a mere pocket at the edge of the vast oilfield that underlays Alberta between the north and south branches of the Saskatchewan. Albertans themselves were not surprised to wake up one morning in 1948 and find they had made a discovery as important to Canada as the discovery of gold in northern Ontario. They will accept it as their due if the field near Edmonton rivals the rich West Texas area.

Ever since Dingman first blew in at Turner Valley, big companies and enterprising individuals have been prospecting Alberta for oil. Thousands of surveys have been made. Hundreds of wildcat wells have been drilled. During the summer of 1948 forty-six parties were spending an average of $700,000 a month searching for likely oil and gas deposits below the wheat and coarse-grain fields and the ranch lands of the third prairie steppe. They represented firms with assets worth many millions of dollars. Albertans looked upon it all as part of their favored destiny. No need to be excited about oil when their province's coal reserves are estimated at forty-seven billion tons!

But they were excited, even for Albertans. Wainwright had been producing heavy oil consistently for over twenty years. At Lloydminster, just when pioneer promoters had decided they must quit for lack of funds, a wildcat well had blown in to start off a field, which for a time was Canada's top producer. Lloydminster wells, which find pay at less than two thousand feet, could be drilled and equipped for as little as $25,000 as compared with $150,000 at Turner Valley. Like mushrooms, derricks reared up to rival the long-familiar grain elevators against the wide prairie horizon. And then Imperial Oil discovered Leduc to start a boom worthy of Alberta.

Leduc had been a small farming center ever since the railway came through some fifty years before. Its land brought prices comparable to millions of other acres in the prairie provinces. As at Lloydminster, only grain elevators cut into the horizon. But all that changed, even the sky line. Suddenly land prices soared. Offers were made and refused, perhaps to be accepted eagerly next morning after the farmer had had time to think things over, and regretted again when oil equipment and oil ruined rich wheat land. Liquid gold was pouring money into Alberta's treasury and Albertans' pockets. The market soared. In Edmonton a new well scarcely merited a headline, so frequently were wells blown in. And then Atlantic No. 3 went wild.

Atlantic No. 3 lived up to the province's high-wide-and-handsome oil philosophy. Barely had it gone into production than it was completely out of control, spewing out thousands of barrels of oil a day. Gas bubbling through the surrounding acres looked like rain on still water. Great clods of oil-soaked mud shot into the air. Streams of oil channeled wheatfields. Within a few weeks a great, green-black lake had formed, a lake so vast that trucks and the Imperial pipeline could not begin to drain it. To lessen the appalling fire hazard, increasing daily, the Alberta Petroleum and Natural Gas Conservation Board closed down the entire field of over sixty wells. Even airplanes were warned to stay away lest a spark touch off a conflagration unequaled in the country's oil history.

Relief wells half a mile apart were drilled at an angle. Water from the North Saskatchewan River was pumped in at the rate of 40,000 barrels daily only to increase the wild flow from 7,000 to some 14,000 barrels a day. Men worked day and night to keep the pipeline at capacity. Others, using bulldozers, threw up earth dikes to hold an estimated 75,000 barrels. It was twenty-three days before the field could be reopened, even temporarily. Sufficient oil had been blown out of the well and its surrounding craters to last eight years at Alberta's conservation allowance of 150 barrels a day. During the well's first six seeks 300,000 barrels had been saved by pipeline and truck and another 50,000 barrels pumped back into adjoining wells. At the end of three months its output was valued at better than $2,000,000 and everyone was counting the cost. Trying to estimate how much Atlantic No. 3 would cost before it could be tamed and how much damage was being done to the surrounding area was a nightmare to the conservation board and the oil interests. John Rebus, who for years had been farming the site of the wild well, surveyed an 80-acre oil-soaked field and tried to figure how many years would elapse before the soil would again grow wheat.

The Rebus family certainly struck it rich. In Alberta only freehold land held since early pioneer days carries mineral rights. The Alberta government and large companies such as the railways and the Hudson's Bay Company sell only surface rights. Oil companies pay a 12½% royalty. In the case of the large Rebus family the royalty has reached $4,000 a day, as much as modest farms earned in a year before Imperial, after spending millions of dollars on surveys and wildcat drilling, discovered the Leduc field.

Another farmer, living on the North Saskatchewan fifteen miles upstream from Edmonton, promptly accepted an offer to sell his quarter section sowed to wheat. The field was just green then. By the time what was left of the wheat had ripened plans were drawn for a model town, trucks were bringing in supplies, streets were laid out, and a great sign, "Simpson's Folly," informed all concerned that the farm's erstwhile barn was now headquarters for resident engineer Simpson. Simpson had come to build a model town.

Never before had there been a model town on the Saskatchewan. Towns and cities just grew. In time more imposing buildings replaced the original false-fronted wooden structures, which haphazardly lined the plank sidewalks with gaps here and there like the gaps in a small boy's smile. The model town of Devon has a planned business and residential area, parking lots, theater, hospital, and recreation building. It also has four oil wells within its borders. Anyone may build there who complies with planning restrictions and does not mind the warning that future wells may be drilled on locations already selected, even in his back yard.

Also on the North Saskatchewan, at beautiful Woodbend, another oil center is developing. Like Devon, this is no stark desert country. Central Alberta's rich parkland lies above the oilfields. The Rockies are to the west. Down north there is all the Mackenzie River traffic. Railways have lines ready to haul both crude and refined oil south and east and west. And because it is Alberta and there are always dreams, at least one man has a scheme for building dams and locks on the North Branch and the main river to barge oil down to Lake Winnipeg and even to the Great Lakes. In Edmonton there was never so much excitement, not even when waiting wives and sweethearts ran up to the H.B.C. flag to greet returning fur brigades a hundred years before, nor when more than six hundred oil-hungry planes landed at the municipal airport in a single wartime day.

The town of Devon received its name from the Devonian limestone in which oil was found. The great field is underlaid by Devonian rock, rimmed by a coral reef left by the ancient semitropical seas that existed before the Rocky Mountains were thrown up and long before the Ice Age. Geologists point out that similar conditions exist in the richest Texas fields, and promoters make the most of the suggestion. Leduc field is estimated as already showing reserves of over a hundred million barrels and the proven area is being extended rapidly. The Imperial Oil Company plans to apply some eighty million dollars recently converted from holdings in Peru, Colombia, and Venezuela to large-scale activities in the Saskatchewan River country. A refinery costing over seven million dollars is under way to bring further impetus to Edmonton. Cracking plants are part of the near future.

Oil and gas deposits between the North and the South Branch are as yet an unknown quantity. Some geologists are confident that the entire area is underlaid from the foothills to the Alberta-Saskatchewan boundary and possibly farther east. Vast beds of natural gas are being used at Medicine Hat, Lethbridge, Calgary, and adjoining towns. Oil has been discovered at Turner Valley, at Edmonton, 300 miles north, and at Lloydminster, 180 miles east of Edmonton. Now oil and gas surveys are investigating crown-owned lands in the Cypress and Great Sand Hills extending along the interprovincial border north from the International Boundary, and east of Medicine Hat's 500 billion cubic feet of natural gas. All signs point to another natural resource in which Canada can be self-supporting. Obviously, to Albertans this is no surprise.

III

Waterway

CHAPTER TWENTY-FIVE

Best In the West by a Dam Site

DURING the spring of 1921 an eloquent legal contract, fully attested, lay in a Medicine Hat safe-deposit box. The contract was an agreement between members of Medicine Hat's United Agricultural Association and Charles M. Hatfield, California rain-making wizard. Hatfield disclaimed all right to the title of rain maker, but he took credit for showers which had fallen on parched lands in California following what he referred to as "offering Nature certain aids." Showers, good, heavy, soaking showers, were what the people of southern Alberta needed more than anything else in the world. In fact, showers were the only thing they needed. They had good, rich soil and long days of sunshine. They had breeding cattle and plenty of seed. So eight thousand of them each put up a dollar and the association sent for Charles M. Hatfield.

The agreement read:

It is hereby understood and agreed that (in respect of) all rain falling from the first day of May, 1921, to the first day of August, 1921 (in an area within a hundred miles of Chappice Lake) that said Hatfield, through efforts of his operation upon the atmosphere, shall be given credit for one-half the precipitation that falls at a uniform rate of $4,000 per inch up to four inches or fraction thereof, the maximum consideration of this contract being $8,000 for a four-inch rainfall.

Chappice Lake is about twenty miles northeast of the city of Medicine Hat. Results were to be secured over a 100-mile radius, with gauges placed fifty miles apart.

Meteorological reports indicate how desperate were the farmers and ranchers living on the parched land along the South Saskatchewan, and how good were Hatfield's chances of pocketing his money. There were only six years when the rainfall was not four inches or better during the thirty-seven years in which official records had been kept at Medicine Hat. The average for the months of May, June, and July was 6.22. Just to avoid any misunderstanding, Charles M. Hatfield, having had a wide experience with the difficulties of producing rain artficially, took care to remind all concerned that his contract called for four inches of rain and not four inches above the average.

The drought cycle that hit the prairies immediately following World War I was not unusual, except to the many people who had arrived since the last one. Old-timers had the comfort of having survived others without the aid of a rain-making wizard. They, and the Indians, had warned farmers against the folly of turning the prairie sod "wrong side up."

Hatfield erected his fragile-looking tower beside Chappice Lake, white rimmed with alkali. It was only about twenty feet high, with an open tank or vat on top. Into the vat he placed certain chemicals compounded according to his secret formula, the only secret thing about the whole affair. The people of Medicine Hat and the entire Northern Plains waited hopefully and, possibly, a little skeptically. Would the gases generated by the chemicals in that small vat actually cause moisture in the clouds to condense? Could Hatfield make the "skies weep at will," as he had promised to do, within the first six days of May?

Men and women looked up and saw the typical cloud banks that had appeared so often in recent years only to be blown away without letting down more than a few provocative drops of rain. Those who had come from down East repeated the statement they had repeated so often since coming out west.

"It rains much easier in Ontario than in Alberta," they said, looking at their thin cattle on the dried-out range or at fields where they hoped wheat would grow.

For three days they waited, some looking frequently at the clouds, others trying not to look at them because, "Well, because it might bring bad luck. Watched pots never boil, you know!"

And then it came! On May 4 there was .33 inch of rain. On May 6 twice as much fell. On the 11th .26 inch made up a total of 1.31 inches. A few farmers decided to ask Hatfield to hold back until they got their seeding finished. Some commented that the rain maker was going to get rich quick at that rate. But he was undoubtedly Medicine Hat's uncrowned king, even at $4,000 an inch of rainfall. Another shower brought the May total up to 1.62 inches.

June did not start so well. Days passed without a drop of rain. Hatfield complained that every time he got the clouds all set for a real downpour a chinook blew them away. Farmers who had talked about holding off till seeding was finished wished they had not spoken so soon. They became anxious. A delegation went to see Hatfield at his shack out at Chappice Lake and firmly reminded him of his contract. It is even said that one or two perched on the hills surrounding the lake and spied with their field glasses to see if he really was at work. In the churches there were the prayers for rain so familiar to churchgoers on the prairies. Hatfield, prayers, or just plain nature—a general rain of over an inch relieved anxiety for a time. Another on July 4, which was general from Winnipeg to the Rockies, cheered everyone, including the rain maker.

July brought its typical hot, dry, days when the sun burned down from a copper-colored sky and the thermometer registered a temperature of 98 degrees in the shade. Soon the effects of prolonged drought began to tell. There was no deep moisture for the plants to draw upon. Another good rain, the one which would make up Hatfield's four inches, would be worth millions of dollars. Everyone in the vicinity of Medicine Hat talked much more of that aspect than about the $8,000 the rain maker would forgo, though they did try to think up a few jokes or wager an occasional brave bet. At last the rain came, well toward the end of July, truly a million-dollar rain. Some said the showers that year were softer and more penetrating than usual. The United Agricultural Association voted in favor of re-engaging Charles M. Hatfield for the next year. Mr. Hatfield refused to accept a cent more than $5,000 for his services. He could have produced much more rain for Medicine Hat, he said, if his tower had been erected northwest of the city instead of northeast resulting in a lot of free rain for Leader community, near the Alberta-Saskatchewan provincial border.

The eyes of the prairies were on Medicine Hat and Charles M. Hatfield. Along the South Branch every town council discussed rain making at meetings which lasted twice as long as usual. Swift Current, which in 1921 had an official rainfall of 6.83 inches for the months of May, June, and July as compared with Medicine Hat's 4.80, offered Hatfield $10,000 for three months of good soaking showers. Hatfield turned down the offer because he could not possibly guard the secret of his formula without being on location day and night. There were other substantial offers, all turned down. Perhaps Medicine Hat's extreme drought was a challenge that could not be ignored. The town of Leader, having enjoyed, at no cost whatever, rain which was intended for Medicine Hat, rejoiced to learn that its neighboring community had re-engaged Mr. Hatfield. Down in Ontario, Sir Frederick Stupart, then chief of Canada's Meteorological Bureau, pronounced the whole episode the "most absurd thing ever perpetrated in the West!"

Perhaps it was absurd to Sir Frederick, living down East where it rains easier than in Alberta. People living in an area with an average rainfall of less than ten inches look at rain with different eyes. They regard every shower as a blessing. They listen with sympathy to every scheme which might condense the great cumulus clouds, so familiar in early summer, into heavy, penetrating rain.

Enormous deposits of coal and natural gas underlying the Great Northern Plains and the relics of dinosaurs and similar prehistoric animals indicate that there was a time when the territory was semitropical with high humidity. That was long before the era of the Indian and the white man. When Captain Palliser explored western Canada, or Rupertsland, as it was in 1858, he outlined what he termed the arid plains as distinct from the areas he considered to be fertile. A triangle, famous as Palliser's Triangle, was drawn on a map and described as extending from what is now Coutts, Alberta, on the International Boundary to near Saskatoon, Saskatchewan, and then southeast to the International Boundary in southwestern Manitoba. Captain Palliser referred to the triangle as the central desert. Through it flows almost the entire South Saskatchewan and a stretch of the North Branch in the vicinity of the Battlefords.

Severe drought is not new to the territory where the short grass once supported millions of buffalo. Explorer John Macoun wrote of it in his autobiography: "In 1879 I found a parched surface, dried and withered grass . . . in 1890 there were numbers of dried creeks in each line of travel . . . in

1894 the country was drying up, the lakes were disappearing . . . nearly all streams on the prairie had ceased to flow."

But the Saskatchewan has never ceased to flow. There has aways been a flow, even in dry years when shoals and sand bars show in August and the water from spring runoffs and mountain streams has raced down to Lake Winnipeg and joined the Atlantic Ocean. In good years no one thinks about the river. In dry years, ever since the first rancher trailed in a few head of cattle and the first farmer plowed virgin sod, prairie folk have looked at it longlingly and, sometimes, bitterly. Pioneers living along the deep-valleyed South Branch regarded the river as useless, except for a few flats; they had no means of raising water from three to five hundred feet. Much more fortunate were the men who took up land along the foothills tributaries, which are almost all surface streams.

Among these was John Glenn, who settled at Fish Creek soon after the first detachment of North West Mounted Police arrived to build their stockaded fort at McLeod. The police and the Hudson's Bay Company people at Fort Edmonton, three hundred miles apart, were his first white neighbors. John Glenn had to depend on his own resources. When he lacked natural hay for his horses and cattle he thought of irrigation. Slowly and laboriously he dug a ditch and diverted water from Fish Creek to irrigate fifteen or twenty acres. From an engineering point of view the project was not a great success. From the point of view of a man who wanted feed for his cattle and, possibly, a few vegetables for his own table it worked very well. Those few irrigated acres put John Glenn on his feet. They kept him a going concern in dry years.

About the same time another early rancher, John Quick, diverted water from Sheep Creek in the general vicinity of today's Turner Valley and the Duke of Windsor's EP ranch. Within a couple of years Quick had a hundred acres under irrigation, and had plans for extensions.

From the very first those small, ingenious, trial-and-error irrigation ditches have been the means whereby many farmers and ranchers staved off disaster during dry cycles similar to the drought of the thirties, which gave the prairies the shocking name of "Dust Bowl." Few were large enough to be termed projects. Many were complete failures because of lack of surveys, and tell some of the bitterest stories of pioneering heartache. All provided plenty of backache, the phase of irrigation that made wheat growing look so easy.

The only way to bear the backache of digging an irrigation ditch by hand is to think of glistening water flowing through ditches and across future acres of alfalfa for the cattle and potatoes and strawberries for your own table. There's a certain exaltation about the whole business, if you can keep your mind on the dream, an exaltation reserved for the few who have tried it. For no one but the man, or woman, who has lived through drought and watched the sides of his once-fat cattle shrink to a washboard fully appreciates the value of water flowing through well-tilled fields. Perhaps that is why there is scarcely a ranch- or bunkhouse in the country which has not at some time had hung on its walls a reproduction of cowboy artist Charlie Russell's painting entitled "The Last of 5000."

Hard winters, as well as dry summers, alternate with extremely good cycles in the South Branch country. Those who cannot face the bad cycles leave. Most stay and put in the time as best they can. Charlie Russell couldn't bear the sight of a herd of five thousand cattle dwindling day after day during the terrible winter of 1886, so he took a piece of charcoal from the stove and sketched his report to his employers, the picture that eventually made him world famous. It depicts a lone, surviving cow, her ribs showing through her hide like slats, facing two wolves across the snow. Unlike some animals, cattle do not paw through deep snow to the underlying grass. Plenty of stacked hay could have saved the entire herd.

The people of Medicine Hat go in for rain-making experiments in dry cycles, probably because Medicine Hat is in one of the driest areas of the Great Central Plains. After years there is still a lot of conjecture as to whether Charles M. Hatfield actually earned his money or not. But citizens of "The Hat" are willing to spend more money on similar projects. The latest has to do with the effect of a couple of magnets on the moon. More likely to succeed are experiments conducted by the Royal Canadian Air Force working with the National Research Council, and employing planes to bombard fluffy cumulus clouds with dry ice.

Efforts to cope with drought occupy a lot of time and energy and dreaming in the territory drained by the Saskatchewan River and its tributaries. Down at Mountain View, in the southwest corner of Alberta, a group of typically enterprising farmers and ranchers secured the right to develop a small irrigation project on their own, so great was their need for water in the dry cycle after World War I. They organized under the Provincial Irrigation Act, chose a committee from among themselves, secured the services of a surveyor, laid out their plan, and allotted a portion of the work and expense to each man according to his acreage. Then they commenced work.

They used their own horses and mules and handled their own scrapers and fresnos. Brush and trees were uprooted with nothing but horse- and mule- and manpower and the dream of water flowing through ditches. Often it was discouraging work, slithering through the mud and up and down greasy banks, working not when they were fresh and eager but when the regular day's work was over. In their spare time they felled and hauled logs and cut them into lumber for the headgates and other ditch structures. Working in their spare time and with limited equipment, they took ten years to complete their community project. And when the headgates were finally in place men's tears mingled with the first flow of water, so great was their relief.

Total cost for the original 3,600 acres of the Mountain View project, 9 per cent of which can be irrigated, was $7.10 an acre. That included the surveyor's fee. There is no debt and the current charge for maintenance and operation is 20 cents an acre a year. The community of Mountain View, even during the terrible drought of the thirties, was self-supporting, growing its own hay, with a small surplus to export to neighboring areas, and its own vegetables.

"Water!" They say the word reverently as they look at the ditch winding through the valleys. "Water is not only gold. It is life itself."

When there is not enough moisture to grow crops in the South Saskatchewan country, its people do a variety of things. Some pray. Many grumble and join new political parties. Rain-making experiments, with gases, moonbeams, or more scientifically, by peppering potential rain clouds with dry ice, are very popular. Everyone talks about irrigation, whether it is feasible in his community or not. The one thing they do not do, during a very dry cycle, is to listen to or read the weather forecasts. The *probs* are *out.*

Land about the foothill streams, where irrigation first started in Alberta, never needed extra water as much as the dry short-grass country farther east, the prairies where they used to allow "forty acres to a critter." In years of adequate moisture, maybe fifteen or sixteen inches, the prairies literally blossom with fragrant wild roses, purple and yellow vetch, and the tough grass, or prairie wool, on which cattle do so well. That combination of quick, lush growth with adequate moisture inevitably attracted big business interests. Often these interests were represented by companies financed by British capital and holding vast grants of land suitable for ranching.

The McLeod Irrigation Company received the first charter less than twenty years after the North West Mounted Police had built their stockaded headquarters in the land of the Blackfoot Indians. Next year the High River & Sheep

Creek Irrigation Company started work, followed by the Alberta Irrigation Company, the Calgary Hydraulic Company, and William Pearce's Calgary Irrigation Company. Irrigation quickly became so popular in Alberta that the Canadian government enacted the North West Irrigation Act, placing all surface water under control of the dominion.

Sir Alexander Galt, one of the Fathers of Confederation, played an active part in settlement about Lethbridge, on the Old Man River. The Galt interests originally called themselves the North-Western Coal & Navigation Company. Very quickly disillusioned by the variable supply of prairie streams, they changed the name of their company and substituted irrigation for navigation. It was a sound move. It led to an agreement with the heads of the Mormon Church down in Utah and brought to southern Alberta a group of settlers familiar with the various processes of irrigation. At first the citizens of Alberta looked askance at the Mormons and declared they wanted no polygamous customs in their community. The Mormons declared they were behind none in respecting the laws of the country in which they lived, and in no time the original citizens of the territory were respecting the incredible crops produced by the newcomers. Polygamy was forgotten.

About the turn of the century the Galt company distributed fifty pounds of sugar-beet seed to settlers on the newly irrigated land about Lethbridge and with it the seed of a new economy. Down in Utah, Mormon Jesse Knight tested some of the beets grown from the seed. The results tallied well with inquiries he had already made concerning land along the Old Man and St. Mary's rivers. As a result he purchased a tract of 30,000 acres near Spring Coulee and a couple of years later built the first sugar-beet factory in western Canada. There was no great rush among the settlers to grow sugar beets. Wheat, they soon discovered, was an easier crop and, seemingly, one which paid much better. The original sugar-beet factory had to be closed. Yet the idea never quite died. Another drought brought widespread failure of the wheat crop, and turned farmers to irrigation and its more laborious though more consistent harvest. After a few decades of trial and error, growing and processing sugar beets in southern Alberta has become a flourishing industry. The "forty acres to a critter," which had grown 250 pounds of beef in a year, irrigated and sown to beets increased the owner's income nearly two-hundredfold.

The Saskatchewan and its tributaries proved as unco-operative to those who sought to use it as a waterway as to those who had used it as a highway. The sixty years in which engineers, ranchers, farmers, financiers, and politicians have been trying to tame it is a series of failures, losses, and heartbreaks. Nothing but a combination of necessity and that optimism born of the altitude and climate kept men at it. The wonder is that they did not abandon the river and its country. Yet, true to the Blackfoot saying, they had drunk of Saskatchewan water and they couldn't stay away.

There was the Canada Land & Irrigation scheme in which a one-time governor-general of Canada, Earl Grey, is said to have lost heavily. The company was financed with English and Scottish capital, as were many of the large land companies of the western United States and Canada. From men who could afford large sums on speculation right down to those who risked their last pound or dollar, money invested in this and other irrigation projects disappeared as quickly and as surely as though it had been washed away by the white waters of springtime floods. At least $12,000,000 have been invested in the Canada Land & Irrigation Company over the years with only about one third of the originally planned acreage of 165,000 acres yet in use. The company, with a grant of 500,000 acres of land, undertook to irrigate 200,000 acres northwest of Medicine Hat, taking water from the Bow River, east of Calgary. One of the main ditches collapsed. That and the subsequent financial strain necessitated several reorganizations.

The Canadian Pacific Railway irrigation ditch at Strathmore has cost many times the sum originally estimated, and is far from a success. Another project resulted in the abandonment of a ditch almost a hundred miles long; because of the porous nature of the soil, not a drop of water flowed through to the proposed outlet. No one now cares to discuss it. In fact, most of the Saskatchewan River failures are a little too recent and a little too painful for anyone to know anything about them at all!

Up near the mouth of the Sturgeon River, close to Fort Saskatchewan and downstream from Edmonton, thousands of dollars in the form of a dam were washed away by the first spring flood following its completion. At La Colle, or, as it is known today, Cole Rapids, below Prince Albert, an unfinished dam remains an ironic monument to the river's traditional lack of co-operation. The project was planned and supervised by competent engineers. Yet only one large concrete span remains to divert the swift flow of spring waters and form a local tourist attraction. When tourists ask what happened, there are numerous dark references to the old slippery mud on the river bottom, the absence of solid rock, and the devastating power of swirling, bucking, ice-laden spring floods. Down East a few people mention the money they, or their fathers, lost at Cole Rapids. In Prince Albert the dam nearly wrecked the city's financial structure and for a time seriously delayed the city's progress. Looking back over the river's story, it looks as though Cole Rapids had been cursed, more or less legitimately ever since the first weary voyageur put himself in tracking harness to haul a York boat from its shore line. There is something about those old river failures akin to bad medicine in the days of the Crees and the Blackfeet because they cast a shadow of doubt over even modern projects.

"You can't do anything with that river," state some of the people living along its banks. "Might as well save your money as try to harness the Saskatchewan. Boats beached, bridges and dams washed out, folks drowned every summer . . . Maybe it ain't supposed to be used!"

Fortunately that attitude is not too widespread. Most people living in its basin regard the difficulties more as a challenge than as a deterrent, especially those living in Alberta, where the streams are almost all on the surface instead of down in the deep valley common to the main streams. You can tell when you are coming to an irrigation area long before you see the glistening ditches or the lush green fields. Gradually the air softens. The fragrance of water welcomes every traveler who has passed through the dry, gritty air of the arid prairies. It is a symbol of the way in which the Saskatchewan's challenge is being met. In fact, each of the increasing irrigation areas might use the slogan of the town of Bassano, which proudly tells the world that it is "Best in the West by a Dam Site." Even the birds know the areas about Bassano and nearby Brooks, irrigated by Bow River water. Year after year they drop down from the Central Flyway in such numbers as to bring thousands of hunters to the community—and a second harvest. That annual duck or goose hunt pleases everyone, the sportsmen who come to shoot over the stubble and the farmers and their wives who turn their homes into temporary hunting lodges.

Yet, challenging as it is, the Saskatchewan continues to dictate its terms to even the most realistic and the most scientifically minded. It has enforced caution to such an extent that modern engineers bend over backwards to avoid taking chances. Whether they admit it or not, the bad medicine of the river's record adds to the struggle and delays success. Politicians make great use of it. Some farmers continue to insist that the river's water as employed for irrigation will never pay; it won't—for hard wheat. And there is the old antagonism that prevents existing irrigation schemes from being used to capacity as though the river resented the good years in which it was ignored. Perhaps it is all tied up in the very nature of the river. From the time the first settler arrived, the Saskatchewan, flowing through its deep valley, has been regarded as useless. Reasonable people will insist that a river has no personality, that it cannot be resentful. Such people do not know the Saskatchewan. Probably it should be referred to as she, and treated as though it had distinctly feminine characteristics. For that river never will be won until it is wooed and understood and its terms faithfully met. Then it may give as generously to the country through which it flows as a woman greatly in love.

CHAPTER TWENTY-SIX

Today and Tomorrow

THE Saskatchewan River basin drains an area of approximately 145,000 square miles. At the Manitoba-Saskatchewan border, below the Forks, the average annual flow is 18,000,000 acre feet. After the spring runoff and when mountain snows are melting, flood conditions are common. By August the river is so low that in places it can be waded. Shoals are common. Two hundred years after its discovery people living along its banks face a struggle for survival almost as great as that of the earliest voyageurs, the problem of how to conserve waste waters of spring and early summer for use during dry months.

Time has evened interest in the two branches. The North Branch, draining an area of 59,000 square miles, has been relatively unimportant since its great days as a highway, though there is one ambitious plan to use its water if not its channel. After a hiatus of settlement, the South Branch has become the important stream, the waterway of the dry high plains and prairies. Nearly three million of its 40-odd million acres could be irrigated. If and when this acreage is under the ditch, sufficient food and feed could be produced to offset the worst sociological and economical disasters of drought cycles. The upper main river flows through park and forest belts where rainfall is higher and less variable than on the prairies. Along the lower main river, drainage is a more pressing need than irrigation.

A lot of figuring has been done on sheets of fresh white paper and the backs of old envelopes about the acreage that could be irrigated by the Saskatchewan. The hopeful enthusiast invariably starts out with that eighteen million acre-foot figure. Maybe it could not all be used, he concedes, but why not try to use half of it? Why not try to conserve even three-quarters in storage dams? These are the natural questions of a man who has watched heat waves dance across his fields until his dreams become hallucinations. Unfortunately the dreams lack even the reality of a mirage. Grain elevators fifty miles away, which sometimes can be seen clearly above the horizon, are the atmospheric reflection of real elevators. Engineers and surveyors claim there is no basis for hoping that more than three million acres can be irrigated by Saskatchewan water, no matter how great the need or how exciting the dreams. Even the three-million figure may be too high.

Actually the accumulated flow in the basin would be sufficient for nine million acres if all of it could be used. But only that portion which can be stored in reservoirs and diverted during the open-water season by canals of reasonable capacity can be used economically for irrigation. This would require a storage capacity of three and a quarter million acre-feet, plus a substantial diversion from the North Saskatchewan. The North Saskatchewan diversion is one of the earliest local irrigation schemes.

The main source is the old glaciers and new snows of the eastern slopes of the Rocky Mountains. The question of how long the glaciers will last is under investigation. Some men, like Jim Simpson of Bow Lake who has watched them recede for fifty years, allow only twice that time until most remnants of the Ice Age will have disappeared. Whether that would make a great difference to the Saskatchewan's flow or whether it would be compensated by melting snows remains to be seen. In the meantime it provides as interesting a topic for the comparative few familiar with the river sources as the annual gambles about when the ice will go out or that popular figuring on the backs of old envelopes.

The main streams in the South Branch system are the Waterton, Belly, St. Mary, Old Man, Highwood, Bow, Elbow, and Red Deer. With the exception of the Waterton, the Belly and the St. Mary, which rise in Glacier National Park in the United States, all these streams start in Canada. The only allocation problems facing irrigation engineers are those dealing with the three provinces of Alberta, Saskatchewan, and Manitoba. The Milk River, rising in Montana, has presented more allocation problems than the three other international streams. Rivers respect no man-made boundaries, the Milk River not only rises in Montana and flows across a good deal of southern Alberta just above the boundary, but after doing so it turns south to join the Missouri. Only that part which is diverted for irrigation joins the Saskatchewan system.

In 1899 the Alberta Railway & Irrigation Company secured rights to divert from the St. Mary River the low-water flow, plus sufficient to make a total of two thousand second-feet during high stages. This was used in the Lethbridge area with great success for several years until the United States Reclamation Service proposed to divert water, in the United States, from the St. Mary to the Milk River for use on projects in Montana. Following their traditional policy of being as good neighbors as possible the two governments negotiated their problems. As a result the Boundary Water Treaty was signed in 1909, soon to become the International Joint Commission.

International water problems of the Great Plains have been handled generally in a manner to be expected of self-governing, self-respecting peoples. In Alberta and Montana water is more precious than gold. That statement cannot be repeated too often. Each community needs every acre-foot of water it can procure. Perhaps that is why each, though populated largely by individualists with thoroughly rugged tendencies, gives and demands fair play so far as water is concerned.

In 1921 the International Joint Commission met to apportion the flow of the St. Mary and Milk rivers, Canada's share of the Milk River to be 40,600 acre-feet and of the St. Mary 362,600; the United States' share of the Milk to be 75,400 acre-feet and of the St. Mary 248,100. By 1940 the United States had constructed storage and irrigation works capable of utilizing its entire share of the two streams. Canada was employing only 165,000 of its allotted 403,000 acre-feet. Citizens of the areas drained by the Canadian portions of the two streams as well as elsewhere in Canada began to think that their neighbors across the border might well claim right to the water if it was not being used. They began to agitate for complete development. The result has been the St. Mary-Milk River Irrigation Project, under construction to safeguard Canada's share of these International streams. The cost is to be divided between the dominion government, the province of Alberta, and the water users.

Prior to commencement of work on the St. Mary-Milk River project there were nineteen major projects capable of irrigating a little over half a million acres, all in Alberta. Less than four hundred thousand acres were actually under the ditch. Numerous small projects, most of them privately owned dams or dugouts constructed under the Prairie Farms Rehabilitation Administration, irrigated at least a hundred thousand acres to make a total of not more than half a million.

A lot of controversy preceded work on the St. Mary-

Milk River project. In common with most large irrigation schemes, there was the argument that it would never pay. The cost would be much too high to levy on the farmers and ranchers who would use it, and why should the rest of the country have to pay the shot? Why bother to reclaim arid lands when there are millions of acres in the Canadian West where insufficient moisture is not a factor? And—the old bad medicine working again—why risk fifteen million dollars on a project which would likely go the same way as most former Saskatchewan River schemes, downstream with the next spring flood? The controversy raged in the press, on the radio, and in Parliament. It was discussed beside the kitchen stove while a 90-mile blizzard raged and in July when the sun blazed down from a burning copper sky. Especially was it discussed when the sun blazed down from a copper sky, licking up every last drop of moisture in the parched soil.

Many of the questions have been answered. Nearly everyone is agreed that large-scale irrigation on the Saskatchewan is a project almost as important to Canada as the St. Lawrence Waterway, and that because it will benefit so many people eventually construction should be regarded as a national responsibility.

The charge that farmers and ranchers should be moved from what are often called submarginal lands is answered by the reminder that the Canadian government has an obligation to the farmers whom it invited to take up free land and who made the Canadian West the granary of the world. As for the bogey of bad medicine, every effort has been made to study the Saskatchewan and to meet its variations. Scientists who do that are not fearful of old bogeys, political and otherwise. The St. Mary-Milk River Irrigation Project is beng constructed as the logical first stage in an over-all development not only of the streams in the vicinity of these rivers but of the entire Saskatchewan River system.

Many and involved were the delicate human considerations that had to be met before construction of the St. Mary

River dam could be commenced. In their way surveys and costs were no more difficult than negotiations with the owners of homes and land which would be flooded. Blood Indians living on their reserve to the west of the river knew the value of the 5,800 acres they held by treaty right. Two Hutterite colonies owning more than five thousand acres, and seventy or eighty buildings with sewer and water facilities, had no desire to see the results of many years of communal effort at the bottom of a great lake. The Hutterites had their own schools and their own customs. In Lethbridge and the surrounding towns no one paid much attention to Hutterite men in their shapeless black suits followed by their women in long, full skirts and kerchiefs. A new community might present unwanted publicity. More easily settled than either the Blood Indian or Hutterite claims was compensation to the Canadian Pacific Railway for a bridge on the line between the predominantly Mormon towns of Raymond and Cardston.

First stage of the $15,000,000 project was construction of a diversion tunnel on the St. Mary above the dam site. The concrete-lined tunnel, 2,100 feet long, and driven through sandstone and shale, had to be 20 feet in diameter to take care of spring floodwaters. As soon as it was completed, work commenced on the dam, a rolled earth fill 186 feet high, 2,600 feet long at the crest, and having a base width of approximately 1,450 feet. Some four million cubic feet of fill went into the construction. The reservoir, which will cover about 11,600 acres of land, eventually will become a lake 17 miles long and as wide as 6 miles where it fills cross coulees. Irrigation water is to be diverted through a horseshoe tunnel 2,600 feet in length, its inlet end controlled by four gates, its capacity 3,200 cubic feet a second. The concrete spillway is designed to discharge 50,000 cubic feet a second.

The St. Mary River will supply the main source of water for the project, with additional water diverted by canal from the Waterton and Belly rivers during the period between

April 15 and October 15 each year. The Milk River will provide irrigation for an additional 18,000 acres. When the project is complete, probably in 1950, there will be storage reservoirs varying from the 15,000 acre-feet of the Pot Hole Coulee to the St. Mary's 290,000 acre-feet. These are the cold figures, setting no world records. Human interest considerations are much more imposing.

The St. Mary-Milk River Irrigation Project will bring an additional 345,000 acres to the 500,000 already under the ditch in the South Branch country. On the Bow River, some 55,000 acres are already under the ditch, most of it developed by the Canada Land & Irrigation Company. Now plans are under way to provide another 180,000 to this tract of potentially highly productive soil. The Bow River basin below Calgary has similar climate and soil conditions to those in the area of the St. Mary-Milk River project. Both have long days of sunlight. Both have the advantages of almost unlimited natural gas. Rightly the people of southern Alberta are in a happy mood. The foothills with snow-capped mountains are over their right shoulders as they face south. Great hope is in their hearts as they face the future.

The Red Deer is the most amazing of South Saskatchewan tributary streams. It has cut deep into the soft rock to provide geologists with one of the finest hunting grounds on the continent. At the coal-mining center of Drumheller it has re-created Dante's inferno in a valley which beggars description. In spring the Red Deer floods. In summer it looks like any other prairie river. Yet its banks and shoulders are layered and fissured to resemble a miniature Grand Canyon. Beehive hills dot its valley, their tops as flat as though a giant plane had leveled them. Bones of dinosaurs and other prehistoric lizards protrude from the rock of the cretaceous Upper Edmonton formation. Oyster shells glisten in the sun light. Tiny fossils of seeds and nuts and tropical fruit lure the geological enthusiast with his delicately poised ax. In gardens bright with summer flowers, fossilized femurs and jawbones and the roots of prehistoric trees provide borders and rockeries. Yet the most important feature of the Red Deer is not its prehistoric wonders. Today the important feature of the Red Deer is water.

William Pearce rode up and down the Red Deer early in the century. He studied its levels and those of the country for hundreds of miles. He watched the muddy water flooding the flats in spring, ripping trees from the banks, washing away shack homes. Thinking of the dry short-grass high plains and prairies, he drew a careful plan for irrigation. William Pearce died before his plan had a chance of fruition. For years it was forgotten except by a few enthusiasts and dreamers. But at last the dreamers have persuaded the engineers and statesmen and politicians to blow off the gritty dust of three or four decades of windstorms and have a look at it. A few people are referring to the revised Pearce Scheme as the Red Deer Development. Others call it the North Saskatchewan Project. The enthusiasts and dreamers remember to associate it with the man who first saw its potentialities.

If the Pearce Scheme ever becomes a fact, water from the North Saskatchewan will be diverted to the South Branch by way of the Clearwater River. Below the town of Red Deer there will be a rolled earth dam 175 feet high, creating a reservoir with a storage capacity of 300,000 acre-feet of usable storage. A main canal will carry water to the vast natural storage basin of Buffalo Lake. Hydro power would be an obvious development. Such figures as an annual output of 30,000,000 kilowatt-hours are mentioned as a result of surveys. Further storage in the mountains would have to be constructed. And, suggest certain enthusiastic engineers, there is always the possibility of blasting a tunnel through the short divide between the Pembina and the North Saskatchewan to divert water which now flows to the arctic. More realistic authorities regard the Pembina diversion as being fantastic.

"Who's going to pay for it?" they demand, generally including the Pearce Scheme in the same blanket query.

There is more agreement concerning the Bow River. The Bow is regarded as being the most important river in Alberta for irrigation and power purposes. But most of the flow of the Bow is required to irrigate adjoining lands. If the power facilities of the Bow could be used for economical pumping purposes, it could pump water from the distant Red Deer, which has excellent storage facilities. Since some of the Red Deer country which could be irrigated is above the general elevation of reservoirs, the two rivers might work in double harness, the Bow's waste summer power used to pump water to land along the Red Deer while that river's flow could be stored for winter use. Already there are surveyors' figures, drawings, and even blueprints for this ambitious project.

The biggest dream of today on the Canadian prairies is that of constructing a high dam on the South Saskatchewan, a project which would likely revive the old Alberta slogan of "Back to the land, but don't forget the water!" Though there are surveys and plans for utilizing South Branch water which date back to 1912, it is expected that at least two years would be required to complete surveys for the project, which is receiving so much attention today.

During World War I there was an interesting scheme to pipe water across the prairies to the cities of Moose Jaw and Regina. That never got beyond the paper stage. During the thirties an open ditch was constructed to carry water to Moose Jaw's natural reservoir at Caron. Professor Hind of the University of Toronto, making a survey for the Canadian government in the seventies, envisaged a dam and diversion works at the Elbow and the possibility of traveling by boat all the way from Winnipeg to the then Fort Calgarry, spelt with two R's. Professor Hind's plan was eclipsed by construction of the Canadian Pacific Railway. The plan of John R. MacNicol, M.P., to make the old fur trade route navigable for coal and oil transport may meet a similar fate. So long as the Canadian Pacific and the Canadian National Railways can handle the traffic there is little support for the expensive system of dams, locks, and canals necessary to the MacNicol Plan. Tomorrow it may not appear so impractical.

Dreams and surveys and blueprints are all part of the South Branch project, for which two sites have been selected, both a few miles downstream from the Elbow, the point below Saskatoon where the river, after flowing east, makes a sharp bend to flow north. Flood regulation is considered. Water for Regina and Moose Jaw receives high priority, since those cities are now too large to be moved. So does cheaper power for all the large and small clusters of lights that brighten the prairies at night. Present plans call for one of the highest earth-filled dams on the North American continent, a fill at least two hundred feet above the river bed. If and when the project is completed it will be a magnet attracting prairie tourists for hundreds of miles. Just as they thronged to view the wonder of Duncairn dam on the tributary Swift Current Creek and other smaller reservoirs, they will come to watch the river rise and back up into the lake, which will spread upstream until, so it is estimated, the great reservoir will be some 135 miles long with a depth of 190 feet.

It is a great vision, as clear to those who see its completion, perhaps in fifty or a hundred years, as the potential reflection of white cumulus clouds in the blue water. For when collected in such a lake the waters of the Saskatchewan will at last become blue. Some beautiful ranches would be at the bottom of the lake, a fact which eases the sense of regret at inevitable delay; those who developed and loved those ranch sites will be spared heartache and, possibly, bitterness. Certain beloved picnic and camping sites would disappear, perhaps to become good fishing grounds. The lovely valley of the Elbow would be lost in the glories of the new lake.

The South Branch project is part of the Saskatchewan conservation plan, whose development would be one of the largest on the continent. When it is completed it will have brought about a great revolution. Agriculture in the dry tract of Palliser's Triangle will have been stabilized to a degree unknown in the era when bumper crops alternated with frustrating failure due to prolonged drought. Then, as water spreads through ditches here and there across the prairies so cultural and economic improvements will spread to the rest of the country.

So much for the vision that realists refer to as a pipedream. Apparently all successful water developments are built on a combination of the two characteristics. There is no shortage of realism concerning the Saskatchewan, especially the South Branch.

"What if the Soils Department of the University of Saskatchewan has tested soils along the lower South Branch?" demanded the realists. "What if they have found eight hundred thousand acres of suitable types and levels? Has one single farmer offered to put his name on paper as desiring it? Is there one who wants to swap a big, mechanized farm, growing mostly wheat, no matter how uncertain, for high boots and a shovel and backache? No! The farmers don't want it. Maybe in a generation or two—but not today. No, sirree!"

Experts among the realists point out the danger of frost on irrigated land north of the Saskatchewan. They refer to the variable water supply and stress the need for prior reforestation in the mountains and foothills. Most are willing to concede the success of a minor project to divert some water to the Qu'Appelle valley to flow by way of the Assiniboine and the Red River back to Lake Winnipeg and the Nelson. There is another snag, they continue, the serious loss of valuable soil by water erosion, which will probably require extensive pipe and sprinkler installation and so increase the cost to a point where it is insupportable. The cost is the high wall against which most of the realists eventually stop, or the gorge they cannot cross.

"A hundred million dollars won't see that South Branch project completed," they insist with authority. "The small population doesn't warrant such an outlay. Maybe, when the population increases . . ."

"Then get on with it and double or treble the population," exclaims the eager visionary. "Give the South Branch country water and they'll come! Anyway, what's a hundred million dollars? Canada spent more than that on only one depression, the last one."

Possibly another depression or a severe drought will have to occur before these contentious projects are developed. No one, not even the realists, most of them men of wide experience and sound judgment, doubts but what eventually full use will be made of every available acre-foot of water that flows naturally or can be diverted to flow through the South Branch channel. In the meantime a lot of attention is being given to less pretentious though nonetheless important projects.

Since the dark days of the dry thirties the Prairie Farms Rehabilitation Administration has lent cultural and financial support to the development of small, individual water-conservation schemes. Some thirty-five thousand of these dugouts and small dams, ranging from an acre or two to more than a hundred acres in extent, hold back a little rain and spring runoff. On the flat plains about Moose Jaw dugouts are common, a simple excavation with the earth thrown up about the sides and a fence or, eventually, a windbreak or hedge, to catch snow. Each is a tiny oasis on the vast flat prairie. Each ensures water for the household and stock, a garden and a little green beauty, things which, in that typically variable climate, mean all the difference between being able to maintain a home through good and bad cycles or going on relief.

In the more rolling country, coulees and cross coulees provide large areas from which runoff water may be collected to a smaller area, sufficient for irrigation of feed crops. Even in dry years the total precipitation, snowfall and rain, averages from 640 to 920 acre-feet on each square mile. Most of it runs off before it has a chance to soak into the rich soil. In spring when the first crocus blooms on southern slopes northern slopes are still frozen and the melting snow courses down to the rivers unimpeded. No natural trees provide even temporary storage. The result is the dual curse of insufficient water on the fields and floods in every stream channel.

A coulee is an excellent dam site, provided it has a large surface-drainage area and the earth-fill dam is constructed at the most effective level. Often a reservoir of this kind will collect thousands of acre-feet of water in a season, securing sufficient by gravity irrigation for gardens, feed, and stock and by pumping for home uses. The experimental farms have developed berrybushes and small-fruit trees able to withstand the freezing and thawing common to the country. Slowly a new word is coming into the vocabulary of prairie farmers. The word "orchard" means much to housewives, who delight to survey rows of bottled fruits, jams and jellies, luxuries hitherto unknown to many who could not afford imported fruits. For it is in comparatively little things that enough water means most to people living on nearly arid farms, little things like not having to carry every dishpanful of water to the garden, not having to listen to the baby fret from diaper rash because there was not enough water for proper rinsing.

Necessity has suggested many means whereby water may be delayed from reaching the Saskatchewan. In good years, those lush exciting periods when two crops of oats can be cut in a season and wheat averages forty bushels to the acre, farmers and ranchers withhold water by growing a maximum of feed and hay. Then the granary, the feedbin, and the haystack become their reservoirs. Windbreaks and hedges borrow a little more water from the flow that ultimately reaches the river. But whether the reservoir consists of plant life or a dugout or a large or small dam it enriches life and adds security and beauty. Perhaps nowhere does beauty reach more closely to the core of human emotion than on the dry prairies, whose color and size as well as beauty are never adequately reproduced. Not often does beauty mean so much as to those people who alternately face comparative wealth and the ancient threats of hunger, thirst, and cold. To such men and women the sight of a sunset or the Northern Lights reflected in the water of a crude dugout is an experience too moving and too intimate for the sacrilege of words.

The Saskatchewan, they say, drains the Rocky Mountains into the Atlantic Ocean. The statement tells its brief, historic story, of which only the first few chapters have been written. The future promises to be much more exciting and far more complex. Late among great North American rivers, it is resuming its place in world affairs, a place as important as when it was the highway of discovery for a continent. Oil, for which the nations are constantly sparring, will play a part. Illimitable coal may attract large industries, as will natural gas. But the Saskatchewan country has greater assets than any of these. They are bread and meat and the natural and synthetic wherewithal to clothe a country, assets as fundamental as man and the needs of man.

Acknowledgments

LIKE the other volumes in the Rivers of America Series, I suppose, *The Saskatchewan* is the result of the effort—and fun—of hundreds, perhaps thousands of people. The Honorable J. L. Phelps, one-time Minister of Natural Resources in the Saskatchewan government, arranged for me to fly the main river with provincial fire ranger L. A. Stewart. Ed. McLean, manager of the Hudson's Bay Company store at Cumberland House, and Mrs. McLean maintained the traditional hospitality of their post as initiated by Samuel Hearne in 1774. A truck driver, whose name I never knew, stopped his truck during a dust storm and did an expert first-aid job on the car I had been loaned; when he realized that the carburetor needed priming he invited me to share his bottle of wine before using the only available container to transfer the necessary gas.

Bruce Peel, curator of the Shortt Library of Canadiana at the University of Saskatchewan, Saskatoon; Deane Munro, who worked with Professor A. S. Morton, and Dr. D. P. Miller of Prince Albert have answered every query presented in person or by mail, often at some inconvenience. L. B. Thomson,

Director of Prairie Farm Rehabilitation, Department of Agriculture, provided information, introductions, leads and moral support with the generous flair for which he is famous. At the Royal Ontario Museum Professor T. F. McIlwraith discussed anthropology; Dr. Madeleine A. Fritz and Dr. L. S. Russell gave guidance in geology, and Mr. Kenneth Kidd concerning the Paul Kane collection.

W. Stewart Wallace, chief librarian, and his staff, of the Library of the University of Toronto, made available pamphlets and books, journals and periodicals with an enthusiasm which was an inspiration. *The Encyclopedia of Canada*, edited by Mr. Wallace (University Associates of Canada, Limited, Toronto, 1935), has been used extensively for fact and spelling. And on many an occasion Mr. Wallace gave generous and well-informed advice.

There was the assistance of librarians and the facilities of the Toronto Public Reference Library; Calgary Public Library; the Library of the University of Alberta; of the *Free Press*, Winnipeg; the *Daily Star*, Toronto; the Archives of the Dominion of Canada, Ottawa; and others.

Mr. Clifford Wilson of the Hudson's Bay Company, Winnipeg, answered many queries, as well as offering the use of the company's library. The Geographic Board of Canada passed on the authenticity of certain place names.

For hospitality, information, and/or guidance this book must be associated with the names of many people including: Dr. E. S. Archibald and Dr. A. Leahey, Experimental Farms, Ottawa; Dr. Marius Barbeau, the National Museum of Canada; Harold Long, Dr. W. H. Fairfield, Dr. W. L. Jacobson, Frank Wilkins, Lethbridge; Mrs. Alex. McCorquodale, J. N. McKeage, and ex-game warden Sam Smith of High River; W. R. Fulton, Drumheller; Kenneth Coppock and W. Henry McKay, Calgary; Mr. and Mrs. Campbell Innes, Battleford; Alice (Mrs. Douglas) MacKay, Winnipeg; Mr. and Mrs. Albert Parsons, Rocky Mountain House; Captain James Bell, D. E. C. Campbell, Ben Russell, and Mayor H. D. Ainlay of

Edmonton; Dr. George W. Simpson, Provincial Archivist, Saskatoon, for permission to use the facilities at his disposal; Floyd Glass, Mr. and Mrs. Burton Lewis, and Mrs. John G. Diefenbaker of Prince Albert; Miss Helen Mitchell, Medicine Hat; A. J. Dalrymple, Vancouver; Jim Greenblatt and "the Coopers," Swift Current; Mrs. Margaret Arnett McLeod, Winnipeg; Sidney Norman of the *Globe and Mail*, Dr. J. B. Tyrrell, Professor Griffith Taylor, John R. MacNicol, former MP, and Dr. H. Hoyle Campbell of Toronto; George Shepherd, of West Plains, Saskatchewan. There are many more, the list of whose names could go on for a page or so, and some whose names I never knew.

There was the late Irene ("Dinty") Moore who had planned a book on the Saskatchewan and who was called to cross the great river to the other world just when she was ready to commence writing. Her vision and perhaps her spirit are part of the heritage of all who write about the country she loved.

Frances Shelley Wees pointed the way.

Dr. Grant MacEwan, Dean of the Faculty of Agriculture and Home Economics, University of Manitoba, read the modern half of the Manuscript and made comments which lend authority to that section of it.

And, if it hadn't been for one person the book might never have seen completion. Dr. Angus A. Campbell, my husband, listened to every chapter and commented on and checked the entire Manuscript painstakingly.

To them all—my heartfelt thanks. I hope they enjoyed doing it as much as I did!

Bibliography

BOOKS

ADAM, GRAEME MERCER, *The Canadian North-West.* Toronto: Rose Publishing Co., 1885.

BALLANTYNE, ROBT. MICHAEL, *Hudson's Bay or Everyday Life in the Wilds of North America.* Edinburgh: Blackwood, 1848.

BEGG, ALEXANDER, *History of the North-West.* (3 vols.) Toronto: Hunter-Rose, 1894-1895.

BLACK, NORMAN FERGUS, *History of Saskatchewan and the Old North-West.* Regina: North-West History Company, 1913.

BRYCE, GEORGE, *The Remarkable History of the Hudson's Bay Company.* London: Low, 1900.

BURPEE, LAWRENCE JOHNSTON, *The Search for the Western Sea.* Toronto: Musson, 1908.

———, *Journals and Letters of Pierre Gaultier de Varennes de La Vérendrye and His Sons.* Toronto: Champlain Society, 1927.

BUTLER, WILLIAM FRANCIS, *The Great Lone Land.* London: Low, 1874.

CAMERON, ARTHUR PHILEMON, *Canadian Rockies, New and Old Trails.* London: Unwin, 1911.

CHEADLE, WALTER BUTLER, *Journal of a Trip Across Canada, 1862-63.* Ottawa: Graphic Publishers, 1931.

COCHRANE, CHARLES NORRIS, *David Thompson, The Explorer.* Toronto: MacMillan, 1924.

COWIE, ISAAC, *The Company of Adventures.* Toronto: William Briggs, 1913.

COUES, ELLIOTT (ed.), *Alexander Henry, the Younger.* Manuscripts and Journals of Alexander Henry and David Thompson. (3 vols.) 1897.

DAVIDSON, GORDON CHARLES, *The North-West Company.* University of California Pubs., 1918.

DENNY, SIR CECIL EDWARD, *The Law Marches West.* Toronto: Dent, 1939.

DUGAS, GEORGES, *The Canadian West.* Montreal: Beauchemin, 1905.

EGGLESTON, WILFRED, *The High Plains.* Toronto: MacMillan, 1939.

FARIES, VEN. R., *Dictionary of the Cree Language.* General Synod of the Church of England in Canada, 1938. (London, 1824.)

FRANKLIN, SIR JOHN, *Narrative of a Journey to the Shores of the Polar Sea*, 1819-20-21-22. (2 vols.) London: Murray, 1823.

———, *Narrative of a Second Expedition to the Polar Sea*, 1825-26-27.

GIBBON, JOHN MURRAY, *Steel of Empire.* Toronto: McClelland and Bobbs-Merrill, 1935.

GRIESBACH, WILLIAM ANTROBUS, *I Remember.* Toronto: Ryerson, 1946.

GUNN, HON. DONALD, and TUTTLE, CHARLES R., *History of Manitoba from the Earliest Settlement.* Ottawa: MacLean, Roger & Co., 1880.

HARMON, DANIEL WILLIAMS, *A Journal of Voyages and Travel in the Interior of North America.* Toronto: Courier Press, 1911.

HEARNE, SAMUEL, and TURNOR, PHILIP, *Journals.* Toronto: The Champlain Society, 1934.

HEMING, ARTHUR, *Spirit Lake.* New York: Doubleday, Page & Co. Toronto: MacMillan, 1907.

HENRY, ALEXANDER, SR., *Travels and Adventures in Canada and the Indian Territories*, Boston: ed., James R. Bain. Toronto: Morang, 1901.

HOPKINS, J. H., *Deep Furrows.* Indianapolis: Bobbs-Merrill, 1915.

HORAN, JOHN W., *West, Nor'West.* Edmonton: Northgate Books, 1945.

HUGHES, KATHERINE, *Father Lacombe, the Black-Robed Voyageur.* New York: Moffat, Yard & Co., 1914.

INGSTAD, HELGE MARCUS, *Land of Feast and Famine*. New York: Knopf, 1933.

INNIS, HAROLD, *Peter Pond, Fur Trader and Adventurer*. Toronto: Irwin, Gordon, Ltd., 1930.

———, *The Fur Trade in Canada*. New Haven: Yale University Press, 1930.

JAMES, NORMAN B., *Autobiography of a Nobody*. Toronto: Dent, 1947.

KANE, PAUL, *Wanderings of an Artist*. Master-Works of Canadian Authors, 1925.

KELLEY, L. V., *The Rangeman*. Toronto: William Briggs, 1913.

KENNEDY, HOWARD ANGUS, *The Book of the West*. Toronto: Ryerson Press, 1925.

LACOMBE, ALBERT, *Dictionnaire de la Langage des Cris*. Montreal: Beauchemin, 1874.

LAUT, AGNES C., *Conquest of the Great North West*. Toronto: Musson, 1914. New York: Macmillan, 1914.

LINGARD, CHARLES CECIL, *Territorial Government in Canada*. Toronto: University of Toronto Press, 1946.

LYSENKO, VERA, *Men in Sheepskin Coats*. Toronto; 1947.

MACINNES, CHARLES MALCOLM, *In the Shadow of the Rockies*. Rivington, 1930.

MACKAY, DOUGLAS, *The Honourable Company*. Indianapolis: Bobbs-Merrill, 1936. Revised by Alice MacKay, 1948.

MACKENZIE, SIR ALEXANDER, *Voyages From Montreal to the Frozen and Pacific Oceans*. London: Cadell, 1801. Toronto: Morang, 1902.

MACLEOD, MARGARET ARNETT, *Letters of Letitia Hargrave*. Toronto: Champlain Society, 1947.

MACOUN, JOHN, *Manitoba and the Great North West*. Guelph: World Publishing Co., 1882.

MASSON, L. R., *Les Bourgeois de la Compagnie du Nord-Ouest*. (2 vols.) Quebec: Cote, 1889–1890.

MCDOUGALL, JOHN, *Saddle, Sled and Snowshoe*. Toronto: Briggs, 1896.

MERK, FREDERICK, *Fur Trade and Empire*. George Simpson's Journal, 1931.

MILTON, WILLIAM FITZWILLIAM, and CHEADLE, W. B., *North West Passage by Land*. (4th ed.) London, 1865.

MITCHELL, WILLIAM ORMOND, *Who Has Seen the Wind?* Toronto: MacMillan, 1947. Boston: Little, Brown & Co., 1947.

MOBERLY, J. H., and CAMERON, WILLIAM BLEASDELL, *When Fur Was King*. Toronto: Dent, 1929.

MORRIS, ALEXANDER, *Treaties of Canada with the Indians of Manitoba and the North West Territories*. Toronto: Belfords, 1880.

MORTON, ARTHUR S., *A History of the Canadian West to 1870-71*, London: Nelson, 1938.

———, *Under Western Skies*. Toronto: Nelson, 1936.

———, *The Journal of Duncan McGillivray of the North West Co. Fort George on the Saskatchewan*. Toronto: MacMillan, 1929.

———, *Sir George Simpson*. Binfords-Mort for the Oregon Historical Society, 1944.

MUNDAY, LUTA, *A Mounty's Wife*. London: Sheldon Press, 1930.

NEWTON, WILLIAM, *Twenty Years on the Saskatchewan*. London: Stock, 1897.

NUTE, GRACE LEE, *The Voyageur*. New York: Appleton, 1931.

———, *Documents Relating to North West Missions*. St. Paul: Minnesota Historical Society for the Clarence Walworth Alvord Historical Society, 1942.

NIVEN, FREDERICK, *The Flying Years*. London: Collins, 1935.

PINKERTON, ROBERT E., *The Gentlemen Adventurers* (In England: *The Hudson's Bay Co.*). Toronto: McClelland, 1931.

QUEENEY, EDGAR MONSENTO, and BISHOP, RICHARD EVATT, *Prairie Wings*. Philadelphia: J. B. Lippincott, 1947.

RYERSON, JOHN, *Hudson's Bay, or a Missionary Tour in the Territory of Hon. Hudson's Bay Company*. Toronto: G. R. Sanderson, 1855.

SCHOOLING, SIR WILLIAM, K.B.E., *The Governor and Company of Adventurers of England Trading into Hudson's Bay during 250 years between 1670-1920*. Pub. by Hudson's Bay Co., 1920.

SELKIRK, 5TH EARL OF, *A Sketch of the British Fur Trade in North America*. London: Ridgway, 1816.

SIMPSON, SIR GEORGE, *Narrative of a Journey Round the World During the Years 1841-42*. London: Henry Colburn, 1847.

SOUTHESK, 9TH EARL OF, *Saskatchewan, and the Rocky Mountains*. Toronto: Campbell, 1875.

STANLEY, GEORGE F. G., *The Birth of Western Canada*. London: Longmans, 1936.

Stevens, Wayne Edson, *The Northwest Fur Trade, 1763-1800.* University of Illinois 1928. (Studies in Social Sciences.)

Steele, Sir Sam Benfield, *Forty Years in Canada.* Toronto: McClelland, 1915.

Tache, Mgr., Alexander, *Vingt Années de Missions dans le Nord-Ouest de L'Amerique.* Montreal: Senechal, 1869.

Taylor, Griffith, *Canada.* London: Methuen, 1947.

Thompson, David, *Narrative of His Explorations in Western Canada.* Edited by J. B. Tyrrell. Toronto: Champlain Society, 1916.

Thorington, James Monroe, *Glittering Mountains of Canada.* Philadelphia: Lea, 1925.

Traill, Henry Duff, *The Life of Sir John Franklin R.N.* London: Murray, 1896.

Tucker, Sarah, *The Rainbow in the North.* New York: Carter, 1852. London: Nisbet, 1858.

Wade, Mark Sweeten, *MacKenzie of Canada.* Edinburgh: Blackwood, 1927.

Walker, Ella Jacoby, *Fortress North.* Toronto: Thomas Allen, 1947.

Wallace, W. Stewart, *Documents Relating to the North West Company.* Toronto: Champlain Society, 1934.

Watkins, Rev. E. A., *Dictionary of the Cree Language as Spoken by Indians in the Hudson's Bay Company Territories.* London, 1865.

Weekes, Mary, *The Last Buffalo Hunters,* as told by Norbert Welsh. Toronto, 1939.

Willson, Beckles, *The Great Company.* Toronto: Copp, 1899.

NEWSPAPERS, ESPECIALLY ANNIVERSARY ISSUES

Battleford *Saskatchewan Herald* (early copies)
Edmonton *Bulletin*
Edmonton *Journal*
Lethbridge *Daily Herald*
Medicine Hat *News*
The Pas *Northern Mail*
Prince Albert *Daily Herald*
Regina *Leader-Post*

Saskatoon *Star-Phoenix*
Swift Current *Sun*
Winnipeg *Free Press*

PERIODICALS AND QUARTERLIES

Agricultural Institute Review
Alberta Folklore Quarterly (discontinued)
Beaver (Hudson's Bay Company)
Bulletin Canadian Mining Institute
Canadian Historical Review
Canadian Cattlemen
Canadian Geographic
Economics and Political Science Journal
Scarlet and Gold (Royal Canadian Mounted Police)
Saskatchewan History
Transactions of the Royal Society of Canada

JOURNALS, PAMPHLETS, ETC.

C. M. STERNBERG, *Canadian Dinosaurs*. National Museum Bulletin 103.
Hudson's Bay Company Record Society Publications.
Hudson's Bay Company Journals, notably:

Batt, Isaac
Cocking, Matthew
Henday, Anthony
Kelsey, Henry
Pink, William.

DIAMOND JENNESS, *Indian Treaties of the Plains*. National Museum of Canada Publication.
SIR HENRY LEFROY, *Journey to the Northwest*. Edited by W. Stewart Wallace F.R.S.C.
CHARLES BRAMBLE, *Land of the Lobstick*.
Northwest Historical Society Pamphlets.
A. S. MORTON & CHESTER MARTIN, Pioneer Settlement Series.
L. BLOOMFIELD, *Sacred Stories of the Sweet Grass Cree*. National Museum of Canada, Bulletin 60.
GENERAL SIR FRED MIDDLETON, *Suppression of the Rebellion in the North West Territories*, 1885. Edited by G. H. Needler.

Index

, M.
The Saskatchewan